Readings in Teacher Development

The Teacher Development Series

Readings in Teacher Development

Katie Head
Pauline Taylor

MACMILLAN
HEINEMANN
English Language Teaching

Macmillan Heinemann English Language Teaching, Oxford

A division of Macmillan Publishers Limited

Companies and representatives throughout the world

ISBN 0 435 24055 2

First published 1997

Series design by Mike Brain
Cover design by Pentacor

Printed in Hong Kong

2003 2002 2001 2000 1999
7 6 5 4 3

Contents

About the authors

Pauline Taylor

I have been a teacher and teacher trainer of English as a Foreign Language for 18 years, training teachers and trainers in the United Kingdom, Turkey and New Zealand, and assessing teachers' courses around the world. I am currently a Joint Chief Assessor for the RSA–UCLES CTEFLA scheme. I was also Events Co-ordinator for the IATEFL Teacher Development Special Interest Group for 4 years. I particularly enjoy integrating what I learn for my own personal development into my teaching and learning, and working with teachers in various countries on many of the themes outlined in this book. I have learnt so much from these teachers and workshops, and from collaborating on this book. I am about to undertake some change inspired by writing about it! I'm moving from South Devon College to the Christchurch College of English Language in New Zealand, where I grew up. To relax I do yoga and I'm learning the violin.

Katie Head

I am a senior teacher at Eurocentre Cambridge. My present job involves me in both classroom teaching of English (to adult groups of mixed nationalities) and pedagogic support to other teachers. My understanding of what teaching is, and of what it can be, has been greatly enriched by the ideas of teacher development as I encountered them through the Teacher Development Special Interest Group of IATEFL. This book is in part a celebration of Pauline's and my involvement in that group. I am very interested in classroom (and staffroom!) dynamics, peer observation and team teaching, and encouraging teacher reflection and teacher research. Having taught English in Taiwan for some years, I also have a particular interest in how Oriental students can be helped to learn English.

The Teacher Development Series

TEACHER DEVELOPMENT is the process of becoming the best teacher you can be. It means becoming a student of learning, your own as well as that of others. It represents a widening of the focus of teaching to include not only the subject matter and the teaching methods, but also the people who are working with the subject and using the methods. It means taking a step back to see the larger picture of what goes on in learning, and how the relationship between students and teachers influences learning. It also means attending to small details which can in turn change the bigger picture. Teacher development is a continuous process of transforming human potential into human performance, a process that is never finished.

The Teacher Development Series offers perspectives on learning that embrace topic, method and person as parts of one larger interacting whole. Katie and Pauline help us to explore these ideas by offering us short selections from a wide range of writers, some from within ELT, some from education generally and some from the field of self-development. Constantly recurring themes are those of learning from our own experience, working with and learning from the experience of others and becoming more active in our own continuous development.

The chosen extracts are woven together with discussions, commentaries and activities through which Katie and Pauline share with us their own insights and enthusiasm, and invite us to participate in bringing out the full possibilities of our own teaching.

As with the other titles in the series, we encourage you to observe, value and understand your own experience, and to evaluate and integrate relevant external practice and knowledge into your own internal evolving model of effective teaching and learning.

Adrian Underhill

Other titles in the Teacher Development Series

Learning Teaching Jim Scrivener

Inside Teaching Tim Bowen and Jonathan Marks

Sound Foundations Adrian Underhill

The ELT Manager's Handbook Graham Impey and Nic Underhill

Introduction to *Readings in Teacher Development*

"Wherever you want to go, you have no choice but to start from where you are." (Karl Popper)

The original idea for this book was inspired by our own experience of professional growth through contact with the 'Teacher Development' movement which emerged in the context of EFL (English as a Foreign Language) teaching in the UK in the mid-1980s. Through involvement in this movement, and specifically in the Teacher Development Special Interest Group of IATEFL (the International Association of Teachers of English as a Foreign Language), we have become aware that teachers all around the world are eager to learn about teacher development and ready to take on more responsibility for their own professional growth.

At the outset we sent letters to a number of teachers personally known to us, who are involved like us in teacher development but in a variety of different countries and institutional contexts, inviting them to send us their 'top ten' list of readings that had made an impact and helped shape their own ideas about teaching. This book started life as a mosaic of such readings, and the many sources on which we have drawn have provided us with insights into the rich variety of meanings of teacher development. As the book has taken shape, it has become more our own, and reflects our own journey in and around the material that has inspired teachers to develop themselves.

Our own teaching experience is that of working with adult learners of English as a Foreign Language in the UK and other countries, and of training EFL teachers. We have both been employed in this field since the late 1970s. Nevertheless, as we have worked with some of the ideas in this book at conferences and workshops, and as we have discussed earlier versions of the manuscript with other teachers, it has become clear that this approach to teacher development has a relevance and an appeal beyond the confines of English language teaching. So we hope that teachers of any subject will find their way into this book and enjoy using it; and as far as possible we have structured the activities so that they open up paths for reflection and action in whatever teaching context you find yourself.

Our purpose has been to weave a colourful tapestry using material from many sources that combine together to make a picture, our picture, of teacher development. We have included:

- material that is relevant and thought-provoking, whether intended for EFL readers or not;
- books and authors that you may have heard of but perhaps not read;
- material that you may not have access to, for example articles from the *Teacher Development Newsletter* (of the IATEFL Special Interest Group) or books that are difficult to find or expensive;

- some writers that you have probably not heard of, but who have given inspiration to other teachers.

Sometimes the reading itself demanded inclusion; sometimes we felt ourselves that a particular idea should be included and then looked around for a suitable reading to accompany the idea.

We have suggested some activities within each chapter to invite you to make personal connections with the ideas presented. They may be used in various ways:

- You can simply read them without stopping to do them. This in itself can be beneficial. Just reading them can trigger ideas.
- You can work on them in more depth, incorporating what you find into your own 'map' of teacher development.
- You may find that you begin to incorporate aspects of the activities into the ways you talk to your students about both *their* learning and *your* learning. You may also decide to use some of the excerpts with your learners.
- Most of the activities can be done by one person working alone. But all of them can benefit from being done as group activities, with participants sharing and challenging each other.
- The activities are designed to connect with each other, so you will find that some overlap. They are also designed to be accumulating, so that they build on each other, and lead towards a deeper understanding of personal development for teachers.

The book contains eight chapters, each with its own focus contributing to the rich and varied picture of teacher development. Each chapter is constructed more like a jigsaw than in a logically ordered sequence. This has always been envisaged as a book to be dipped into, rather than read from beginning to end, and we hope that the division of the material into 'pocket-sized chunks' will allow readers to pick out and use individual pieces of the jigsaw even when time is short. We would rather see the book kept in a handy spot and dipped into briefly but often, than read right through once and abandoned to a top shelf!

The ordering of the chapters has been the result of some shifting around of the material in order to guide the reader from the most basic question of what 'teacher development' actually means (Chapter 1), through its interpretation in the context of work and relationships (Chapters 2 to 5), to concern with the personal well-being of the teacher (Chapter 6). Along the way you will perceive a gradual shift towards the inclusion of more material from sources beyond and outside teaching. Chapter 7, which focuses on ways of managing your own change, embraces the fact that change is a fact of life, and looks at the role of teacher development in the wider context of educational and social change. Chapter 8 looks at some approaches to self-monitoring and appraisal.

We have met regularly and worked as closely together as has been practically possible, given the fact that we live on opposite sides of England and are both working full-time. Each of us contributed a different shade of experience and personal involvement in the area of teacher development. In writing the book, our own ideas and skills have changed and developed, and the process has contributed to our own learning in unexpected ways.

We have aimed to bring together a range of approaches to and ideas about teacher development in a practical and inspiring way. We hope that the enquiring reader who hasn't explored the field before will find here some attractive ideas to provide a direction for their development, and that the teacher who is already familiar with our sources will be glad to have a collection of good readings to dip into and be refreshed by. We have tried to give a broad focus to the area in which we are interested; and while inevitably our selection will reflect a bias towards our own particular understanding of what teacher development is, we hope we have not excluded significant contributions in the wider context of what others in education have said about 'good' teaching and 'good' teachers.

A frequent comment from those teachers who suggested readings for the book was that they experienced their greatest moments of inspiration in learning from other people, either from colleagues around them at work, or in a conference workshop, or even in a classroom event in which something said or done by students provided a spark of deeper understanding. We offer this book as an added resource. We know that it is also common for teachers to experience professional isolation, and that not everyone is able to attend teachers' conferences or have easy access to libraries. We particularly hope that something included in this book will speak personally to you, whatever your situation.

Thanks

This book is a collection of many people's ideas. We are grateful to all those authors and teachers, including our own past teachers, who inspired us and allowed us to use their work.

We would also like to say thank you to all those people who offered us ideas and suggestions of readings that have inspired them. Their generosity and support, together with that of colleagues and friends, helped us to get started and continually refocused our thinking as the book progressed. In particular, we would like to thank Susan Barduhn, Rod Bolitho, Allan Bramall, Rachel Collingbourne, Ros Draper, Julian Edge, Martyn Ford, Bärbel Fink, Richard Hopper, Chantal Kickx, Dave King, Diana Lubelska, Sue Mace, Angi Malderez, Jonathan Marks, Maggie McNorton, Felicity O'Dell, Dave Owen, Maria Elena Perera, Jon Roberts, Jayagowri Shivakumar, Rosie Tanner, Linda Taylor and Rowena Whitehead.

Special thanks to Adrian, Jill and Alyson, our patient editors, for believing in us and encouraging us all the way. Without their expertise and insight we might never have succeeded in shaping our ideas into book form.

Katie Head and Pauline Taylor
Cambridge and Buckfastleigh, Devon

Chapter 1 Defining teacher development

1 Introduction
2 What are the key characteristics of teacher development?
3 What kinds of activities are developmental?
4 What do developing teachers and their students have in common?
5 What's new about teacher development?
6 How are 'training' and 'development' different?
7 How can training and development complement each other?
8 Why is development an important concept in teacher education?
9 How can development be built into initial teacher training programmes?
10 How can outside change become a spur to personal development?
11 Why is it helpful for learners to see that their teachers are capable of developing?
12 Conclusion

1 Introduction

Development means change and growth. Teacher development is the process of becoming 'the best kind of teacher that I personally can be' (Underhill 1986 p1). To the extent that teachers are regularly asking themselves 'How can I become a better teacher?' 'How can I enjoy my teaching more?' 'How can I feel that I am helping learning?' they are thinking about ways of developing. They are acknowledging that it is possible to change the way they teach and perhaps also the preconceptions that they have about teaching and learning.

In this chapter we will look at some of the ideas that have helped to shape *development* as a distinct concept in our thinking about teachers' learning. In giving it a name we seek to define a way of learning which is complementary to *training*, and which is motivated by teachers' own questioning of who they are and what they do, rather than by any external training agenda.

Teacher development, as we understand it, draws on the teacher's own inner resource for change. It is centred on *personal awareness* of the possibilities for change, and of what influences the change process. It builds on the past, because recognizing how past experiences have or have not been developmental helps identify opportunities for change in the present and future. It also draws on the present, in encouraging a fuller awareness of the kind of teacher you are now and of other people's responses to you. It is a *self-reflective* process, because it is through questioning old habits that alternative ways of being and doing are able to emerge. Through the activity below, and those which follow later, we aim to help you experience this process.

Activity

This activity suggests a way of thinking about your own teaching experience up to now, and of noticing the things that have particularly influenced your development.

- Can you identify the particularly important stages in your development as a teacher?
- Which of them were triggered in some way by external events, or by contact with other people?
- Which were brought about by your own accumulating experience?
- You may find it interesting to draw a time line representing the time you have been in teaching, and mark these 'significant phases' on it. Look at the following examples, drawn by two teachers at the end of their first year of teaching, to see what a time line can look like.
- Can you see any patterns or threads in your own development?

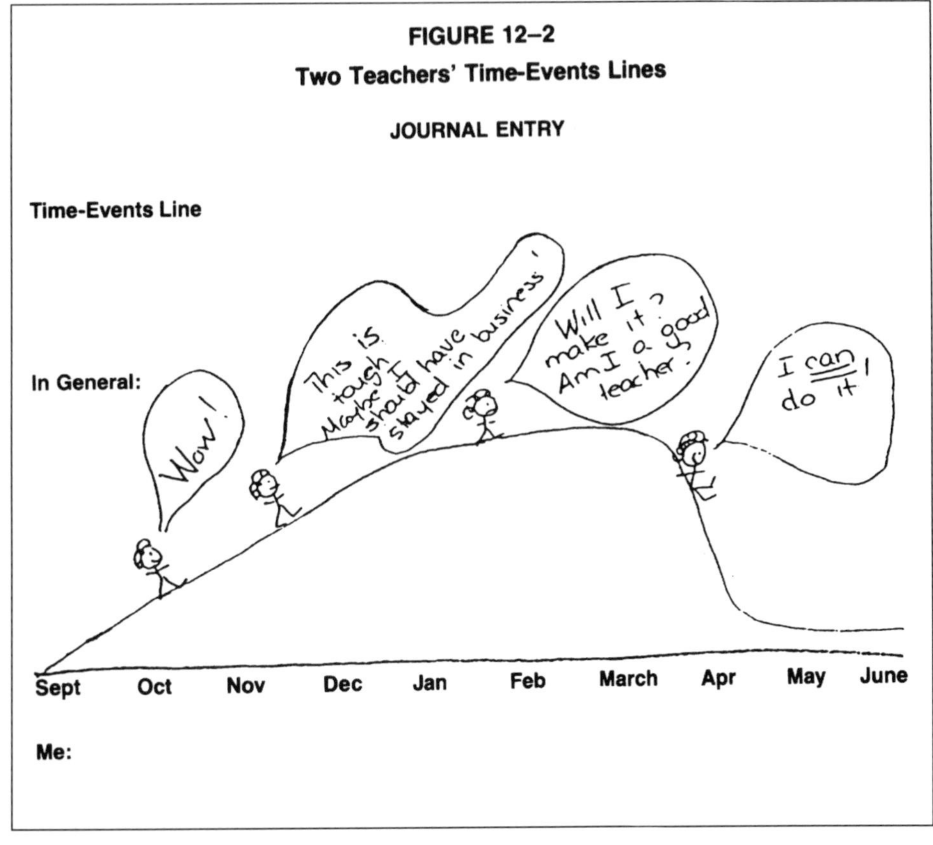

FIGURE 12–2
Two Teachers' Time-Events Lines

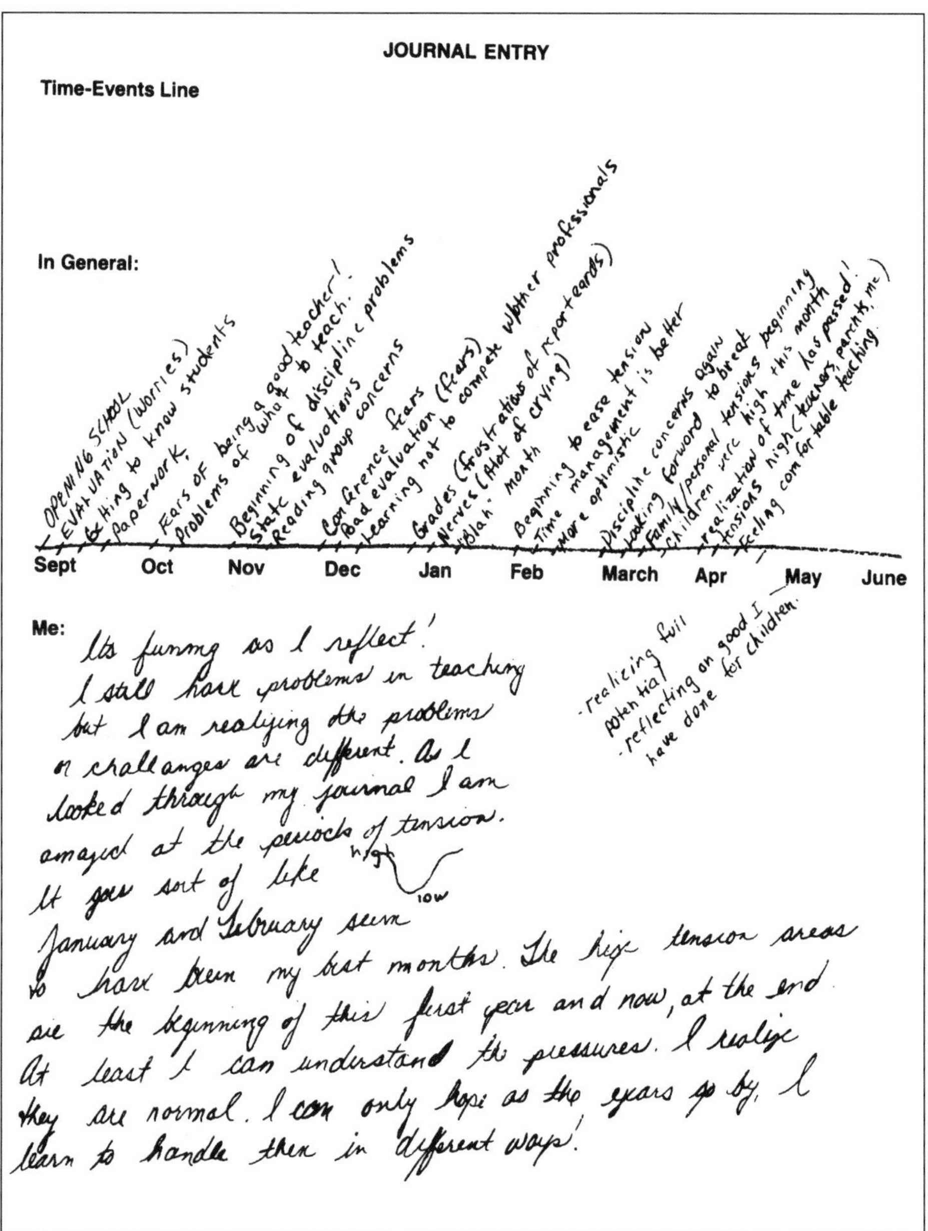

JOURNAL ENTRY

Time-Events Line

In General:

Sept: OPENING SCHOOL / EVALUATION (worries) / Getting to know students / Paperwork

Oct: Fears of being a good teacher! / Problems of what to teach.

Nov: Beginning of discipline problems / State evaluations / Reading group concerns

Dec: Conference fears (fears) / Bad evaluation (fears) / Learning not to compete w/other professionals

Jan: Grades (frustrations of report cards) / Nerves (A lot of crying) / 'Blah' month

Feb: Beginning to ease tension / Time management is better / More optimistic

March: Discipline concerns again / Looking forward to break / Family/personal tensions / Children were high this month

Apr: realization of time has passed! / tensions high (teachers, parents, me) / Feeling comfortable teaching

Sept Oct Nov Dec Jan Feb March Apr May June

Me: It's funny as I reflect! I still have problems in teaching but I am realizing the problems or challanges are different. As I looked through my journal I am amazed at the periods of tension. It goes sort of like [high / low] January and February seem to have been my best months. The high tension areas are the beginning of this first year and now, at the end. At least I can understand the pressures. I realize they are normal. I can only hope as the years go by, I learn to handle them in different ways!

- realizing full potential
- reflecting on good I have done for children.

Holly 1989 pp168–9

There have almost certainly been occasions in the past when your teaching has been strongly influenced by someone you have met, by a new approach or idea, by a change of job or a course you have attended. Perhaps you have also observed periodic shifts in your own approach, when you have decided that something is no longer working for you and that you will try doing things differently. Examples of this might be a decision to trust your learners more and encourage them to give you feedback; to manage your time differently and be more careful about what work you take home with you; or to give particular attention to a skill or area of expertise that interests you. Thinking about the way that you have experienced change and new learning in the past could give you insight into what kind of development you would like for yourself now, and how to go about it.

2 What are the key characteristics of teacher development?

Although development can happen in many different ways, it seems that certain core characteristics emerge when teachers are asked what they think teacher development is. Richard Rossner was interested in finding out what these characteristics were. He conducted an informal survey among EFL teachers both in the UK and other countries. One of the questions he asked the teachers was, *'What do you personally understand by the term "teacher development"?'* Their responses indicated that it has at least the following four key characteristics in teachers' minds.

A It is about dealing with the needs and wants of the individual teacher in ways that suit that individual. The needs may be many and diverse – from confidence-building to language awareness or technical expertise.

B Much of TD is seen as relating to new experiences, new challenges and the opportunity for teachers to broaden their repertoire and take on new responsibilities and challenges. This helps them to fight a feeling of jadedness and also to develop their careers as well as themselves.

C TD is not just to do with language teaching or even teaching: it's also about language development (particularly for teachers whose native language isn't English), counselling skills, assertiveness training, confidence-building, computing, meditation, cultural broadening – almost anything, in fact.

D TD, in most teachers' opinions, has to be 'bottom-up', not dished out by managers according to their own view of what development teachers need. This doesn't mean to say that managers have no role in it ... Nor does it mean that managers should stop organising in-service or other training courses.

Rossner 1992 p4

Because teacher development focuses on individual needs, it takes on different specific meanings and forms depending on where you are working and what your desired direction for development is. Richard Rossner also asked the teachers to describe their *'best teacher development experience'*. Here are some of their responses:

"I was working as a 'foot-soldier' in Madrid, churning out run-of-the-mill, solid stuff. Then my Director of Studies got me involved in giving seminars on a teachers' course. My confidence sky-rocketed, ideas flooded in, I was on my way."

"... my MA course – ... time to reflect and read/talk about my attitudes to learning, teaching, etc."

"A series of seminars in Cairo run by two Egyptian teachers explaining Egyptian culture and particular linguistic problems ..."

"... sitting down with another teacher and planning for a class I was having problems with ..."

"... in the Philippines, I worked on teacher training workshops in the provinces – impoverished areas often caught in the middle of civil war."

"Without a doubt, the use of Total Physical Response ..."

"... a talk on 'teacher guilt' ..."

ibid p5 (abridged)

Activity

Looking back to the previous activity, it may be helpful to ask:

- What were your best development experiences? Can you identify one that was particularly significant?
- What was it about these experiences that helped you to experiment and perhaps change your teaching?
- Do your experiences confirm what Rossner found to be the key characteristics of development?
- And since you know that you can learn from experiences of this kind, can you identify any ways of using opportunities, in the present or in the future, to help you go on developing?

It seems a simple question, but it is important to get to know what helps you to actualize your potential as a teacher, and to keep asking 'What does the concept of development mean to me?'

---

3 What kinds of activities are developmental?

It is a common experience among teachers to feel, after several years of teaching, that they need a fresh impetus to encourage them to go on learning and developing. Most teachers can recognize a point in their career when they have mastered the technical skills. Some believe, having reached that point, that they have attained their own personal best and have nothing more to learn. Some decide to go on to a further course of academic study such as an advanced diploma or Master's degree, or some kind of in-service training.

Many other teachers who are keen to understand more about teaching and learning find, however, that academic courses either are not an option, or seem not to provide an appropriate way of developing themselves. The questions that motivate such teachers to go on learning come from the sense that they have the potential within themselves to become better teachers through deepening their own understanding and awareness of themselves and of their learners.

Development can mean many different things and take many different forms, as teachers find ways of responding to the inner desire that motivates them to learn. In an article written to illustrate the concept of teacher development, Alan Maley uses a series of short sketches to exemplify this variety.

Teacher development explained

What is TD? Since no single definition will suffice, examples may help to characterise a 'family resemblance'.

1 Teacher A feels constantly under stress, is sleeping badly and is off her food. She decides to act. After reading articles/books on stress and on personal organisation she decides to set aside 30 minutes 'quiet time' daily and to use this to make lists of personal action points.

2 Teacher B finds a good practical idea [in a teachers' magazine]. He decides, with a colleague, to try it out for a month and to discuss progress once a week.

3 Ten teachers from school X decide to meet once a month to discuss a book or article all have agreed to read.

4 Eight teachers from school Y decide to meet once a month to talk over problems individuals have encountered. There is no agenda but the group is tolerant and mutually supportive.

5 Teacher C decides to take a course on a non-ELT subject, which she thinks may give new insights for her teaching. (For example, a course on counselling skills, Neuro-Linguistic Programming, photography, and so on.)

6 Teacher D decides to improve his qualifications. He enrols on a RSA Dip. TEFL* course.

7 Teacher E has never written for a publication. She decides to review a recent book she feels enthusiastic about. She seeks advice from more experienced colleagues on how to write it and who to submit it to.

8 Teachers G and H decide to implement ideas they have on learner independence. They set up a small action research project. They present their findings at the next IATEFL** Conference.

Maley 1990 p67

* Royal Society of Arts Diploma in Teaching English as a Foreign Language
**International Association of Teachers of English as a Foreign Language

One characteristic that all these stories have in common is that the teachers themselves decide what they are going to do. They are in charge. It seems that an activity is likely not to be developmental unless it takes on a real personal value for the people involved. Setting yourself a development agenda, irrespective of whatever external constraints are operating (low pay, long hours, inadequate resources, etc) is an important way of acknowledging your own inner needs and desires and of making your experiences more worthwhile.

4 What do developing teachers and their students have in common?

As a model of teacher learning, the kind of development we have described parallels the kind of learning experience that, as teachers, we want to provide for our students. Adrian Underhill sees it like this:

Development means ... keeping myself on the same side of the learning fence as my students. This is the only way that I can keep alive a sense of challenge and adventure in my career, and avoid getting in a rut. If I am in a rut, then so is my teaching, and then so are my students, and learning from a rut is tedious, slow and uninspiring.

Underhill 1988 p4

Activity

Are there times when you have felt that your teaching was in a rut?

- How did this feeling come about?
- How did it affect your teaching?
- How did it affect your self-image?
- How do you think this affected your students?

Are there other times when your teaching has felt fresh, inspiring, interesting?

- What causes you to feel one way or the other?
- And what is the result for you and your learners?

It is important to notice and act on messages from your feelings as well as those which are rationalized by your mind. There is a difference between feeling OK about being where you are and being in a rut. Ruts are difficult to climb out of, because they sap your energy and limit your vision. When you are in a rut, you are not in a learning mode, and this means that you are not keeping yourself on the same side of the learning fence as your students.

5 What's new about teacher development?

It is sometimes claimed that teacher development is nothing new. Certainly, some of the ideas that have most influenced our current thinking about teacher development were first put forward long ago and have been much debated over the years by philosophers, psychologists and educationalists.

There were, however, a number of quite specific reasons why, during the 1980s, English language teachers began to feel the need for some form of self-motivated professional development, and to express this in various ways, through journals, conference papers and workshops, and teachers networking informally together to share ideas.

Within IATEFL, the *Teacher Development Special Interest Group* was formed in 1985 to provide a forum for interested teachers to exchange ideas and to reach a wider audience of teachers all over the world. Adrian Underhill was its founder and first co-ordinator. The information exchange which took place in the *Teacher Development Newsletter* and in correspondence between members revealed that two things were happening: first, that some teachers were already working on their own and in groups, independently of the IATEFL movement, in a variety of ways, on similar issues; second, that many teachers were ready and eager to join in this exchange, which addressed relevant issues concerning their own development, with the support and focus that the Special Interest Group could provide. It became clear that the concerns that led to the formation of the Special Interest Group were not confined to the context in which it was formed initially, but were already engaging very many teachers worldwide who found that personal self-awareness and reflective practice were the key to professional growth.

In an article considering the reasons for the emergence of 'teacher development' as a distinct concept in English language teaching, particularly in the UK, Rod Bolitho identified a number of background factors as significant. They are summarized below from his original paper:

1 The huge expansion of the language teaching industry, bringing large numbers of teachers into the profession, and the lack of a career structure offering opportunities for variety and promotion.
2 The 'mid-life crisis' experienced by many teachers after ten or more years in the field.
3 Low pay and poor conditions of service in many institutions, and many teachers working on temporary or part-time contracts, leading to low morale, low self-esteem, and often a sense of frustration and isolation among teachers.
4 An increasing preoccupation with qualifications. British ELT needed to professionalise itself, yet higher academic courses seldom have the kind of practical orientation that many teachers hope for, and there are no guarantees of a permanent job at the end of them.
5 The influence of 'humanistic' views of language teaching, while from a more academic base studies of second language acquisition were also beginning to focus on the learning process, spawning new ideas of a more learner-centred approach to teaching.

Bolitho 1988 pp2–4 (summarized)

From the demand for workshops and contributions to the newsletter Bolitho concluded that teachers need to convince both themselves and others that they are doing a job which is valued, and that they can take control of the direction of their own development. The kind of teacher development we are talking about in this book provides a conceptual framework for this to happen. Its vitality is centred in the power it gives teachers to make real choices.

6 How are 'training' and 'development' different?

In what has been said up to now, an implicit distinction has been drawn between *training* and *development*. We would now like to make this more explicit.

It has become customary, among people concerned with the definition of what teacher development is *not*, to list the respective merits of training and development in terms of polar opposites. Tessa Woodward points out, however, that comparisons of this kind, while perhaps helpful in drawing attention to some differences of emphasis between types of teacher learning, can also separate and polarize approaches rather than helping to build a fuller, more complete picture.

teacher training	**teacher development**
compulsory	voluntary
competency based	holistic
short term	long term
one-off	ongoing
temporary	continual
external agenda	internal agenda
skill/technique and knowledge based	awareness based, angled towards personal growth and the development of attitudes/insights
compulsory for entry to the profession	non-compulsory
top-down	bottom-up
product/certificate weighted	process weighted
means you can get a job	means you can stay interested in your job
done with experts	done with peers

(Similar to a diagram by Paul Davis in an unpublished paper: What is TD and is it really different to TT?)

With bi-polar scales something has to be on the left and something has to be on the right. Is left dominant? We do belong to a left-to-right reading culture and the dominant or most important elements do tend to come on the left ... the mid points of scales can tend to get de-emphasised and the poles re-emphasised so that ideas and attitudes are gradually crystallised into two opposite and extreme positions ... this crystallisation *can* help us to see our own practice anew and to reflect on its assumptions, but a greater tendency is for the poles to become detached from each other, separated, and for one pole to be labelled 'better' than the other. When this happens, teacher and trainers are dumped into guilty corners or feel 'holier than thou' and the arguments start!

Woodward 1991 pp147–8

It is more useful to see training and development as two complementary components of a fully rounded teacher education. Teacher training essentially concerns knowledge of the topic to be taught, and of the methodology for teaching it. It emphasizes classroom skills and techniques. Teacher development is concerned with the learning atmosphere which is created through the effect of the teacher on the learners, and their effect on the teacher. It has to do with 'presence' and 'people skills', and being aware of how your attitudes and behaviour affect these.

Adrian Underhill has been an important influence within the EFL teaching community in identifying and naming this distinction. In the following excerpt, he defines the difference as he sees it:

The argument for training in this sense may go like this: 'I believe that my effectiveness as a teacher depends largely on my pedagogic skills, and my knowledge of the topic I am teaching, and on all the associated methodology. My teaching is only as good as the techniques or materials that I employ, and I improve by learning more about them. I acknowledge that the kind of person I am affects my teaching, but I don't really see what I can do about this other than by further training and by gaining experience.'

The part of me that argues for development may say things like: 'I believe that my effectiveness as a teacher depends largely on the way I am in the classroom, on my awareness of myself and my effect on others, and on my attitudes towards learners, learning and my own role. I value my facility with pedagogic skills and my knowledge of the topic, but it is the 'me' who operates them that primarily influences their effectiveness. I teach only as well as the atmosphere that I engender. I believe that education is change and that I will not be able to educate unless I am also able to change, otherwise my work will come to have a static quality about it that is not good for me or for my students.'

Underhill 1988 p4

Activity

It may seem artificial to make a distinction between development and training, but it may also be helpful, especially if you can identify distinctions that fit your own experience, as Underhill did in the reading above.

- How do you distinguish training from development?
- Can you make a short 'rough and ready' definition of each for yourself?
- Now, with reference to these two definitions of your own, can you find an example of a change in your teaching that has resulted from 'training', and another that fits better the definition of 'development'?

Perhaps you can easily distinguish training and development effects in your own teaching, or perhaps not. Ideally the two influences go hand in hand, and are two aspects of the same thing – the external knowledge or skill accompanied by the internal insight. But since this often does not happen, we, and others like us who promote the ideas and activities of teacher development, feel the need to draw attention to the possible absence of development by naming it, discussing it, identifying it.

7 How can training and development complement each other?

Some of the dangers of too narrow an emphasis on 'training', in the sense defined above by Adrian Underhill, are examined in the following article by Rod Bolitho. While writing from his own personal perspective about teacher development, he summarizes much of what we have been saying so far. He also raises some important questions about the relationship between teacher needs and institutional needs. In the activity which follows the article, there are some questions to help you focus on a number of issues arising from it. You may find it helpful to look at them before you start reading.

Teacher development – a personal perspective

Although teaching is a skill, the rudiments of which can be acquired by study, imitation of models, evaluation and other means, it is not an activity which can be successfully conducted in a way which is extrinsic to a person's being. The best teachers I know are all people who have achieved an integrity of personality; the best teaching I have been aware of has been at moments when the barriers between teachers and students, between the classroom and the world, have become unnoticeable or irrelevant. Conversely, I have seen technically brilliant teaching which has been devoid of any lasting significance.

These perceptions have consequences for teacher training and teacher development. Affective factors are often neglected on training courses, on the grounds that personalities represent an unwelcome variable, or that they will possibly encourage too much concentration on unpredictable fringe issues. On the other hand, maybe it is wrong to expect too much of training courses, especially initial ones. Most of them take place at a time when trainees are still squaring up to life, and most, too, have a limited amount of time available to achieve minimum stated aims. The problem is that for some teachers, these courses represent an end: 'Now that I am qualified, my professional education is over.'

An alternative view would be: 'Now that I am qualified, the door is open to a new and exciting period of personal and professional growth.' This view would at least partially relegate the initial training course to the status of a skills programme, which is, I believe, its most valuable function. The problem is what follows. Teachers may attend in-service training courses, even MAs in Applied Linguistics, in quest of external solutions and stimuli, with a sharp focus, still, on knowledge and skills. The discontent or ambition which leads them to take such a course may colour their view, preventing them from seeing other ways forward. For the training of teachers (leading to their qualification and certification), usually has very little to do with development; or if it does, the effect is all too often coincidental.

This is not to say that development cannot be planned or budgeted for. In all the debate about quality in education, we often overlook the fact that initial training is massively funded, that in-service training and the acquisition of qualifications are well institutionalised, but that teacher development opportunities are rarely supported. Stale or narrowly subject-bound teachers are a menace to the profession, yet a career structure which emphasises training at the expense of development means that such teachers proliferate. Just how do teachers grow and develop? Some, of course, don't. Some do benefit from further training, though I suspect that the thinking time afforded by a break in routine is at least as valuable as the specialist input. But what about the others? Several teachers I know have benefited enormously from taking yoga courses: the increasing physical confidence and awareness acquired on the courses helped them to combat stress and cope more effectively with their students' demands. Others have attended drama courses, not only to 'add a string to their bow' but also to learn more about themselves. Many 'related disciplines' have a lot to offer teachers in terms of perspective, self-discovery and sensitivity to others.

> Others still have job-swapped or taken leave of absence to work on an overseas contract, bringing them into touch with fresh personal and professional influences ... Paid sabbaticals seem to be a luxury in our cost-conscious age, but a teacher needs breathing space, time to consider fresh ideas, an escape from the downward spiral of weekly routine, for his students' sake as much as his own.
>
> Growth implies space to grow into. As we all know only too well, growth cannot take place if such space is constantly cluttered with aids, materials, demanding students, examinations ... the list is endless. [We need] to examine ways in which the space needed for growth can be offered to teachers, thus helping to redress the balance between training and development.
>
> *Bolitho 1986 p2*

Activity

Rod Bolitho's article raises some interesting questions that you may like to reflect on in relation to your own experience:

- What aspects of your present job did your initial training not prepare you for?
- What did you do/have you done about this?
- What else would have been helpful in your initial training?
- What kind of in-service training would be most helpful to you now?
- What can you do to help bring this about?

Thinking about these questions is likely to raise other questions about how much responsibility you can take upon yourself for initiating change. As Rod Bolitho points out, the best way forward is not always the most obvious one, and there can be risk involved in setting your own development agenda. Questions that are raised include these two: What do I need to change in my teaching/school environment? What do I need to change in myself?

8 Why is development an important concept in teacher education?

Teacher development has sometimes been unhelpfully identified as a further step beyond training, and as being particularly concerned with the needs of experienced teachers as opposed to those in initial training. By keeping it separate from training, we imply that development is something distinct and unusual, and that people who have little or no experience of teaching are not ready to deal with the issues it raises. Yet this is to misrepresent the essential nature of teacher development, which is a reflective way of approaching whatever it is that we are doing as teachers, and at whatever level of experience we are doing it. When better to learn the attitudes and intentions of a developmental outlook, than when we are starting out?

The focus of teacher education is already being extended from a narrowly based training model towards a broader approach in which developmental insights are learned alongside classroom teaching skills. The implications for 'teacher educators' (ie the people who design and implement teacher education programmes both at pre-service and in-service levels) are discussed in the excerpt below by Martha Pennington, a lecturer in teacher education in the US. She argues that viewing teaching as a profession provides a motivation for continuous career growth, and that teacher educators have a responsibility to prepare teachers right from the start to adopt a developmental perspective.

Within the framework of teaching as a profession, teacher preparation aims at the development of competency standards for the field and for the attainment of a certain level of competency for all individuals, while underscoring the importance of individualized professional growth throughout the teaching career. Professional teacher preparation programs will have as goals the development of an extensive repertoire of classroom skills and the judgement to apply these skills as needed. In this way, teacher preparation moves beyond 'training' in the narrow sense to enabling an individual to function in any situation, rather than training for a specific situation ...

For long-term professional development, education can provide the confidence and the knowledge to continue to reach and to grow, while a practicum* or prepracticum* course can, for example, provide experience in accepting feedback and implementing suggestions offered as feedback by another professional – a colleague or supervisor. Education provides the background for helping the teacher to understand what type of feedback is appropriate in different situations; training can teach the candidate how to give that feedback, both to students and to colleagues, in a way that will be most beneficial. Education also aims to build tolerance in future teachers and teacher supervisors, reminding them that there are many different perspectives on teaching, all of which may be equally valid. Practical training experiences can also assist in the development of attitudes that are open to differing perspectives and to modification through experience.

Pennington 1990 pp134–5

*American English terminology for in-service and pre-service training

---

Activity

Martha Pennington draws attention to the importance for teachers of becoming competent in these areas:

1 Individualized professional growth throughout their career

2 Ability to exercise judgement and make choices appropriate to the situation

3 Confidence to reach out towards new goals and objectives

4 Feedback skills

5 Tolerance towards a variety of perspectives on teaching

Think back to your own education as a teacher.

- How far did your teacher education provide you with preparation in each of these five areas?

- If you are a teacher trainer, or someone with responsibility for the development or professional well-being of other teachers, how are you building or would you build such preparation into your work?

---

9 How can development be built into initial teacher training programmes?

Jonathan Marks, an EFL teacher and teacher trainer, proposes some concrete steps that can be taken by those who implement initial training programmes. While they are based on his experience of running courses for native speaker teachers of EFL, he believes that they can be applied to any training context where the trainees have little, or no, previous training or teaching experience. Trainees who are encouraged to adopt a developmental perspective will take away from the course learning which will inform not only their teaching, but also their social skills and attitudes generally.

The following is a summary of the suggestions contained in Jonathan Marks' paper.

Teacher development – right from the start

Teaching practice

1 Allow plenty of time to prepare for and give feedback on teaching practice, if necessary at the expense of reduced seminar time.

2 Encourage trainees to make their own suggestions about lesson content and procedures.

3 Get the trainees to specify lesson aims for themselves as well as for the learners, eg to give equal attention to all the learners in the class, or to ask questions only once and avoid repeating or reformulating them.

Seminars

1 Avoid giving models of 'correct' teaching, as they can be threatening.

2 Use seminars to discuss and review different types of lesson observed or taught by trainees, and guide the discussion towards a typology of appropriate procedures based on the trainees' own observations.

3 Devote some seminar time to discussing ways of developing after the course finishes, eg peer observation, self-observation using video or audio recording, teaching diaries, teachers' groups, professional conferences, etc.

4 Devote some seminar time to 'process reviews' which look at the trainees' feelings and reactions to being a course participant: topics such as coping with tiredness, confusion, what's happening in the group, etc.

Observation

1 Make space for the tutors to teach the learners with the trainees observing. Trainees can use the same procedure for observation and feedback that the tutors are using when they observe a trainee. In this way it can be seen that the tutors, too, acknowledge the value of exploring and developing their own role as teachers and trainers.

2 Give the trainees practice in observing and describing, not only evaluating, what they see, and learning not to mistake the one for the other.

Feedback and assessment

1 Encourage trainees to self-assess their teaching right from the start.

2 Set up a framework for the trainees to get feedback from the learners as well as from other trainees and the tutors.

3 Learn to use good counselling and feedback skills, such as Six Category Intervention Analysis*.

4 Focus on the developmental process happening as the course progresses, rather than getting too distracted by the product of an individual lesson.

Personal support

1 Allow some space on the course for unstructured time when trainees can just be together, eg during coffee breaks, so that they can talk about whatever they need to talk about, and be mutually supportive.

2 Invite teachers with around one year's experience to visit and discuss with the trainees how they have fared, and how they have dealt with the challenges of their first year of teaching.

3 Realise that some trainees will need more help than others, and try to treat each one as an individual.

Marks 1990 pp9–10 (summarized)

*Six Category Intervention Analysis is an interpersonal skills training model designed for professional people whose job requires them to listen, support, guide and give feedback in ways that are honest, direct and supportive. It was developed by John Heron. For a fuller description see Chapter 4.

Activity

With reference to the strategies suggested by Jonathan Marks:

- Which of them were part of your own initial training?
- Which of them were not, but would have helped you if they had been?
- Are there any suggestions in his list which would not have helped you?
- Are there any suggestions in the list which can be helpful to you now?
- Which of these strategies are you already using?

Whether you are involved in teaching or teacher training, you will probably find that Marks' suggestions are worth bearing in mind whenever you are helping a group of learners. All learners bring with them an expectation of what they will be taught and how they will be taught, based on previous learning experience. By encouraging them to reflect on what is going on for them, and to describe precisely and concretely what this experience is, you help them to acquire new learning and integrate it into their way of working.

10 How can outside change become a spur to personal development?

Change is inevitable in the life of any group or institution. Adopting a developmental outlook helps teachers to cope better when they are facing change within and around their work environment. It is important for people to retain a sense of personal control over the extent to which outside change affects them personally.

Michael Fullan has written a number of books based on studies of the effects of educational change on institutions and the people who work in them. He believes that it is essential for teachers to find ways of managing and responding positively to change, not only so that they themselves are not left behind as the world moves on, but also because they have a responsibility to prepare their students to cope with a world in which change is the norm. He writes:

> ... the secret of growth and development is learning how to contend with the forces of change – turning positive forces to our advantage, while blunting negative ones ... It is not possible to solve 'the change problem', but we can learn to live with it more proactively and more productively ... Teachers' capacities to deal with change, learn from it, and help students learn from it will be critical for the future development of societies.
>
> *Fullan 1993 pp vii–ix*

Activity

Consider an occasion when you have had to respond to a change introduced in your workplace.

- How was the change introduced?
- How did you respond to it? Did you welcome it, or did you resist it? Why?
- What are the factors that have an important effect on your response to change?
- Would you like to improve your capacity to cope with change?

Chapter 7 of this book deals more fully with the topic of *change*, and suggests ways of developing your capacity to manage it.

11 Why is it helpful for learners to see that their teachers are capable of developing?

Teachers who have the capacity to go on seeing and doing things in new ways are a powerful example to their students of how it is possible to embrace the opportunities that change brings with it. Michael Fullan sees this as an important role for teachers. He suggests that there are four core capacities which are necessary for dealing positively with change. These are *personal vision-building*, *inquiry*, *mastery* and *collaboration*.

Capacities for managing change

Personal vision-building

It is not a good idea to borrow someone else's vision. Working on vision means examining and re-examining, and making explicit to ourselves why we came into teaching. Asking 'What difference am I trying to make personally?' is a good place to start ... To articulate our vision of the future ... forces us to come out of the closet with doubts about ourselves and what we are doing ... It comes from within, it gives meaning to work, and it exists independently of the particular organization or group we happen to be in ... Once it gets going, personal purpose is not as private as it sounds ... The more one takes the risk to express personal purpose, the more kindred spirits one will find ... Individuals will find that they can convert their own desires into social agendas with others ... When personal purpose is present in numbers it provides the power for deeper change.

Inquiry

Inquiry is necessary at the outset for forming personal purpose. While the latter comes from within, it must be fuelled by information, ideas, dilemmas and other contentions in our environment ... Reflective practice, personal journals, action research, working in innovative mentoring and peer settings are some of the strategies currently available. Inquiry means internalizing norms, habits and techniques for continuous learning.

Mastery

The capacity of mastery is another crucial ingredient. People must behave their way into new ideas and skills, not just think their way into them. Mastery and competence are obviously necessary for effectiveness, but they are also means (not just outcomes) for achieving deeper understanding. New mindsets arise from new mastery as much as the other way around ...

Collaboration

Collaboration is the fourth capacity ... There is a ceiling effect to how much we can learn if we keep to ourselves ... People need one another to learn and to accomplish things. Small-scale collaboration involves the attitude and capacity to form productive mentoring and peer relationships, team building and the like. On a larger scale, it consists of the ability to work in organizations that form cross-institutional partnerships such as school district, university and school-community and business agency alliances, as well as global relationships with individuals and organizations from other cultures ...

We need to go public with a new rationale for why teaching and teacher development is so fundamental to the future of society ... To do so we need the capacities of change agentry.

ibid pp12–18 (headings added)

Activity

Teachers sometimes ask their learners to complete sentences in a way that is true for them. Here are some sentences for you to think about and complete for yourself.

- The difference I am trying to make through my teaching is

  ....

- The kinds of inquiry I use for my continuous learning are

  ....

- The new ideas and skills I am working on mastering are

  ....

- Opportunities that exist for me to work collaboratively with other teachers are

  ....

(They might include setting up peer activities with your colleagues, joining a local or national network of teachers, writing newsletter articles, etc.)

Michael Fullan makes the point that when you begin to communicate your personal vision, you might be surprised to find that other people want to share and extend it. If you keep your ideas to yourself, you are unlikely to be able to push them to the limits of their potential. Working with other people provides the power to accomplish things and to convert your vision into reality.

12 Conclusion

This chapter has looked at what *teacher development* means, in terms of teachers' own understandings of how they go on learning and becoming better at what they are doing. We have presented a view of development which is distinct from training, and which is centred on the teacher's own awareness of himself or herself as a person as well as a teacher. This kind of development involves the teacher in a process of reflecting on experience, exploring the options for change, deciding what can be achieved through personal effort, and setting appropriate goals. It is based on a positive belief in the possibility of change. Development is not only a way forward for experienced teachers who believe that they have unfulfilled potential and who want to go on learning. If its attitudes and beliefs can begin in pre-service training, where trainees can be encouraged to learn from their own developing awareness and reflection alongside feedback from tutors and fellow trainees, then it can continue as a basis for career-long learning.

Chapter 2 Learning about ourselves as teachers

1 Introduction

Not all the knowledge that you bring to your teaching has been learned in formal training. Much of it accumulates from experience. The different teaching or learning situations that you have been in, from childhood onwards, will all have left their mark on the kind of teacher you are today, and on your subjective picture of what 'good' teaching and learning are. Your understanding of yourself and of teaching are shaped not only by the teacher training you have received but also by contact with people (your students, other teachers, your family and friends), by working with different kinds of materials and resources, by all the many different experiences that shape your life and make you the person – and the teacher – that you are.

Teachers, when asked *why* they do what they do in order to help their students learn, often find it hard to articulate the beliefs and attitudes which underlie the way they teach. But change may not be developmental unless it involves a challenge to these beliefs, and a willingness to recognize that they may no longer be serving you well. This is why it is important to examine those beliefs, to think about why you hold them and where they may have come from, as a first step in deciding what you would like to change and how.

In this chapter we look at what teachers know and how they use that knowledge. We consider some ways of using a reflective approach to deepen your awareness of what it is that you know about teaching and learning and why, as a teacher, you do what you do. Teachers who take time to reflect on such questions find that they are constantly discovering more about themselves and the way they teach. We will look at some common beliefs and patterns of behaviour which can block development, and suggest some approaches to changing them.

Underlying this approach to teacher development is a belief that the way we experience what is going on, and the feelings that we have about it, provide us with important information about ourselves which can be useful in deciding on next steps. This is what we refer to as paying attention to *process* (see Chapter 3 for more about this). The rationale for teaching and learning through attention to personal needs and goals, and supporting the individual's own search for solutions, has a basis in humanistic psychology. As you work with the material in this chapter and make your own personal connections through the activities suggested, you may also want to consider how far, in the way you teach, you in turn provide this kind of learning experience for your students.

2 What do teachers know?

What kind of knowledge do teachers have? How is that knowledge organized? How do they use it to do what they do in classrooms? Donald Freeman, a teacher educator and researcher in the US, has been interested in these questions for a number of years. In the following extract he compares three different views of teachers' knowledge. He calls them *teaching as doing things*, *teaching as thinking and doing* and *teaching as knowing what to do*, and he argues that only the third of these views accounts properly for the context-dependent way in which teachers apply what they know.

Three views of teachers' knowledge

... In the society at large, teaching is generally seen as doing things – as behaviors and actions which lead hopefully to other people's learning. ... The problem is that this view of teaching as doing vastly simplifies an extremely complex process. It simplifies the process of teaching by not attending to the role that the teacher as a thinking person plays in it. ...

We reframe our view in important ways when we see teaching as thinking and doing. Now teaching includes the crucial cognitive and affective dimensions which accompany and indeed shape the behaviors and actions which teachers do in classrooms. ...

To understand how teachers cope with the complexities of their work ... we have to adopt a view which takes into account not only what teachers do, but also what they think about. This means looking at teaching from a different perspective.

Perhaps an example is useful here. Take planning, for instance. When teachers-in-training are taught about lesson planning, they are usually introduced to the notion of objectives, of specifying the content of what they are teaching, and of blending that content into appropriate activities. The aim of teaching novice teachers to plan in this way is to help them organize what they will do in the lesson, to identify what actions or behaviors will carry out their purposes most efficiently and effectively.

However, in the late seventies, when teacher-thinking research began to probe the actual planning processes which teachers use, some interesting findings arose. ... The findings are that teachers do not naturally think about planning in the organized formulae they are taught to use when in training. Further, if they do plan lessons according to these formats, they often do not teach them according to plan. Teachers are much more likely to visualize lessons as clusters or sequences of activity. They will blend content with activity, and they will often focus on their particular students. In other words, teachers tend to plan ways of doing things for a given group of students, rather than to plan for a particular objective. ...

Teaching is not simply thinking and doing, it involves context – who you are teaching and why – in profound ways. This may be why, when you ask experienced teachers about aspects of their work, they will often preface their responses with 'It depends ...' The following vignette illustrates this contingent sense of 'it depends' knowledge.

> At a conference last year, I remember running into a colleague in the hall between sessions. This woman is a senior teacher and teacher educator, who I seem to only see once a year at such conventions. As we talked, she mentioned that she had just come from a session which she found interesting. The presenter had asked people to rate various common techniques on a Likert scale from one to five, according to whether they should use them as teachers and whether they would like to have them used as students. The intent was to illustrate the parallels and discontinuities between what we do as teachers and what we prefer as learners. My friend said she found the exercise extremely frustrating. 'How can I respond in that sort of exercise as a teacher?' she said. 'So much of which technique I use depends ... it depends on so many things.'

If we stick to the view of teaching as behavior, we may be tempted to see such 'it depends' responses as reflections of the imprecise nature of what teachers know ... difficult to measure, let alone assess.

If we see teaching as thought linked to behavior, we may see such 'it depends' statements as evidence of the individual and subjective nature of what teachers are thinking about. This can make measuring such knowledge according to some general standard, as groups which are creating professional standards for teachers attempt to do, very difficult and messy.

But if teaching is seen as knowing what to do, then the classroom context and the people in it become central and crucial. They are not just settings for implementation; they provide frameworks for knowing. In this third view, the 'it depends' statements which teachers often make are evidence of the highly complex, interpretative knowledge which they must have in order to do their work.

Freeman 1992 pp1–3

Activity

Donald Freeman says that 'knowing what to do' is a complex process of continually adapting your lessons to the needs of the particular classroom situation, some of which cannot be known in advance.

Reflecting on the way you plan and teach lessons:

- Can you think of an occasion when your teaching was based on 'doing' what someone else had suggested or decided, using the lesson material or technique as given, without adapting it in any way? Can you suggest some situations in which this is an acceptable, or even correct, way to teach? How does it make you feel?
- How much 'thinking' do you typically do in advance of a lesson, and how carefully do you plan your lessons? What are the advantages of advance planning? Are there any disadvantages? Is it more important to plan for some kinds of lessons than for others?
- When you are teaching a prepared lesson, to what extent are you able to allow learners' reactions to influence and even redirect the lesson content? How do you balance the need to cover the curriculum with the need to be responsive to your learners as people?
- Do you feel that 'knowing what to do' is an appropriate description of the way you use your knowledge in teaching? Can you think of any points of conflict between what you were taught on teacher training courses and what you have learned from experience?
- What effect do the teachers' books that accompany published coursebooks have on the above?

3 Knowing-in-action

Much of the knowledge that teachers have is acquired through experience of actually doing the job. Donald Schön, an American sociologist who has studied the habits of thinking and acting that professional people use, calls this kind of knowledge *knowing-in-action*, and sees it as characteristic of the way that professionals work. Knowing-in-action means teachers being able to make the necessary on-the-spot practical decisions to cope with problems as they arise while a lesson is in progress. Schön defines it as the skill of making spontaneous yet appropriate responses in 'situations of unavoidable uncertainty'.

When we go about the spontaneous, intuitive performance of the actions of everyday life, we show ourselves to be knowledgeable in a special way. Often we cannot say what it is that we know. When we try to describe it we find ourselves at a loss, or we produce descriptions that are obviously inappropriate. Our knowing is ordinarily tacit, implicit in our patterns of action and in our feel for the stuff with which we are dealing. It seems right to say that our knowing is *in* our action.

Similarly, the workaday life of the professional depends on tacit knowing-in-action ... In his day-to-day practice he makes innumerable judgements of quality for which he cannot state adequate criteria, and he displays skills for which he cannot state the rules and procedures. Even when he makes conscious use of research-based theories and techniques, he is dependent on tacit recognitions, judgements, and skillful performances.

Schön 1983 pp49–50

4 Reflection-in-action

Professionals who combine the skill of making on-the-spot decisions with a reflective approach, who take some time to review the moment of decision, to examine what influenced it and what the alternatives might have been, engage themselves in a process of self-directed learning based on personal experience. Schön calls this learning process 'reflection-in-action'.

... both ordinary people and professional practitioners often think about what they are doing, sometimes even while doing it. Stimulated by surprise, they turn thought back on action and on the knowing which is implicit in action. They may ask themselves, for example, 'What features do I notice when I recognize this thing? What are the criteria by which I make this judgement? What procedures am I enacting when I perform this skill? How am I framing the problem that I am trying to solve?' ... There is some puzzling, or troubling, or interesting phenomenon with which the individual is trying to deal. As he tries to make sense of it, he also reflects on the understandings which he surfaces, criticizes, restructures, and embodies in further action. It is this entire process of reflection-in-action which is central to the 'art' by which practitioners sometimes deal well with situations of uncertainty, instability, uniqueness, and value conflict.

ibid p50

5 Applying a reflective approach in teacher training and development

Michael Wallace, who has worked in ELT teacher education for many years, acknowledges that most training courses do not prepare teachers for the kinds of situations that involve on-the-spot responses. Teachers develop skill in dealing with these situations through actual classroom experience, and are far more likely to explain their actions in terms of what was happening at the moment of decision, and of the feeling that they had about it, than to refer back to the received wisdom of their past training. For this reason Wallace favours encouraging a reflective approach in teaching and in teacher training and development at all levels.

Activity

This activity is from Michael Wallace's book *Training Foreign Language Teachers: A Reflective Approach (1991 p14).*

Think back to some incident or development that happened in class which you had not planned for, eg

- a disciplinary problem
- an unpredicted error made by a student
- an unexpected lack of understanding
- a decision on your part that you would have to teach the lesson differently from what was planned, etc.

1 What was the problem or development exactly?

2 How did you handle it?

3 Why did you handle it the way you did?

4 Would you handle it in the same way again? If not, why not?

5 Has the incident changed your general view of how to go about the practice of teaching? (For example, you may have decided in general to be more strict, to use groupwork less, to ask more questions, etc.)

Getting behind the action, to an understanding of how the action came about, gives us information about ourselves and our handling of the situation which we can usefully reflect on. Whether we decide that we handled the situation appropriately, or that we would like to do things differently next time, by looking at the alternatives in this way we find out what it is that we really want for ourselves.

6 The theory of experiential learning

As soon as you begin to engage in the kind of reflective process described above, you will notice that there are aspects of your teaching that you would like to change, and alternative courses of action that are open to you. D. A. Kolb, who has studied the theory and origins of experiential learning, believes that this pattern of examining and modifying your existing beliefs and habits leads to the most effective learning.

Kolb defines experiential learning as 'the process whereby knowledge is created through the transformation of experience' (Kolb 1984 p38). Key characteristics are:

1 Learning is conceived as a process, not as a series of outcomes.

2 This process is continuous, and grounded in the learner's own experience.

3 It involves bringing out the learner's existing beliefs and theories, testing them against new experiences and insights, and reintegrating the new, more refined ideas that evolve through this process of examination and reflection.

4 It is a process of ongoing adaptation to an environment which is constantly changing.

Activity

Although experiential learning has been advocated and written about since ancient Greek times, it is only recently that it has been so systematically and widely discussed.

- Was your own learning at school typically characterized by 'being told things by teachers who knew more than you' or was there also a significant element of experiential learning? Can you recall examples?
- Are you able to say whether either approach was more helpful, or successful, or enjoyable than the other?
- Whatever your answer to the first two questions, have you found that once you started teaching you wanted, or were required, to teach in a way that was more experiential than the way you were taught at school?
- If so, what challenges has this presented to you?
- And what do your students seem to prefer?

If you were a successful learner in a traditional school environment where the teacher was 'the expert' and the motivation to learn what he or she already knew was enough for you, you may find it hard to imagine a different basis for structuring your own learning or that of your students. You may like a teacher who takes charge of the learning programme and decides for you what you need to know. On the other hand, if you found it hard to relate what you learned in school to your own personal interests and needs, you will probably be unsympathetic to the kind of teaching that offers an expert view. Whichever learning style you prefer, it is important to be aware that learning happens on the inside, and to acknowledge that the choice you are making is not the only possible one. Quite possibly you find a flexible and sympathetic blend of both approaches to be the most helpful.

7 Making the connection between past and present

Memory aids development by enabling us to learn from past experience and to recognize links with present behaviour patterns. John Dewey, one of the earliest advocates of experiential learning, wrote:

> ... the principle of continuity of experience means that every experience both takes up something from those which have gone before and modifies in some way the quality of those which come after ... As an individual passes from one situation to another, his world, his environment, expands or contracts. He does not find himself living in another world but in a different part or aspect of one and the same world. What he has learned in the way of knowledge and skill in one situation becomes an instrument of understanding and dealing effectively with the situations which follow. The process goes on as long as life and learning continue.
>
> *Dewey 1938 pp35, 44*

8 Recognizing your 'ghosts'

Memories of some of your own teachers can exert a powerful influence on your mental picture of the kind of teacher you would like (or not like!) to be. Acknowledging the presence of these 'ghosts' can help you examine how you appear to your students, and how classroom rapport can be affected by the teacher's personality and behaviour.

An effect of recalling memories of past teachers is that you are likely to become aware of certain things that you also do when you are teaching, and you may decide that you would like to change some of them. In an account of a teachers' workshop, Ephraim Weintroub describes one participant's memories of her old Latin teacher. As she recalled her feelings about this teacher's presence in the classroom, she managed to confront negative aspects of her own teaching behaviour.

> A teacher sitting across the circle in the small group twisted awkwardly and then joined the debate for the first time. I was relieved to hear her voice because others had long since broken the barrier of silence. 'I once had a teacher of Latin whom I remember vividly,' she began hesitantly. 'He was a wonderful teacher – so knowledgeable, so strong ... er ... but ...,' she hesitated, 'he terrified me.' She stopped as if in shame. We waited and held our breath. Our silent support encouraged her.
>
> 'He was so cynical and so sarcastic, a cruel hurting tongue. Any mistake would earn you a tongue lashing. On the one hand, I was terrified, but he also angered me enough that I forced myself to excel ... to beat him at his game. I became his best pupil. For years, he used to say that he had never had a pupil like me. And yet he terrified me and every lesson had its own terrors for me.' ...

In recalling the effect that her Latin teacher's behaviour had had on her, this teacher was taking a first step towards identifying something significant about her own teaching.

> As the workshop progressed, participants were asked to describe their own modes of work in their own classes. After giving the matter a great deal of thought, she said, 'I think many pupils must admire me because my lessons are brilliant. I make my pupils think and I stretch them to the limit. There are, I suppose, moments when they fear my caustic wit. I have such a sharp tongue ...' It was at this moment that her previous words echoed in our minds. She had adopted the mode of the teacher who had so terrorized her. This man whom she had admired had become integrated into her teaching persona. The sheer force of his teaching presence had led her to unconsciously adopt a similar stance, ignoring the consequences of this kind of behaviour. Now that she had had to remember the negative effects and to realize their impact on her childhood, she would of necessity have to deal with this in her own classroom.
>
> *Weintroub 1993 pp24–5*

Activity

- Recall a teacher from your own past. Picture the place, the time, how old you were and what you were doing, and the other people (if any) who were there with you.

- What were the particular qualities of this teacher?
- What were your feelings while you were working with him/her?
- Now imagine what it is like to be a student in a class taught by you.
- Can you identify any echoes of 'ghosts' from the past in your own teaching?

Being able to relate to our own 'teaching ghosts' and acknowledge how they have influenced our teaching is an important aspect of personal learning. We would also do well to pay attention to the feelings that emerge from this reflection, as they will still be around today in the relationships we build with our own learners. If recalling a teacher from your past brought back feelings of pain or anger, you may find it useful to think about whether you have noticed similar feelings in your learners and how something *you* do, perhaps unconsciously, might have led to these feelings. How do you then respond to learners who show these feelings? Is it the kind of response you would have liked from your own teachers? If the recollection was a happy and satisfying one, you can draw on this memory to heighten your awareness of the importance of establishing trust between teacher and learners.

9 Getting out of the groove

One thing which can hinder the lifelong learning process that Dewey describes in section 7 is a person's own assumption that things will not change, or that they cannot create the kind of change they would like for themselves. A reflective approach to your work can help you become aware of where these unconscious beliefs come from and how they influence your behaviour. Replacing a disabling pattern of beliefs with an enabling one may be all that is needed to move you on. In his book *The Inner Game of Tennis*, Timothy Gallwey uses analogies from the world of tennis to explore the power of inner motivation to influence the quality of outer performance. He points out that developmental learning is very often a process of 'unlearning' old habits and recovering a childlike interest in experimentation and discovery.

> There is a far more natural and effective process for learning and doing almost anything than most of us realize. It is similar to the process we all used, but soon forgot, as we learned to walk and talk. It uses the so-called unconscious mind more than the deliberate 'self-conscious' mind ... This process doesn't have to be learned; we already know it. All that is needed is to *un*learn those habits which interfere with it and then to just *let it happen*.
>
> *Gallwey 1974 p12*

Tennis players often need to unlearn old habits of play in order to improve their game. One of the keys to this is mastery of the 'inner game' which keeps repeating negative mental messages and reinforcing the old patterns of behaviour which are preventing change. As with tennis, so too in teaching our old habits are sometimes hindering us from being as effective as we could be, and it is only our inner fears and uncertainties about what might happen if we gave them up that stand in the way of our trying out alternatives which might serve us far better.

One hears a lot about grooving one's strokes in tennis. The theory is a simple one: every time you swing your racket in a certain way, you increase the probabilities that you will swing that way again. In this way patterns, called grooves, build up which have a predisposition to repeat themselves ... Every time an action is performed, a slight impression is made in the microscopic cells of the brain, just as a leaf blowing over a fine-grained beach of sand will leave its faint trace. When the same action is repeated, the groove is made slightly deeper. After many similar actions there is a more recognizable groove into which the needle of behavior seems to fall automatically. Then the behavior can be termed grooved.

Because these patterns are serving a function, the behavior is reinforced or rewarded and tends to continue. The deeper the groove in the nervous system, the harder it seems to be to break the habit. ... If you watch a player trying to correct the habit of rolling his racket over, he will usually be seen gritting his teeth and exerting all his will power to get out of his old groove ... Usually the battle is won only after a great deal of struggle and frustration over the course of some time.

It is a painful process to fight one's way out of a deep mental groove. It's like digging yourself out of a trench. But there is a natural and more childlike method. A child doesn't dig his way out of old grooves; he simply starts new ones! The groove may be there, but you're not in it unless you put yourself there. If you think you are controlled by a bad habit, then you will feel you have to try to break it. A child doesn't have to break the habit of crawling, because he doesn't think he has a habit. He simply leaves it as he finds walking an easier way to get around.

Habits are statements about the past, and the past is gone. I'm not even sure it exists, since I don't experience it except as a memory or a concept in the present ... In short, there is no need to fight old habits. Start new ones. It is the resisting of an old habit that puts you in that trench. Starting a new pattern is easy when done with childlike disregard for imagined difficulties. You can prove this to yourself by your own experience.

ibid pp67–9

Activity

With reference to the excerpt from Timothy Gallwey, it can be interesting and helpful to identify such 'grooves' in our teaching. The trouble is that when you are in a groove it's usually difficult to recognize it! It's easier to spot grooves that others are in. So try this:

- What teaching habits might a student, sitting in your class now and being taught by you, identify as being your 'grooves'?
- How can you find out more about this?

---

10 Breaking your own rules

Breaking rules is a way of increasing the number of choices you have, and of liberating yourself from the grip of your habits. John Fanselow wrote a whole book for teachers advocating *Breaking Rules* (Fanselow 1987). Tessa Woodward, who is a teacher trainer, found that Fanselow's approach provided a way of exploring and developing her own teaching, and that she was also able to incorporate this into her workshops for teachers. In the following text she describes what happened during one workshop.

Some teachers attending a workshop came up with the following set of rules that they took for granted:

- I never leave the door open.
- I never move the furniture.
- Teachers mustn't leave the room during class.
- Only one student can approach the teacher's desk at a time.
- Students must put their hands up before speaking.
- I always carry chalk with me, in my pocket.
- I always put my materials and books to the right of the room as I face the students.
- No two-language dictionaries are allowed in class.
- The students must only speak English in class.
- No student corrects another student.

The teachers who gave these rules generally stuck to them closely. In some cases (eg carrying their own chalk) the rule had been formed to create a feeling of security and safety (this teacher felt bereft if he forgot his chalk and so couldn't use the board). Some rules had been formed as a result of colleague pressure (eg no furniture moving – my colleague doesn't like the noise). Other rules had been handed down subconsciously from watching teachers years ago (eg leaving the door shut). Yet others had never been thought about consciously before.

In some cases the teachers felt that the ground rules made good common sense. They were happy with them and wanted to keep them. In other cases the teachers felt that some interesting things could happen if the rules were broken. One thing I noticed was how much laughter there was as people mentioned their own rules: everybody else's rules sounded idiosyncratic, our *own* rules sounded sensible! ...

Since then I have been watching myself and thinking: I have lots of routines, some of which are useful, some are pure habit. I am now starting to break some of my own rules to see what will happen and talking to others about rules they have broken ... It seems that even tiny changes can have interesting results.

Woodward 1989 p19

Activity

- What are some of the 'rules' that have become ingrained in your teaching?
- How does each one affect your teaching?
- What do you think would happen if you broke each of the rules?
- Choose one, decide exactly how you could break it, and then do so for the next week. Monitor yourself.

- How easy or difficult was it to stick to breaking the rule?
- Did anybody else notice or comment?
- Do you want to stay with the new behaviour, go back to the old rule or try something different?
- Whatever you decide, it may help to think about *why* you are making a particular choice, and what it implies about your teaching.

This kind of activity has all the characteristics of a mini classroom research project (see Chapter 8) and is quite a useful way of getting started with research. It is worth noting down what happens at each stage, and the reasons for your decisions, so that you can reflect on them later and review the extent to which the process has been developmental.

11 Disabling feelings: guilt

Opening up to the possibility of changing our existing ideas and beliefs about teaching is often a risky business, and it is not made any easier by anxieties about what we are already doing. A sense of guilt and failure is common among teachers, and we rarely take the time to consider what gives us confidence in our teaching. In this next article, written for the *Teacher Development Newsletter*, Keith Ricketts explains some personal tactics that he uses. At the time of writing Keith was teaching in a private EFL school in the UK.

During a recent discussion among colleagues, a feeling that kept arising was that of guilt, exemplified by such remarks as 'I know I could do more' or 'Everybody seems to be doing a good job except me'. These anxieties that we are not quite up to the job in some way often seem to characterise discussion among teachers about our work.

I notice that everybody carries something like this around with them, but it is patently false. Feelings of inadequacy breed guilt and lead to individuals becoming 'frozen', i.e. we cannot change either ourselves or our working environment if we feel less than worthwhile for much of the time. To shift guilt means developing our perceptions of ourselves as people. Guilty feelings prevent us from seeing who we really are. Here are a few tactics I have used to overcome the effects of TEFL-induced guilt.

1. Stop putting myself down. I am a trained teacher who is intelligent, creative and with the potential for positive influence on the lives of my students and so of the world.
2. Interrupt those who put themselves/others down.
3. Don't moan. Moaning equals gathering in corners to say how bad something is, rather than taking positive steps about real grievances. Try it for a week and see the effects.
4. In class itself, ask students to say what they have learnt and liked about lessons as well as what they want to change. If I do this openly, honestly, and without defensiveness, I may be pleasantly surprised.

5 Review for the day/week the things I have done well in and outside the classroom.

6 Share with others my successes as a teacher and why I enjoy being a teacher.

7 Recall all the compliments I have been paid implicitly and explicitly by students/colleagues. Treat them as having definite validity. There can't be that many liars in the world!

Ricketts 1986 p9 (abridged)

Activity

- Do you carry around guilt about aspects of your work?
- What effect does this have on you?
- Try monitoring your own behaviour during the next week, and resolve to arm yourself against feelings of guilt using one of Ricketts' strategies, or one of your own.

---

12 Disabling feelings: fear and anxiety

Many teachers resist changing to a more humanistic approach in class because they are uncertain and afraid of what may happen. Gertrude Moskowitz believes this is largely because they have not prepared for uncertainty in their own learning and professional training. In the introduction to her book *Caring and Sharing in the Foreign Language Class*, she acknowledges the fears that teachers have and explains why they are based on misapprehensions of what is involved.

Some of the fears expressed by teachers take the form of worrying that the foreign language teacher will take on the role of psychologist. In effect, teachers may already be in that role whether they admit it or not. We all have the power to make others feel better or worse about themselves, but teachers, in particular, have this power with every sentence they utter. In using self-awareness techniques, teachers try to *enhance the student's personal growth* along with his growth in the target language. By doing so, they recognize that affective goals are a legitimate part of the curriculum ...

Another fear some teachers have is that they may do some unintentional damage to students, since emotions and feelings are not areas customarily delved into. Their concern is generally unwarranted. Sensitive teachers will deal sensitively in most classroom situations, just as insensitive teachers will be consistent with their own behavior patterns ...

Being innovative does indeed involve some risk-taking, but the need for innovation in the schools is quite pronounced. Generally, schools have not encouraged combining affective experiences with the learning of subject matter. This is no doubt one reason why many youngsters don't find the classroom a place where things that are important to their lives happen.

Moskowitz 1978 pp18–19

Activity

- Can you recall feeling afraid of trying something new in your teaching?
- What exactly was the fear? (failure? ridicule? making a mistake? drying up?)
- Can you say what caused the fear?
  - your inexperience?
  - something in your past learning?
  - some limiting belief from your own training?
  - the influence of a colleague or manager?
- Think about trying something new with your class. What is the worst that could happen?
- What do you know about your learners and about yourself that would counter these fears?

You may find it interesting to look at some of your fears from the angle of the learners as well as your own. In a humanistic approach it is important that you allow your learners opportunities to teach you, and that you are not afraid to learn. In language teaching particularly, drawing on the learners' own personal stories, encouraging them to express real opinions and feelings in class, provides meaningful opportunities for language practice and helps the group to cohere. There is more about this in Chapter 3.

13 'The can of worms'

Chris Aldred, who trains teachers in the UK, has found that all kinds of issues are brought into the open when teachers begin to talk about the difficulties they experience in coping with their own anxieties. She likes to use metaphor and analogy in her teaching and in her thinking about teaching. Here she explains how she uses the metaphor of 'opening a can of worms' as a way of exploring teachers' worries and helping them deal with them. In the activity which follows, she presents a model she uses in her own teacher training, and you are then invited to lift the lid on your own can of worms.

The 'opening the can' metaphor struck me as an appropriate way of thinking about my role in working with teachers. The 'can' here is obviously ambiguous; meaning both building confidence, encouraging the realisation of potential or empowerment of teachers so that they feel they 'can', and also bringing into the public domain aspects of professional and sometimes personal lives from the hidden or known-to-self domains in the 'can'. It will be obvious that I have been influenced by the humanistic movement in education, but I believe I am not alone in questioning its wholesale adoption. For there are many types of 'can', they need to be opened in different ways, as with the sardine can we can easily lose the key, or with the beer can a sudden wrong movement can tear the ring-pull off, leaving the can well and truly sealed.

The initial reflection activities presented here have been developed as a result of a growing recognition that I needed to think seriously about my approach and what seemed to be a too frequent mismatch between my beliefs and the techniques I was using, and the approaches and beliefs of teachers I was

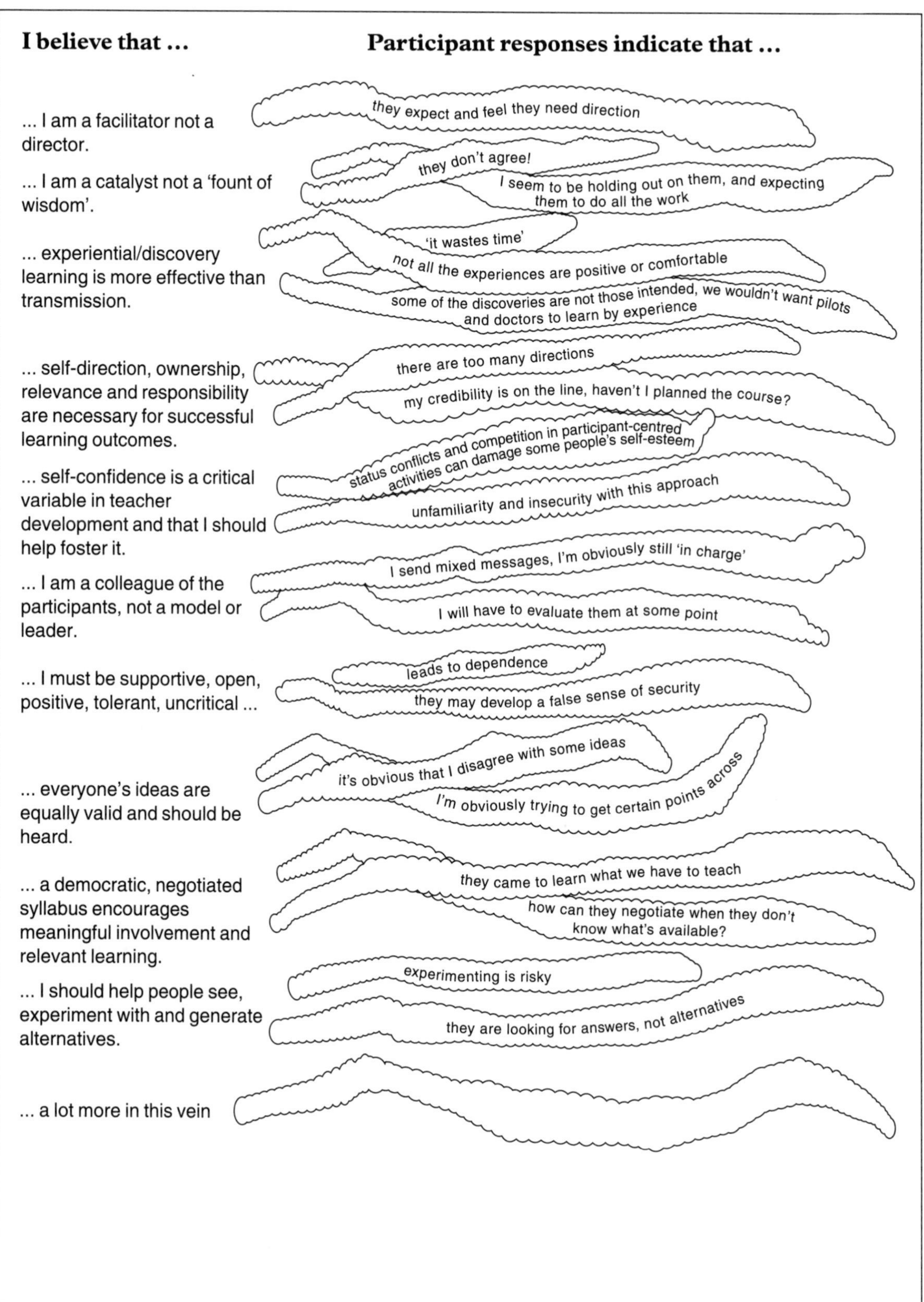
I believe that ...
Participant responses indicate that ...
... I am a facilitator not a director.
they expect and feel they need direction
... I am a catalyst not a 'fount of wisdom'.
they don't agree!
I seem to be holding out on them, and expecting them to do all the work
... experiential/discovery learning is more effective than transmission.
'it wastes time'
not all the experiences are positive or comfortable
some of the discoveries are not those intended, we wouldn't want pilots and doctors to learn by experience
... self-direction, ownership, relevance and responsibility are necessary for successful learning outcomes.
there are too many directions
my credibility is on the line, haven't I planned the course?
... self-confidence is a critical variable in teacher development and that I should help foster it.
status conflicts and competition in participant-centred activities can damage some people's self-esteem
unfamiliarity and insecurity with this approach
... I am a colleague of the participants, not a model or leader.
I send mixed messages, I'm obviously still 'in charge'
I will have to evaluate them at some point
... I must be supportive, open, positive, tolerant, uncritical ...
leads to dependence
they may develop a false sense of security
... everyone's ideas are equally valid and should be heard.
it's obvious that I disagree with some ideas
I'm obviously trying to get certain points across
... a democratic, negotiated syllabus encourages meaningful involvement and relevant learning.
they came to learn what we have to teach
how can they negotiate when they don't know what's available?
... I should help people see, experiment with and generate alternatives.
experimenting is risky
they are looking for answers, not alternatives
... a lot more in this vein

> working with, as conveyed to me by their responses. These responses are the 'worms', initially perceived as problems but nowadays, on reflection, I like to see the 'worms' as the gardener or the fisherman does ... as fertiliser or bait.
>
> I made a list of beliefs I hold about my role in teacher development and rationale underpinning techniques I use in the classroom ... I then recorded what I understood, often inferred, from the responses of teachers I was working with. The gap gave me food for thought.
>
> *Aldred (unpublished paper)*

Chris Aldred represented her own set of beliefs about her role as a teacher trainer, and the 'worms' that gnawed away at them (see overleaf). The worms represent projections of her own uncertainties about whether she is giving her students what they want, as well as things that they have actually said.

Activity

After looking at the way in which Chris Aldred has set out her list of beliefs and the contents of her 'can of worms', you may find it helpful to do the same activity yourself.

- Write down on the left-hand side of a worksheet a list of the beliefs you hold about teaching and learning. Alongside each belief, write some phrases in the worms you have drawn beside it, which reflect the kinds of responses you have had from learners (called participants on the worksheet), or what you predict will be their responses, given the background of your learners.
- Look at your list and the can of worms. Are there any gaps between the beliefs you hold and your learners' responses?
- Can you think of any activities that you use or could use, by yourself or in a group, to help bridge these gaps?

Chris Aldred uses various activities throughout her training courses to help her trainees bridge their gaps. One of them is based around aphorisms. These are some of the sayings that she uses:

A journey of a thousand miles begins with one step.

If you keep on doing what you've always done, you'll keep on getting what you've always got.

If you say you can and if you say you can't, you're right!

If you give someone a fish, you feed them for one day; if you teach them to catch fish you feed them for life.

I hear and I forget, I see and I remember, I do and I understand.

She explains:

I most often give each member of a small group one saying to memorise, present and explain to the group, and then ask the group to talk about the potential significance of each saying.

I remember an occasion while working with some teachers in China, when weeks after we had discussed giving a man a fish, one of the group, frustrated by my refusal to give an immediate answer to his question, was reminded by another member that I was teaching him to catch fish.

ibid

It is important not only to be aware of the gaps between your own understanding of your role and your learners' expectations, but also to continue to address them throughout the course you are teaching, both in your own preparation for teaching and in the way you work with your students. We have found that using activities with our learners which make them more aware of classroom dynamics and different ways of learning and teaching, and encourage feedback within the group about their individual needs and expectations, helps bridge the gap. We look at some of these activities – stories, metaphors and images, for example – in Chapter 3. As Chris Aldred's Chinese anecdote shows, the greatest measure of your own success in bridging the gaps between yourself and your learners may be that your learners begin to deal with them too.

14 The power of metaphor

Chris Aldred is a teacher trainer who likes to use metaphor in her work with teachers. Teryl Lundquist is another teacher trainer who finds that metaphors can help to illuminate and focus her view of teaching. In the following account she describes how watching the movie *The Wizard of Oz* on TV offered her sudden new insights into her own behaviour both as a teacher and as a learner.

Remember Dorothy's odyssey through the land of Oz, encountering curious local characters, unlikely companions, fierce opposition and magical aid as she followed the yellow brick road to find her way back home?

Most of us in the US have seen this delightful movie at least once a year since we were children. I thought I knew the story. Then one evening, as I was making final preparations for a teacher training workshop on 'Empowering ourselves as we empower our students', I became distracted by yet another re-run on the TV. Through senses sharpened by focus on my workshop I saw the story in a completely fresh way: it is all about empowerment!

Since then I have shared and expanded my understanding of this lovely and insightful metaphor for the teaching/learning/empowering process. It is often through such fanciful tales that my own inner child is touched and activated. And it is my inner child, I am convinced, that holds the power of my intuitive, creative, spontaneous wisdom. My new interpretation of the movie has been like a guide, showing me new ways of understanding myself as a teacher and learner, reinforcing principles of empowerment that I already believed on a more intellectual level, and leading me to develop strategies that are an empowering of myself, my colleagues and my students, of whatever age.

First of all, I now recognise some of the limiting beliefs that persist in distracting me on the path to my own empowerment. The Scarecrow's lament, 'If I only had a brain', represents my own nagging doubt about my intellectual abilities, my 'lack' of a PhD and published research. After all, aren't teachers supposed to know everything and trainers supposed to have academic degrees?

The Tinman only wants to find a heart and keep his armour from rusting shut, keeping him locked inside. Don't I also sometimes wear a stiff protective layer over my real self, my emotions, the center and core of my identity? Even though I consider myself to be humanistic and open with students, I also long to feel the freedom to be more open, vulnerable, 'tender, gentle and sentimental' ... in the classroom and out.

In the Cowardly Lion's plea for 'courage' I see my own lack of confidence, my fear of people not liking me, my hesitancy to take risks and follow hunches, my false bravado in the face of the unknown, my frequent inner terror at the role of authority and 'expert' which I take on professionally.

In the witches I see my higher and lower selves. The Wicked Witch of the West is my controlling, judging, self-denying, nasty self that would keep me from realising my own goals, my potential, my dreams.

In Glinda, the Good Witch, I am reminded that I have a higher self, an inner teacher and guide, which enables me to believe, trust, succeed, as well as to empower myself and others. I also notice that Glinda stays out of the way of the learning, providing just enough supportive presence to enable Dorothy and friends to experience their own process.

The Wizard explains sheepishly that he is a good *man*, just a bad *wizard.* He is an illusion, an exaggerated image, a role, a 'humbug', a dazzling audio-visual display of empty power, a puff of smoke and a flash of light ... just what I often find myself creating in my desire to impress: a well-meaning pretense of perfection and control.

And then there is Dorothy. In her I recognise my seeking self, the me that wants to find out what is over the rainbow; to tap my full potential and resourcefulness; to discover the new people, places and experiences out there. Like her, I am willing to share the road with my fellow journeyers and defend their rights to reach their goals too. Yet, also like Dorothy, I feel I want to be 'at home in Kansas' where I feel completely myself and familiar. In one of those paradoxes of life, even as I seek newness I am also nervous about the unknown, reluctant to surrender to the reality that things change.

Having analyzed these analogies and seen the diverse players within myself, I know that I need to develop an accepting, active relationship with each part of who I am. I am an integrated whole, not just one of my parts at any given time.

Like Dorothy and her companions (who, by the way, from the start showed amazing courage, intelligence, loyalty, tenderness and teamwork), I am finding that I already have what I am looking for; it has been with me all along. My mind is intuitive and capable, my spirit is brave and adventuresome, my heart is both open and full, my home and truth wherever I am. It is not the Wizard of Oz nor the magic of the witches that will give me my power; it is my own 'readiness' to engage the power within myself and within my community of fellow seekers.

I come away from the elaborate metaphor with two key principles to empowerment that I will call my 'Oz Principles'. First is the support of COMMUNITY as a source of support, strength, joy and talents for the journey. The true spirit of community can tap the best in us, spark our creativity, multiply our experiences, expand our world vision and our self awareness. The experiences we share on the yellow brick road are what teach us about our true possibilities. We don't have time for fear and shyness when helping each other gain our individual and collective liberation. The power of the group allows for individual growth and the realisation of personal goals, while it also develops team spirit, cooperation, and fun. No one wins unless everyone wins (a powerful truth in Oz).

The second Oz Principle for me is the complete recognition, acceptance and engagement of the WHOLE PERSON as an INDIVIDUAL in the process. It is allowing the deep knowledge we have of ourselves and others to assist in creating our growth and change. It is recognising that we are each knowers and learners, with rich life experiences and cultural identities to draw from. In tapping those internal and external realities and strengths as resources for our learning, we remember that each individual is a weave of different cognitive and affective influences.

How do these two principles help me as an ESL [English as a Second Language] teacher and teacher trainer? For one thing, I can make more effort to see the true heart, mind and spirit of each student. I can look beyond appearances and poor self images to what is true, real, innocent, wise, whole and capable in each person. I can accept the physical energies and realities and cultural/ linguistic uniqueness – the tin, straw, and tail of the learner. I can be less concerned with apparent or perceived lack in each individual and focus on the abundance of knowledge, love, courage, support, truth and willingness to take risks.

I can assist the students in forming a sense of community: of fellow journeyers, companions in a quest, sharers of a goal, collaborators both in the finding of solutions and the vanquishing of foes, pioneers in crossing the boundary between the known and the unknown. It is not what is similar or different in all of us, but what we do together to create a texture, a harmony, a dance, a rainbow. It is our commitment to each other and to the goal that gives us a readiness to stretch and find our true strength.

I can also remember the people that make up the learner's world outside the classroom: the Auntie Ems, parents, siblings, friends, etc. They are a part of the larger community of the learner, the full design of his or her identity.

I can provide challenge and direction, ruby slippers, occasional assistance and especially medals, diplomas, testaments and encouraging words. I can trust my intuition and support other teachers to trust theirs, so that our use of texts, lesson plans, materials, human resources and the physical and social environment, is effective, spontaneous and sparked by joy.

But mostly, I can stay out of the way. The path of learning is full of obstacles and tests of courage, distractors and mistakes, sleep-inducing poppy fields, locked doors and 'impossible' tasks. I can't shorten the path or eliminate the steps for anyone else. All I or anyone else can do is offer support and firm, unbending belief that the learner will learn best from experience and from peers, and especially, that the learner is fully capable of meeting the task – that each learner has 'always had the power' needed – that the power is tapped from within and from the resources of the community.

These are my goals for empowering my students and the teachers I train. But mostly these are the messages I am teaching the many selves within ME that are uniting to be empowered.

Lundquist 1990 pp13–15

Activity

The author finds that characters in *The Wizard of Oz* give her powerful metaphors that deepen her understanding of herself as a teacher.

- Do you have a metaphor or story, or can you think of one now, that helps you understand your teaching?
- Go through the metaphor or story, carefully describing how you relate to each character or each phase.
- What can you learn from this? What particularly touches you?

This activity probably benefits from being talked through with a colleague.

---

15 Giving yourself confidence

Confidence in yourself, as we have seen, is a necessary prerequisite for believing in your potential to develop. The final extract in this chapter introduces some teachers' voices on the subject of confidence. Twelve native and non-native teachers of English, many of whom had not met each other before, came together at a summer school to share their feelings about what confidence meant for them in their own experience of teaching. By the end of the meeting, everyone in the group was energized by finding that they had so much in common in an area not often spoken about openly and sincerely. Here are some of their comments.

Confidence for me means:
- Thinking of my students as individuals with personal backgrounds, particular needs and individual requirements.
- Being a better listener to students and colleagues.
- Letting students take their own responsibility for their learning.
- Believing in myself and my capabilities and spending less time worrying

about how others, particularly my colleagues, see or judge me, either personally or professionally.

- I can't have the perfect lesson all the time. I have to accept that. I need to be less uptight, to find the right quality of personal and professional involvement.
- Honest feedback with my students. Sharing responsibility with them.
- Not taking everything so personally.

Underhill 1986 p9 (abridged)

Activity

- What do you draw on to give yourself confidence *while* you are teaching?
- Can any of the ideas in this chapter help you feel more confident about your own teaching?
- What insights have been most helpful?

---

16 Conclusion

In this chapter we have presented a view of the developing teacher as someone who is continually engaged in learning more about herself and her way of working. We have expressed the view that humanistic approaches offer a positive direction for personal and professional development. Humanistic psychology recognizes that there is in every individual the potential to be self-directing under the right conditions. These conditions include openness to the possibility of change and growth, willingness to break old habits and try out alternatives, and commitment to deepening self-knowledge. The model of the 'reflective practitioner' provides a way for teachers to become conscious of how their own knowledge and skills are shaped by experience. In the ongoing process of reflection, we dispel old myths and acquire fresh insights which can be springboards to further learning.

We have also drawn attention to the importance of process in bringing about change. Any change which is developmental will reach the inner subjective experience of the person affected, and increase their awareness of their own potential to grow. Challenging the attitudes we hold today as teachers, shaped by past experience and learning, can help us achieve greater self-awareness and discover new directions for our development. In the next chapter we look at how this awareness can affect what happens in the classroom.

Chapter 3 The facilitative relationship

1 Introduction

The focus in this chapter is on the interpersonal relationship between teacher and learners, and the role of the teacher in that relationship. It reflects an underlying belief that a good rapport between people in the classroom leads to more effective and enjoyable learning and teaching.

Teachers often define themselves and their way of working in terms of their relationships with learners. Teacher development therefore has a basis in this interpersonal context. The understanding that you have of yourself as a teacher can be complemented by information about yourself that others, such as the learners you teach, can provide. They can help complete the parts of the picture that you cannot see for yourself.

2 The importance of group rapport

Jill Hadfield and Angi Malderez sent out questionnaires to language schools and state colleges all over Britain, inviting teachers to list their most common staffroom moans about problems in the teaching/learning process: 'the kind of preoccupation that fills your head when you have just finished a lesson you were not completely satisfied with' (Hadfield 1992 p7). What they discovered was that teachers were overwhelmingly preoccupied with anxieties about the relationships between the class members, with groups which didn't 'gel' and where the classroom atmosphere was tense and unfriendly. Reflecting on this, Jill Hadfield writes:

In common with the teachers who wrote the cries of despair on the questionnaire, my own most miserable teaching experiences have not been due to the inadequacy of any particular textbook, or lack of proper classroom facilities, but to a negative atmosphere that somehow built up in the group.

Hadfield 1992 p9

The comments made by teachers made it clear that they know exactly what it feels like to teach an unsuccessful learning group. These are the characteristics that Jill Hadfield identified:

- The individuals in the class do not cohere into a group.
- There is an uncomfortable, tense, or negative atmosphere.
- The members of the group are all intent on their individual ambitions and are unwilling to compromise or define group goals for learning.
- Some members of the group will not participate in group activities.
- Some members of the group tend to dominate group activities at the expense of shyer members.
- The members of the group are territorial or cliquey and will not interact equally with all members of the group.
- Members of the group will not listen to one another.
- Group members are not interested in each other and are even antagonistic towards each other.
- Group members are not self-reliant but dependent on the teacher.
- Group members cannot put problems in perspective; trivial things develop into major upsets.
- There may be an 'indigestible' group member who causes problems or creates a negative learning atmosphere.
- Group members will not co-operate to perform tasks.
- Members of the group do not trust each other.
- Individuals in the group are competitive and attention-seeking.
- Members of the group are intolerant of cultural and personal differences.
- Group members have certain fixed or rigid ideas which they are reluctant to modify.
- Members of the group lack responsibility: they are reluctant to make an effort or take the initiative.
- Group members tend to be over-serious with little sense of fun.
- Group members lack confidence in themselves as learners, what they are learning, and the way they are being taught.

ibid p11

Activity

- Write your own description of the characteristics of a successful learning group. You may choose to do this by turning Jill Hadfield's statements on their heads, so that they express positive rather than negative characteristics. Or you may prefer to start with a blank sheet and set down your own ideas.

- How is it that some classes develop into successful learning groups, while others develop negative characteristics?
- Is there anything that teachers can do to encourage the development of a positive group atmosphere, and discourage its opposite? (We will deal with this more fully in Chapter 4.)

Teachers know instinctively that a positive group dynamic can have a beneficial effect on the motivation and self-esteem of everyone in the learning group, including the teacher. The problem is in knowing how far the teacher can influence the group dynamic, and what skills are needed. On the whole, training courses have tended to pay little attention to these subjective issues in the experience of teaching and learning. Yet modern teaching methods which encourage the use of pair and groupwork have greatly increased opportunities for interaction in the classroom. Knowing something about the way groups operate can help the teacher understand what is happening between people in the classroom situation, and make sense of why group activities don't always work as well as we hope.

3 Paying attention to process

A person-centred approach to teaching and learning means that the teacher values and uses the personal knowledge and experience of each group member. What the learners are feeling, as well as what they are processing intellectually, is an important part of their learning experience. Adrian Underhill believes that teachers need to be tuned into the dynamics of process in their class of learners, and in themselves. Here he defines what he means by this, and why it is so important.

> Process concerns the way in which the content of a lesson, syllabus, or curriculum is taught and learnt from the point of view of the learner, and how that content can become directly relevant to the lives of the learners. Process focuses on the immediate subjective reality of the individuals in a learning group, and is concerned with how participants relate to themselves and each other in order to carry out the task. Whatever contributes to the ambient learning atmosphere, including the attitudes, values, and awareness of the teacher and of the learners, is part of the process.
>
> The dynamics of process revolve around issues such as authority and self-determination; co-operation and competition; expectation and motivation; the individual and the group; security and risk; failure and success; self-esteem and its absence; personal meaning; and how participants feel, think, and act in relation to themselves, to each other, and to what they are doing. Teachers who claim it is not their job to take these phenomena into account may miss out on some of the most essential ingredients in the management of successful learning.
>
> Process is important precisely because it affects the quality of the outcome of

the task. The problem for process is that it takes place at least partly beyond our consciousness. But this does not have to be the case, and the aim of a facilitator is to become more awake to process, while at the same time fulfilling the requirements of the task.

Underhill 1989 pp250–2

Activity

- Recall an activity you often use successfully in class.
- Notice the steps involved in setting it up and monitoring it.
- Now consider each step in the procedure in terms of the dynamics of process, as defined by Adrian Underhill above. For example:
  - How do the learners relate to you and to each other?
  - Is the atmosphere competitive or co-operative?
  - How much risk is involved for the learners?
  - How relevant is the activity to them as people?
  - Does the activity take account of individual differences in learning style or motivation?
- Has there ever been an occasion when the activity has not worked as well as it normally does? How far can this failure be explained in terms of process factors?

'Process' is different from 'procedure', which can be seen as the series of steps we take in carrying out a task or activity. Once we become aware as teachers of the importance of attention to process in both ourselves and our learners, we can make different choices and assume greater control over the way we teach and learn. The skill is to be watchful of the way we do things, and of the effect we have on others, and of how and why what we do has this or that outcome.

4 Recognizing that feelings matter

Earl Stevick is a close observer of the ways in which people approach language. In the following text he portrays the complexity of the language class when viewed as a group of living, feeling human beings struggling to relate to each other and to integrate the experience with everything else they know:

... a language class is one arena in which a number of private universes intersect one another. Each person is at the center of his or her own universe of perceptions and values, and each is affected by what the others do ... If approval from one's parent-figures is an important reassurance, then it becomes urgent to please the teacher, and to have frequent tests, and to do well on those tests. On the other hand, it would be intolerable to find that our teacher, no matter how strong, self-confident, and apparently competent, used a style of teaching that contradicted the values that we had picked up from our parents or from earlier teachers ... We may resist the language itself, just for its foreignness, in the same way we resisted the native language teacher who tried to get us to say 'he doesn't' when all our friends said 'he don't' ... To become faithful to this foreign way of speaking would feel like being unfaithful to the group that nourished and supports us ... The need for support from those around us may also prevent us from achieving all that we could, just because we don't want to be regarded as the one who puts our classmates in a bad light ...

Our 'world of meaningful action' ... draws on the power figures in our life, and on our peer groups, and on the more or less tightly integrated set of goals that we have set for ourselves. Other things being equal, we will respond better to a language course that fits into that system, and less well to a course that does not.

Stevick 1980 pp7–9

Activity

- Have you ever taught a student (or group of students) who disapproved of your teaching style?
- In what way did your teaching not meet that person's or that group's expectations? Where do you think their expectations came from?
- Try to put yourself 'in their shoes' and imagine what was going on inside them, what they were feeling.
- What feelings were aroused in you when you became aware of their disapproval? How did you deal with them?
- Now turn this activity around and think of a time when you were a learner in a class where the teacher did not meet your expectations. Recall your own feelings and how you dealt with them. Try to make sense of why the teacher was doing what he or she was doing.

The skilled facilitator recognizes that learners have expectations based on previous experience of formal learning situations, and understands that resistances need to be acknowledged and worked through in a safe and supportive environment.

5 Working with learners' feelings

In deciding what kind of teacher you want to be, you can choose whether or not you want to invite people to bring their feelings into the open, and how you will handle this. Whatever you decide, it is important to recognize their influence on each learner's experience of your lessons. Gertrude Moskowitz, whose book *Caring and Sharing in the Foreign Language Class* contains over a hundred exercises which encourage learners to express their feelings and relate to each other in a personal way, is convinced that her humanistic approach particularly helps people who have failed to learn in more traditional school environments.

Affective education is effective education. It works on increasing skills in developing and maintaining good relationships, showing concern and support

> for others, and receiving these as well. It is a special type of interaction in itself, consisting of sharing, caring, acceptance, and sensitivity. It facilitates understanding, genuineness, rapport, and interdependence. Humanistic education is a way of relating that emphasizes self-discovery, introspection, self-esteem, and getting in touch with the strengths and positive qualities of ourselves and others. It enables learning to care more for ourselves and others. In addition to all this, humanistic education is fun.
>
> As students find that their thoughts, feelings, and experiences are regarded as important in school, school becomes important to them. This type of growth and closeness comes gradually. It is *not* instant intimacy.
>
> Students who fail in school never have had a chance to experience such things – to become aware of their own strengths and to share themselves with others. Those who drop out because of lack of interest do not do so because we haven't given them enough facts. It's just that the facts have no meaning for them.
>
> *Moskowitz 1978 p14*

Activity

- How do you react to Gertrude Moskowitz's suggestion that encouraging students to share personal thoughts and feelings in class helps them to learn?
- What opportunities do you provide in your own lessons for this to happen?
- Do you use particular activities and materials which encourage relating as people, not just relating as students?
- How do you deal with any positive and negative feelings that come up?
- How open are you willing to be in class about your own feelings and experiences?

When students feel that any contribution they make will be listened to and appreciated by the teacher and the other class members, they can relax and lose their inhibitions about participating. This enables them to make the most of their learning opportunities, and to ask for what they want from the class. Drawing on the learners' own experiences and opinions engages their attention and makes any classroom material personally relevant.

6 The teacher's 'presence'

The concept of 'presence' is central to a person-centred view of teaching. The focus here is on the person-to-person way in which teacher and students affect each other. We want to look at two aspects of presence: its uniqueness to the individual and its quality. We will also consider how you can become more aware of the effect of your presence.

The uniqueness of your presence

Firstly, presence can be defined as the unique psychological climate that a teacher creates in the classroom. The difference you make by being there – your characteristic behaviour and attitudes – is what Adrian Underhill calls your 'atmospheric signature'. It is the way in which, ultimately, your students identify and know you. It is important to be aware of the effect of your presence on your learners, so that you have choice and control over the way you want to be with them. Underhill suggests one way of thinking about this:

> We probably all have the impression that any two teachers, teaching the same topic to the same level of similar learners, and using the same teaching procedures, will nevertheless have quite different effects on their learners. And why is this? Think of the good teachers you have had in your past (not always easy for everyone). What was it about them that was beneficial, that left a lasting and positive memory? How did you feel at that time in their classroom? You'll probably come up with a range of answers to this, but I expect that many of them will have to do with the psychological atmosphere created by that teacher, rather than with the topic itself or the teaching procedures used ...
>
> Our attitudes are embedded in all of our behaviours and are transmitted unconsciously, willy nilly. Learners pick them up both consciously and unconsciously, just as you did from your teachers. In my opinion teacher training rarely if ever gives direct feedback in a skilled and supportive manner on the effects of our attitudes on the performance of our learners, and if it does it tends to give the feedback obliquely through comments on either the procedural or the topic aspects of our practice ... But neither of these is the right channel for directly studying the ways in which our attitudes create a more or less facilitative learning climate.
>
> *Underhill 1994 p2*

Activity

- Think back to a good teacher you remember. What was it about them that you especially remember? Was it, as Adrian Underhill suggests, something about the psychological atmosphere that they created, rather than about what they taught?
- Now think of a colleague at work. What is it about their presence or absence that makes the difference?
- And what is it about your presence that other people notice? If you find it hard to answer this question, try putting yourself into the shoes of a student in a class that you are teaching. What do you think the student would write about you in a letter to someone who doesn't know you?

If you actually try writing a letter like this, you may be surprised by all the positive points you put into it! Or you could decide to give yourself a boost by focusing *only* on the good influences that you think your presence has in class. It is possible to do this without wandering off into realms of delusion, and it may help to focus your attention on the attitudes and behaviours that you value.

The quality of your presence

The second way we can define presence is 'the quality of being present with your full attention' as opposed to 'being absent'. It is important for the other person, or group, to feel that you are really there with them, and that they have your full attention. This means putting aside other concerns and making sure that, for the time that is necessary, you can give them this attention.

Activity

This is an activity involving physical movement and contact with a partner. Its aim is to help you observe how easy or difficult it is to stay 'present' with another person. First you lead while your partner follows, and then you change over.

1 Stand facing your partner. Make sure you are comfortable, with your shoulders down and your knees relaxed.

2 Imagine that you are a flexible willow tree. Your roots are going down into the earth so that you are firmly anchored to the ground but still able to bend with the wind.

3 When you are ready, place your hands against your partner's so that the palms are almost, but not quite, touching.

4 (Leader) Begin to move your arms and upper body. Your partner follows and moves with you as you lead. Watch your partner's reactions.

5 Then change roles and repeat the activity.

- When you are leading, try to notice:
  - Are you going at a speed which respects your partner's pace and limits of comfort?
  - Where is your partner's 'creative edge' – that is, the point at which moving in harmony with you becomes difficult? Beyond this limit a little stretching can create positive tension and still be comfortable, but too much will have a negative effect.
- When you are following, try to notice:
  - How easily can I follow?
  - When does it become difficult to follow?
  - Is this difficulty caused by my own lack of attention, or because the leader is stretching me too far?

Developing awareness of the effect of your presence

Adrian Underhill believes that self-awareness on the part of the teacher is an essential complement to understanding what is happening inside the learner, and that developing awareness lies at the heart of our development as teachers.

> Teacher attitudes modify teacher behaviour in lots of subtle ways, and together attitudes and behaviour make up this atmospheric signature. This atmosphere ... is what our learners have to breathe during every lesson, and it shapes the parameters of what is possible for each learner in a lesson.

> Awareness is the instrument I have for getting in touch with how I affect my learners. It is the only instrument I have for reducing the disparity between what I think I do and what I actually do, between the psychological atmosphere I think I create, and the one I actually create, between my experience of myself in the classroom and my learners' experience of me. It is only through awareness that I can cross the bridge and find out what it is like on the other side, and then modify what I do on my side accordingly. I am claiming that awareness is the instrument for teacher (or personal) development, and that this instrument can be tuned into any aspect of our practice that we want to investigate or develop or become more competent at. I am also saying that of the many aspects of our practice that we could study with the instrument of awareness, the study of the psychological learning atmosphere that we create in our classrooms could be one of the most fundamental, the most fruitful, and the most far-reaching in its implications for our development as teachers.
>
> *Underhill 1994*

Developing awareness is a process of reducing the disparity between what you do, and what you think you do; reducing the discrepancy between the psychological effect that you imagine your attitudes and behaviour have on your learners, and the effect that your atmosphere really has on them.

> Here is a map that proposes four stages of development relating the competence of what we are doing to our awareness of our competence. It's like this:
>
> **1** Unconscious incompetence
> I am not aware of something I am not doing well.
>
> **2** Conscious incompetence
> I become aware of doing something in a way that is not what I want.
>
> **3** Conscious competence
> I find that I can do this thing in a better way as long as I keep my attention on it.
>
> **4** Unconscious competence
> This becomes natural, leaving my attention free for something else.
>
> This represents four stages of development regarding any aspect of my teaching behaviour and its impact on the learning of my students. It could be as simple as the way I walk into the classroom, or the quality of my eye contact, or the quality of my listening, or the way that I give instructions, or the quantity or quality of my talk. It could be the impatience that leaks out of me when I am trying to appear patient, or it could be my inner psychological response to different questions. It could be the quality of my joy or disappointment at what happens, or it could be the subtle signals of acceptance or rejection or judgement that I send out to a particular student.
>
> Whatever the focus, there is often a tendency among teachers to miss out

stage 2, since that is the one that hurts. This is where I am likely to feel deskilled and destabilised. But the fact that it hurts is precisely because of the disparity between the effect I think I am having and the effect that I find I am actually having. Once I become defensively identified with a certain self-image it becomes difficult to open up to the risk that I am not what I imagine myself to be, and this is perhaps the biggest single obstacle to my development.

Underhill 1991 pp3–4

Activity

- Read again the four-stage development map in the excerpt above, beginning with 'unconscious incompetence'.
- Take different examples of your own development as a teacher and relate your progress to the four stages. This can be quite insightful.
- What typically is your response when you hit stage 2, 'conscious incompetence'?

---

7 Developing awareness of your learners

As teachers we naturally want to believe that our learners are involved in the lesson, and that what is being taught is being learned. But what we observe from the front of the classroom is often a misrepresentation or only a partially correct picture of the truth. To see what is really happening, we need to view our class from another perspective.

The following excerpt is taken from John Holt's book *How Children Fail*. Although originally published in the 1960s it is still in print and on many teachers' list of 'books that have inspired me' because it was one of the first accounts by a teacher of what he saw actually going on in his classroom. Holt spent a good deal of time observing and team teaching with colleagues, and recorded his observations and reflections over several months. Although it is an elementary school class in the US that is being described, we feel sure you will be able to relate to at least some aspects of the picture, whatever your teaching situation.

Of all I saw and learned this past half year, one thing stands out. What goes on in class is not what teachers think – certainly not what I had always thought. For years now I have worked with a picture in my mind of what my class was like. This reality, which I felt I knew, was partly physical, partly mental or spiritual. In other words, I thought I knew, in general, what the students were doing, and also what they were thinking and feeling. I see now that my picture of reality was almost wholly false. Why didn't I see this before?

Sitting at the side of the room, watching these kids, not so much to check up on them as to find out what they were like and how they differed from the teen-agers I have worked with and know, I slowly became aware of something. You can't find out what a child does in class by looking at him only when he is called on. You have to watch him for long stretches of time without his knowing it.

During many of the recitation classes, when the class supposedly is working as a unit, most of the children paid very little attention to what was going on. Those who most needed to pay attention usually paid the least. The kids who knew the answer to whatever question you were asking wanted to make sure you knew they knew, so their hands were always waving. Also, knowing the right answer, they were in a position to enjoy to the full the ridiculous answers that might be given by their less fortunate colleagues. But as in all classes, these able students are a minority. What of the unsuccessful majority? Their attention depended on what was going on in class. Any raising of the emotional temperature made them prick up their ears. If an argument was going on, or someone was in trouble, or someone was being laughed at for a foolish answer, they took notice. Or if you were explaining something so simple that the rest knew it, they would wave their arms and give agonized, half-suppressed cries of 'O-o-o-o-oh! O-o-o-o-oh!' But most of the time, when explaining, questioning, or discussing was going on, the majority of children paid little attention or none at all. Some daydreamed, and no amount of calling them back to earth with a crash, much as it amused everyone else, could break them of the habit. Others wrote and passed notes, or whispered, or held conversations in sign language, or made doodles or pictures on their papers or desks, or fiddled with objects.

They went on daydreaming, no matter how often they got caught and embarrassed doing it, because the class, despite our efforts to make it interesting and safe, was a boring, confusing, and dangerous place, from which they would escape if they could – and daydreaming was the only way to escape.

There doesn't seem to be much a teacher can do about this, if he is really teaching and not just keeping everyone quiet and busy. A teacher in class is like a man in the woods at night with a powerful flashlight in his hand. Wherever he turns his light, the creatures on whom it shines are aware of it, and do not behave as they do in the dark. Thus the mere fact of his watching their behavior changes it into something very different. Shine where he will, he can never know very much of the night life of the woods.

Holt 1984 pp32–4

Activity

Two of the points that John Holt is making in the above excerpt are:

1 that there is a discrepancy between what the teacher thinks is going on, and what is actually going on.

2 that daydreaming is a natural response for some learners to what is happening in their classroom.

One of the aims of developing awareness is to enlarge your attention to take in more of what is going on in the classroom.

- What enables you to be more observant in your class?
- Does it require you to be less preoccupied with other things, in order to free up some of your attention?

- What are the moments with your current classes when you have more mental space, more possibility to observe without reacting?
- If you observe that some of your learners seem to be daydreaming, why do you think this is happening and what, if anything, would you like to do about it?

John Holt found that observation of a class taught by a colleague provided an opportunity to learn something about his own teaching. Peer observation offers a framework for investigating an aspect of the learning environment and the teacher's role in it that interests or puzzles you. If you are interested, consider what would be involved in setting up a series of observations with a colleague so that you can investigate a question of your own. Chapter 8 suggests some guidelines for conducting peer observation.

A technique for developing awareness: guided visualization

John Holt worked with a picture in his mind of what his class was like. There is a technique for using the power of your mind to create pictures and stories which relate to the real world in new ways and offer fresh insights. This is called 'guided visualization'.

The following activity involves a guided visualization. Visualizations or fantasies are fun and interesting and unusual because they allow you to be very imaginative and to find out what your hopes and ambitions, worries and fears really are. It is important to go into it in the right state of relaxation and openness to the messages of the subconscious mind. Here is one way to get yourself ready to do a visualization yourself.

1 To get into a relaxed state, sit or lie down.

2 If you are sitting down, put your feet flat on the floor. If you can't reach the floor, put a book of the right thickness under your feet to allow your knees to be at right angles. If your legs are longer, put cushions on your seat, again so that your knees are at right angles.

3 Make sure your spine is straight and imagine that someone is holding a string attached to the top of your head, so that your head is loose on your shoulders, a bit like a puppet.

4 Lift your shoulders up and back and let them relax and drop as you breathe out.

5 If you are sitting down, rest your left hand in your right hand, palms facing up and rest them gently in your lap. If you are lying down, rest with your arms a little way from your side, palms facing upwards and fingers lightly curled.

6 When you are ready, lower or close your eyes, whichever is comfortable.

7 As you relax, listen to your breathing. Just notice it, without changing or forcing it.

8 Just concentrate on your breathing, and as thoughts come in, just notice them and, without judging them, let them go.

9 As you relax, notice how your breathing is becoming deeper ... and deeper, as you become more ... and more ... relaxed.

10 Keep breathing in this deep and relaxed way until you feel very calm.

11 Now you are ready to go into a guided visualization or fantasy.

12 Make a picture of anything at all that you want to see. A picture may just come to you, prompted by a reading, for example, or you may want to create a picture of yourself in a new situation which reflects the development you are working towards. If you don't find it easy to see pictures, don't worry. Just let sounds or thoughts come to you, and the more you practise, the better you will be able to make pictures.

13 Make the pictures as clear and vivid as you can, with colour if possible, and a lot of detail. Use all your senses by thinking:
- What can I see?
- What am I doing?
- What are other people doing?
- What am I and others saying?
- What can I hear?
- What can I smell?
- What can I touch?
- What do I feel like?

Create a very positive feeling and atmosphere and hold onto that feeling. Believe very strongly that you want, and can have, this picture, if it is a new situation you are working towards.

14 If the picture fades, gently bring it back. Keep relaxed. Check out your breathing and the parts of your body, especially to see that you have relaxed eyes and chin.

15 When you have a clear enough picture, say goodbye to the scene and, still with your eyes closed and keeping the relaxed feeling, imagine yourself slowly walking away from there and into the building where you are doing this exercise. See every step of the journey and come into the room you are in. Feel yourself sitting in the chair. Think of the room. Listen to the noises outside and then inside. Feel your back against the floor or the chair. Notice the taste in your mouth. When you are ready, keeping the relaxed feeling, *slowly* and gently stretch and open your eyes and get up, if lying down.

16 Sit quietly and think about what you have seen. You could try putting these instructions on tape so that they are ready for you to respond to, and so that you can relax totally. Alternatively, to relax your body before a visualization, you could turn to the relaxation techniques suggested in Chapter 6.

Activity

This is a guided visualization. It helps you to develop awareness by looking at your classroom through the eye of your mind. Before you begin, it is helpful to go through the steps suggested above to get yourself into a relaxed state. Then you are ready to do the following.

- Imagine yourself in one of your own classes. Take time to develop the picture fully in your mind.
  - What are the students saying?
  - Look around at the students' faces.
  - Look at the classroom walls and the seating arrangements.

– What atmosphere is there?

- When you have a very full picture, very slowly imagine yourself walking out of the classroom, out of your school, and back to where you are now.
- If you like, write down what you 'saw' or 'heard' or 'felt'.

---

8 Creating an environment which facilitates learning

Teachers whose approach to learners aims to be person-centred acknowledge and try to make use of the existing knowledge and experience that the learners bring with them into the classroom. They understand that real learning involves adapting old knowledge in the light of new insight. They believe that it is better for learners to discover and evaluate new ideas for themselves, than to be told what they need to learn. Kolb, whose ideas on experiential learning we looked at in Chapter 2, describes it in this way:

> How easy and tempting it is in designing a course to think of the learner's mind as being as blank as the paper on which we scratch our outline. Yet this is not the case. Everyone enters the learning situation with more or less articulate ideas about the topic at hand ... Thus, one's job as an educator is not only to implant new ideas but also to dispose of or modify old ones. In many cases, resistance to new ideas stems from their conflict with old beliefs that are inconsistent with them. If the education process begins by bringing out the learner's beliefs and theories, examining and testing them, and then integrating the new, more refined ideas into the person's belief systems, the learning process will be facilitated ... Ideas that evolve through integration tend to become highly stable parts of the person's conception of the world.
>
> *Kolb 1984 pp26–8*

The concept of person-centred learning is hardly a new one. Around two thousand years ago Socrates was clear that his role as a teacher was to help the learners to answer their own questions.

> I shall only ask him, and not teach him, and he shall share the inquiry with me; and do you watch and see if you find me telling or explaining anything to him, instead of eliciting his opinion.
>
> *Quoted in Brandes and Ginnis 1986 p10*

Socrates sees himself as a kind of companion and guide, facilitating the learner's discovery of knowledge. He also looks forward to acquiring new insights himself from the shared inquiry.

The relationship between teacher and learner is similarly portrayed by the Lebanese writer Kahlil Gibran in his poetic text *The Prophet.*

> Then said a teacher, Speak to us of Teaching.
> And he said:
> No man can reveal to you aught but that which already lies half asleep in the dawning of your knowledge.

> The teacher who walks in the shadow of the temple, among his followers, gives not of his wisdom but rather of his faith and his lovingness.
> If he is indeed wise he does not bid you enter the house of wisdom, but rather leads you to the threshold of your own mind.
> The astronomer may speak to you of his understanding of space, but he cannot give you his understanding.
> The musician may sing to you of the rhythm which is in all space, but he cannot give you the ear which arrests the rhythm, nor the voice that echoes it.
> And he who is versed in the science of numbers can tell of the regions of weight and measure, but he cannot conduct you thither.
> For the vision of one man lends not its wings to another man.
> And even as each one of you stands alone in God's knowledge, so must each one of you be alone in his knowledge of God and in his understanding of the earth.
>
> *Gibran 1992 pp74–5*

Activity

- How far does the kind of helping relationship described by Socrates and Kahlil Gibran match your idea of the 'perfect' teacher–learner relationship? What problems are there for you in it?
- Is there a student you have taught, with whom you have developed a particularly effective relationship? What was the essence of this relationship?

Traditional formal schooling in many cultures tends to adopt the 'blank slate' approach to learning, which assumes that the teacher will tell the students what they need to know, and the students will not question the teacher's expertise. The power of such assumptions on the part of the learner can make it a frustrating task trying to help students to become independent and to identify their own needs and goals. Perhaps part of the frustration is that when they don't take this responsibility, we sense the loss to the learner and to ourselves of the missed opportunity to share in the adventure of learning. This can be compared with the satisfying relationship that develops with learners who are clear about their learning goals, and who draw confidently on the teacher as a source of information and help. The extract we have quoted from *The Prophet* has inspired a number of teachers we know who are working on their own development. Perhaps you can bring to mind an occasion when you have felt inspired by a text, a radio or TV programme, or perhaps a painting or a piece of music, which seemed to deepen your awareness of what being a teacher means for you personally.

9 The role of the teacher as facilitator

The American psychologist Carl Rogers, who was very active in the field of education, also found that the best learning happens when each student is fully involved and developing towards the realization of his or her unique potential. Rogers proposes a shift of focus in education from teaching to learning, and from teacher to facilitator. He writes:

> The primary task of the teacher is to *permit* the student to learn, to feed his or her curiosity. Merely to absorb facts is of only slight value in the present, and usually of even less value in the future. Learning *how* to learn is the element that is always of value, now and in the future. Thus, the teacher's task is delicate, demanding, and a truly exalted calling. In true teaching there is no place for the authoritarian, nor the person who is on an 'ego trip'.
>
> *Rogers 1983 p18*

In his book *Freedom to Learn for the Eighties*, from which the above quote is taken, Carl Rogers describes how many teachers and students have put this philosophy into practice in their own experience. He goes on later in the book to explain why he believes that teachers need to be facilitators rather than instructors, and what the essential qualities of a good facilitator are.

> Teaching and the imparting of knowledge make sense in an unchanging environment. This is why it has been an unquestioned function for centuries. But if there is one truth about modern man, it is that he lives in an environment that is continually changing ... The only man who is educated is the man who has learned how to learn; the man who has learned how to adapt and change; the man who has realized that no knowledge is secure, that only the process of seeking knowledge gives a basis for security. Changingness, a reliance on *process* rather than upon static knowledge, is the only thing that makes any sense as a goal for education in the modern world ...
>
> I see the facilitation of learning as the function that may hold constructive, tentative, changing *process* answers to some of the deepest perplexities that beset humankind today ... We possess a very considerable knowledge of the conditions that encourage self-initiated, significant, experiential, 'gut-level' learning by the whole person ... We know ... that the initiation of such learning rests not upon the teaching skills of the leader, not upon scholarly knowledge of the field, not upon curricular planning, not upon use of audiovisual aids, not upon the programmed learning used, not upon lectures and presentations, not upon an abundance of books, though each of these might at one time or another be utilized as an important resource. No, the facilitation of significant learning rests upon certain attitudinal qualities that exist in the personal *relationship* between the facilitator and the learner.
>
> *ibid pp120–1*

What are these qualities, or attitudes, that facilitate learning? Rogers identifies them as *genuineness*, *acceptance*, and *empathic understanding*.

Genuineness means being yourself, not playing a role in front of your learners:

> When the facilitator is a real person, being what she is, entering into a relationship with the learner without presenting a front or a façade, she is much more likely to be effective ... She can be enthusiastic, can be bored, can be interested in students, can be angry, can be sensitive and sympathetic. Because she accepts these feelings as her own, she has no need to impose them on her students. She can like or dislike a student product without implying that it is objectively good or bad or that the student is good or bad.

She is simply expressing a feeling for the product, a feeling that exists within herself. Thus, she is a person to her students, not a faceless embodiment ... [This] is sharply in contrast with the tendency of most teachers to show themselves to their pupils simply as roles.

ibid pp121–2

Acceptance means regarding each learner as a human being of worth:

I think of it as prizing the learner, prizing her feelings, her opinions, her person. It is a caring for the learner, but a non-possessive caring. It is an acceptance of this other individual as a separate person, having worth in her own right. It is a basic trust - a belief that this other person is somehow fundamentally trustworthy ... Such a teacher can accept the student's occasional apathy, her erratic desires to explore byroads of knowledge, as well as her disciplined efforts to achieve major goals ...

ibid p124

Empathic understanding involves, to use Rogers' own words, 'understanding the student's reactions from the inside'.

This kind of understanding is sharply different from the usual evaluative understanding which follows the pattern of 'I understand what is wrong with you.' When there is a sensitive empathy ... the reaction in the learner follows something of this pattern, 'At last someone understands how it feels and seems to be *me* without wanting to analyze me or judge me.' This attitude of standing in the other's shoes, of viewing the world through the student's eyes, is almost unheard of in the classroom ... But it has a tremendously releasing effect when it occurs.

ibid p125

Rogers found that when, in a group of people, these conditions are achieved, the results are exciting for everyone involved in the learning experience.

When I have been able to transform a group – and here I mean all the members of a group, myself included – into a community of *learners*, then the excitement has been almost beyond belief. To free curiosity; to permit individuals to go charging off in new directions dictated by their own interests; to unleash the sense of inquiry; to open everything to questioning and exploration; to recognize that everything is in process of change – here is an experience I can never forget. I cannot always achieve it in groups with which I am associated, but when it is partially or largely achieved, then it becomes a never-to-be-forgotten group experience. Out of such a context arise true students, real learners, creative scientists and scholars, and practitioners, the kind of individuals who can live in a delicate but ever-changing balance between what is presently known and the flowing, moving, altering problems and facts of the future.

ibid pp119–21

Activity

- Take some time to reflect on the three conditions for facilitating learning described above by Carl Rogers. To what extent do you demonstrate these qualities in your own intentions and behaviour in the classroom? How do you know?

Carl Rogers formulated a set of questions to focus his own thoughts about himself as a facilitator of learning.

1 Can I let myself inside the inner world of a growing, learning, person? Can I, without being judgemental, come to see and appreciate this world?

2 Can I let myself be a real person with these young people and take the risk of building an open, expressive, mutual relationship in which we both can learn? Do I dare to be myself in an intensive group relationship with these youth?

3 Can I discover the interests of each individual and permit him or her to follow those interests wherever they may lead?

4 Can I help young persons preserve one of their most precious possessions – their wide-eyed, persistent, driving curiosity about themselves and the world around them?

5 Can I be creative in putting them in touch with people, experiences, books – resources of all kinds – which stimulate their curiosity and feed their interests?

6 Can I accept and nurture the strange and imperfect thoughts and wild impulses and expressions which are the forerunners of creative learning and activity? Can I accept the sometimes different and unusual personalities which may produce these creative thoughts?

7 Can I help young learners to be all of one piece – integrated – with feelings pervading their ideas and ideas pervading their feelings, and their expression being that of a whole person?

If, by some miracle, I could answer yes to most of these questions, then I believe I would be a facilitator of true learning, helping to bring out the vast potential of young people.

Rogers 1990 p6

Activity

- What are your reactions on reading Carl Rogers' questions?
- Are there times when you could answer 'yes' to one or some of them?
- Do you feel 'Well, this is fine, but ...'? If so, then what are the 'buts'? Try to be clear about your main 'but'. Do you know what causes it? (For example, past experience, fear of change, scepticism.)
- Do you have a question that embodies your own values of teaching or facilitating?

If you are wary of changing your perspective on teaching in this way, and felt some defensiveness as you read through Carl Rogers' questions, it may be worth trying to analyse the cause of those feelings. I (Katie) sometimes find that the problem is in the kind of language used by writers in this area rather than in the actual ideas. By thinking about the ideas and beginning to make sense of them in your own terms, rather than in the language of the authors, you may find that you want to integrate them into your approach to teaching after all. If reading the questions made you feel curious and you would like to know more, notice these feelings too and decide whether and how you can act on them.

10 The right kind of control

In one of his books on language teaching methodology, Earl Stevick proposes the following metaphor of teaching and learning:

> Teaching and learning are two men sawing down a tree. One pulls, and then the other. Neither pushes, and neither could work alone, but cutting comes only when the blade is moving toward the learner. At least, that's how it should be. If the teacher pulls while the learner is still pulling, they work against each other and waste their strength. If, in her zeal to help the learner, the teacher pushes, then the blade will buckle, rhythm will be broken, both will become disheartened.
>
> *Stevick 1980 p16*

Stevick goes on to suggest, however, that there is a kind of teacher control which is necessary to support the learner's self-discovery, and which may answer some teachers' and learners' resistance or fears about lack of control. Like Timothy Gallwey, who we quoted in Chapter 2, Stevick also uses analogies from the world of tennis and coaching.

> We have sometimes talked and written as though an increase in the learner's initiative necessarily requires some reduction in the degree of control that the teacher exercises, and vice versa. We have therefore concluded that all we can do is try for an appropriate balance, or trade-off, between control by the teacher and initiative by the student. In recent years, however, I have come to believe that this is not so. I believe there is a way to define 'control' and 'initiative', not widely consistent with everyday usage, which will allow the teacher to keep nearly 100 percent of the 'control' while at the same time the learner is exercising nearly 100 percent of the 'initiative'. This distinction has proved to be one of the more useful ideas that I have run across.
>
> Some kind of 'control' is necessary for the success of any human undertaking. As far as I can see, 'control' *by the teacher* is legitimate even in 'progressive' or in 'humanistic' education. As I am using the term, 'control' consists of only two essential elements. The first element is the structuring of classroom activity: What are we supposed to be doing? When is it time to stop what we are doing and start something else? In tennis, the teaching professional provides the court, explains the rules, provides suitable models, and sets appropriate goals ...

The other essential element of 'control' consists in making it easy for the learner to know how what he has done or what he has said compares with what a native would have done or said. In tennis, even the novice can generally see for himself whether or not the ball hit inside the line. In a foreign language, the new learner is not immediately equipped to know these things for himself ...

Seen in this way, 'control' is clearly a teacher function, at least in the early part of any course. It is the teacher's necessary contribution toward making this new and bewildering corner of the student's 'world of meaningful action' into a stable, well-lighted place in which to work (or play!) ...

'Initiative', as I am using the word here, refers to decisions about who says what to whom, and when. These decisions consist of choices among a narrow or a very broad range of possibilities which are provided by whoever is exercising 'control'. Seen in this way, 'initiative' and 'control' are not merely two directions along a single dimension. That is to say, 'control' on the part of the teacher does not interfere with 'initiative' on the part of the student: when the teacher tightens her 'control' of what is going on, she need not cut into the student's 'initiative'; often, in fact, she will actually increase it. Similarly, insufficient 'control' by the teacher may reduce or paralyze the 'initiative' of the student ...

The trick, for the teacher, is ... to provide just the right amount of learning space. If there is too little, the students will be stifled. If there is too much, the student will feel that the teacher has abandoned him.

ibid pp17–20

Activity

- Notice carefully Stevick's use of 'control' and 'initiative' in the excerpt above. (You may want to re-read it.)
- Record a lesson you are teaching, or ask a colleague to come and observe you. (Ways of using recordings and peer observation are discussed in Chapter 8.)
- Review a part of the lesson, noting down the ways in which you exercised control and invited initiative.
- Can you spot occasions when you abdicated control? Was it intentional? What happened?
- How does your exercise of control encourage student initiative, and how does it at other times inhibit student initiative?
- Can you spot any moments where your control is either 'stifling' on the one hand or 'abandoning' on the other?
- Do you notice anything in your exercise of control that owes more to a fear of losing control than to an appreciation of exactly what help the student needs at that moment?

---

11 Creating the right amount of learning space

Using an anecdote from his own childhood, Stevick goes on in his book to illustrate how 'the right amount of learning space' enables learners to be adventurous and self-confident in their learning.

When I was growing up, we sometimes played with box turtles. These little animals, five or six inches long as I remember them, could make amazingly good time as they moved along on their stubby legs, head fully extended from the shell. What we liked to do, of course, was to find one of them earnestly marching along somewhere, and touch it ever so lightly on the back. It would immediately retract its head and its legs into its shell, and remain motionless. Then we would pick it up and set it down again wherever we liked. (I have sometimes wondered whether, after it had recovered from its alarm and set out again, it headed for its original destination, or whether it had lost its bearings and had to devise an entirely new trip.)

I think we often see something like that happening in language classes ... Any student can arrive at a correct response in either of two ways: by using his own power, or by complying with the teacher's skillful lesson plan. If he does what he does on his own, and in conformity with his own timing and his own purposes, he knows where he is, and why, and how he got there. If he merely lets himself be carried along by the lesson plan, then what he does will not be truly a part of him, and it may be lost all too quickly.

The analogy breaks down, of course. In a language class, it is possible for the student to travel by both means at the same time: some lesson plans provide opportunities for students to propel themselves along within the overall guidance of the teacher. What is unfortunate is that many lesson plans are based on the belief that we should get the turtle to the destination we have chosen for him as expeditiously as possible, even if we have to take him off his feet. Equally unfortunate, though less common, is the opposite extreme: 'humanistic' techniques that place a premium on student initiative and student contributions sometimes fall flat. When this happens, it usually means that the turtle is being asked to come out of his shell in an environment which, for some reason, he finds alarming. Yet success in getting a new language ... requires the turtle's head and legs to be as far out of its shell as possible. For any method, but especially for the 'humanistic' ones, there needs to be harmony between the two 'selves' of each student, and a minimum of irrelevant tension among the people in the classroom.

Stevick 1980 pp13–14

Activity

With reference to the excerpt above:

- To what extent do your lesson plans require or prefer that learners conform to what you want them to do?
- To what extent do your plans provide an environment in which learners can relate to their own way of working?

- Do you have other, less conscious, expectations of your learners? For example, what do you 'want' or 'prefer' to happen at certain points in a lesson?
- In what subtle ways may these expectations affect your classroom behaviour?

Teachers who propel students through lessons without regard for the individual learner's own purposes or timing, as well as teachers who expect their learners to be capable of organizing their own learning without any direction, may be creating negative tension which interferes with effective learning.

12 Seven steps for developing a more person-centred classroom

Supposing that you want to become more person-centred in your teaching, how can you make the changes necessary to bring this about? Donna Brandes and Paul Ginnis were involved in a large-scale secondary-school project in Birmingham, England, which encouraged teachers to adopt a person-centred approach in the classroom. They developed a seven-stage model for implementing change and monitored its effects on teachers, students and the school institution.

The seven steps are:
1 motivation
2 establishing trust
3 assessment
4 accepting resistance
5 awareness
6 problem solving
7 contracts

The authors emphasize that these do not necessarily occur in any particular order and can sometimes seem to happen simultaneously. We will look at each of them in turn.

Motivation to change could have any number of causes:
- dissatisfaction with your job
- reading a book or professional journal, or attending a lecture or workshop which inspires you with a new idea
- a chance comment from a colleague or student
- a clash of values which limits your ability to act according to your beliefs or values
- management demands for change

Many teachers express dissatisfaction with their jobs. They may be aware that their relationships with the kids could be better, or that their own emotional needs are not being met, or that they are full of knowledge which they want to give, but which the students do not want to receive. Some teachers simply feel that there must be more to teaching than marking, discipline, and getting students through exams. Also, of course, there are many teachers who have developed an intuition about how school ought to be, and for one reason or another find things are not that way. So, for many there is a distinct dissonance between what they want and what they are actually getting ... [and] it has been our experience that for every teacher who is traditionally based and/or resistant to change, there are many others who would give anything to be able to reshape their jobs.

Brandes and Ginnis 1986 p74

Establishing trust means that you decide to be honest and open with your learners about everything that concerns yourself and them. If you want things to change in the classroom, you need to explain to them why you are doing what you are doing, and to get their confidence.

Time and again we have experienced the phenomenon of telling the truth about what we are feeling and thinking at the moment, and being met with increased openness and respect on the part of the student ... A partnership has now begun; as the teacher changes, so the students respond. As trust grows, motivation and responsibility increase. It is a symbiotic progression.

ibid p76

Assessment is the process by which you identify where you are now, and the points at which change is possible. You decide the first achievable steps that can be taken, and the realistic goals to be set.

It is no use coming into the group and saying to its members, be they teachers or students, or even to yourself, 'We're doing things the wrong way; we should be like *that*.' This is a critical attitude which is threatening to all concerned, and usually creates resistance. If the group is invited to take a clear look at the whole picture of the way things are now, the desired changes will make themselves apparent, and will therefore probably be more acceptable. Whatever criteria the group may establish, we have one favourite question we like to ask, and that is: *Does it work?* By this we mean: Is everyone getting what they want, and is the group functioning properly? So, 'Does it work?' is a shorthand way of saying to ourselves, or to the group: Is the strategy we are assessing producing the desired results?

ibid p78

Accepting resistance means acknowledging the fears within yourself, and accepting that support and reassurance will be necessary. There may be resistance on the part of the students too, and this has to be heard and dealt with.

Dealing with anyone's resistance, including your own, does not have to be a battle. In fact, if you fight, it is inclined to harden. If resistance is met with acceptance, it tends to dissipate. Whatever the resistance is, it needs to be first *expressed*, then heard and accepted. There is then no conflict with the source of resistance, be it external or internal.

Beware of saying to yourself 'I shouldn't be feeling this way'; give yourself permission to feel what you are feeling. Do the same for the rest of the group, or you will increase their resistance. Try acknowledging to yourselves: 'It is OK for us to be feeling this way. We can feel resistance and still go ahead.'

ibid p79

Awareness that you are now the 'owner' of the process you are undertaking releases you and the learners to use your capabilities to the full in planning and negotiating the way ahead.

Students and teacher draw the map together. The very act of planning and negotiating together evokes in the learner an awareness that she is now the owner of her learning. If her opinions and ideas are valued, she must be a valuable person. If she is expected to take responsibility, she must be a responsible person.

ibid p80

Problem solving involves turning over to the group the responsibility for making decisions. This does not depend on a certain level of maturity or intelligence in the students; in fact, it helps to develop them.

... the important ingredient is the teacher's attitude. The students quickly detect if the teacher is just pretending to share a problem which he has already solved in his own mind. There must be an inner change on the part of the teacher in which he says to himself *and means* 'This is not my problem to solve; I will have to *ask them.*' The teacher must get out of the habit of solitary problem-solving ...

ibid p82

Brandes and Ginnis suggest the following four steps as a basis for group problem solving:

1 Discuss and *own* the problem.
2 Brainstorm solutions, and select one.
3 Try out the chosen solution for an agreed length of time.
4 Re-evaluate, and start again if necessary.

Any of these steps could be done in small groups, or by secret ballots; there is no need to do all of them together. Also they can, of course, be adapted to your own use ...

ibid p192

The problem solving approach is extremely useful in solving behaviour problems, in planning for group activities and work, in dealing with emotional issues which may arise, and indeed in working on any problem which may affect the group as a whole.

ibid p83

Contracts are formal agreements between yourself and your learners which represent the official acknowledgement of the ground rules for co-operation in the group.

[Contracts] are a means of establishing ground rules and firming up agreements. They are negotiated with the students and established voluntarily with no consequences built in if they are broken. This does not mean that no consequences exist. For example, if five students are working together on a project, and they have made an agreement that each person will do a share of the work and have it finished by Tuesday, and one student has not completed his task, it is not the teacher's responsibility to step in and punish him. The student will have to negotiate with the rest of his small group. If a conflict occurs, the teacher may have to mediate in the negotiations. It may then develop into a problem-solving situation.

ibid p84

13 Practical strategies for introducing change in the classroom

Brandes and Ginnis use the metaphor of a visit to the swimming pool to suggest that there is a range of options for getting started with a new group of students. The 'toes-in' approach means cautiously sticking a toe in and testing the water. The 'dive straight in at the deep end' approach is for those who are confident of their ability to handle resistance and are good at taking risks. In between is the option of going in 'waist-deep' and then moving either towards the deeper water or back into the shallows. The important thing is to feel comfortable and confident about the approach you choose.

If you are uncertain about what becoming a more person-centred teacher would mean for you personally, you may like to try some of these 'toes-in' strategies. We will look at a number of them in more depth in Chapters 4 and 5, which focus on groupwork skills.

1. Sit down with the group.
2. Improve your own communication skills with the group by avoiding sarcasm, and by telling the truth.
3. Be more ready to acknowledge contributions and achievement, avoid putting people down.
4. Begin to offer choices.
5. Sit with the group, and use strategies to break down barriers, and to start building a safe climate.
6. Learn, teach, and use listening skills.
7. Decide on and declare your bottom lines (the points beyond which you are not willing to move).
8. Begin to concentrate on raising self-esteem.
9. Begin to shape up some ground rules, with your groups.
10. Teach the skills of giving and receiving feedback.

11 Encourage people to take risks, learn from mistakes, try new things.

12 Deepen discussions; enable people to explore what they *really* think and feel, *not* what they think will please you.

13 Encourage people to drop old ideas about themselves ...

14 Ask questions to which you do not know the answer, or to which there are many possible answers; encourage lateral thinking, argument, multiple options, divergent viewpoints.

15 Trust the group yourself: 'Nothing can go wrong here, because together we can sort out anything.'

16 Throw some salt and pepper into the pot ... keep your sense of humour.

17 Encourage creativity, spontaneity, and humour in others. Value unpredictability.

18 Freshen up your own thinking: *read, visit, observe, talk, share with colleagues!*

19 Do what it takes to feel centred and open in the group – for instance, take some deep breaths, wait a minute, laugh at yourself, share your feelings, remember whatever it is, it's not the end of the world.

20 Be yourself! There's no point in pretending to be someone you're not.

Brandes and Ginnis 1990 pp61–2

If you think you would prefer a 'deep-end' approach, you need to feel sure that your facilitator skills are good enough to handle student resistance.

[Staying] at the deep end ... would mean that the leader would make it clear that she is not going to take responsibility for the group's learning or achievement, and would consistently refuse to rescue them. A lot of skill may be needed in handling the opting out, the anger, the criticism, the chaos which might ensue ... In the end, it might have been a very efficient way of raising awareness, and of getting to the other end, where people really do take responsibility, not just play around with it. A radical beginning can sometimes produce a radical result. What you might have then is an extremely strong, cooperative group, with the accompanying rise in self-esteem for each individual.

ibid p75

Activity

- How do *you* establish trust and security in a new group?
- Look at the 'toes-in' strategies again. Which of them do you already use in some way? Which could you use better? Which do you not use?

Whatever approach you take, it is wise to plan it well, to be clear about what you propose to do and how you will introduce it, and to anticipate the kinds of problems that might arise and how you will deal with them. Developing the right amount of trust both in yourself and in your learners is the key. New techniques should never be tried out without belief in the underlying attitudes that accompany them.

14 Where inspiration comes from

In *The Tao of Leadership* John Heider offers the following thoughts on how learning happens. They are a helpful reminder that too much conscious concentration on getting things right can block out the inner inspiration.

Unclutter your mind

Beginners acquire new theories and techniques until their minds are cluttered with options. Advanced students forget their many options. They allow the theories and techniques that they have learned to recede into the background.

Learn to unclutter your mind. Learn to simplify your work.

As you rely less and less on knowing just what to do, your work will become more direct and more powerful. You will discover that the quality of your consciousness is more potent than any technique or theory or interpretation.

Learn how fruitful the blocked group or individual suddenly becomes when you give up trying to do just the right thing.

Heider 1985 p95

Activity

- Have you found ways of 'uncluttering' and 'simplifying' as you have progressed from Beginner Teacher to More Advanced Teacher? Can you describe an example of this?
- And can you find examples in your own experience of success coming after you have 'given up trying to do the right thing'?

---

15 Conclusion

At the beginning of this chapter we acknowledged the significance to both teachers and learners of developing a good classroom atmosphere in which people are at ease with each other and work well together. We suggested that it is helpful for teachers to develop an understanding of the kinds of process issues that can affect relationships in the classroom and to be aware of the significance of subjective feelings and responses both in themselves and in their learners. The most effective conditions for learning are facilitated by attention to these interpersonal factors. Carl Rogers has been influential in describing the personal qualities that are needed to facilitate learning, which he identifies as genuineness, acceptance and empathic understanding.

We have also considered other models of the teacher–learner relationship: Stevick's description of the kind of control that enables learners to explore new ideas in safety, and Brandes and Ginnis's analysis of the stages of change. We hope that some of the ideas and activities in this chapter have been helpful in suggesting alternative ways of thinking about the role of the teacher as a facilitator of learning. In the two chapters that follow, we develop the theme of working with and in groups.

Chapter 4 Ways of working with groups

1 Introduction

In Chapters 4 and 5 we focus on groups. This chapter looks at some of the skills and techniques associated with effective groupwork which you may find useful in thinking about the way that you work with groups. We suggest some things that you can do to encourage a positive group atmosphere in the classroom. In the following chapter we move on to consider some of the practicalities of setting up and maintaining a teacher development group.

The kinds of groupwork skills and techniques we describe in this chapter are aimed at establishing trust and co-operation so that people can work together and learn to respect each other. Whether you are thinking primarily of classroom groups, or of teachers' groups, or more generally of other groups to which you belong and for which you have some responsibility, we hope that the readings and activities in this chapter will give you fresh ideas and insights into your way of working with and in groups.

2 Active listening

Good listening skills are essential to effective groupwork. Many people are not very good listeners. They are either too busy and preoccupied or they want to rush in and interrupt with their own story or idea. Active listening means more than just hearing another person talking. It means giving the speaker your full attention, and enabling them to feel that they have been fully understood.

You can learn to listen more effectively by training yourself in the skills of active listening (see below).

At a workshop I (Katie) attended, the facilitator began by asking us to brainstorm all the things that prevent us from listening well. Our responses included:
– time pressure
– boredom
– thinking ahead about what I want to say
– thinking of 'solutions'
– prejudices about the speaker or the topic
– preoccupation with my own concerns
– physical discomfort
– not being able to hear or understand the speaker clearly.

Activity

- How well do you listen?
- How do you know?
- In one-to-one conversations and/or groups, do you tend to listen more than you speak, or speak more than you listen?
- What interferes with the quality of your listening? Can you add anything to the list above?

---

3 Responses that block communication

Because teachers can often be under stress, they can easily develop the habit of answering colleagues and students without really listening to them. You can begin to improve your listening ability by becoming aware of those of your responses which can perhaps put a block on the speaker. Robert Bolton calls these 'communication spoilers'. In his book *People Skills*, which has several chapters on listening, he provides a list of the kinds of response which can have the effect of blocking what another person is trying to say, rather than encouraging them to continue and develop the point they are making. Although we do not feel that this list should be accepted as 'gospel', we think it is interesting and makes a useful statement about the way people can so easily obstruct communication.

Criticizing: Making a negative evaluation of the other person, her actions, or attitudes ...

Name-calling: 'Putting down' or stereotyping the other person ...

Diagnosing: Analyzing why a person is behaving as she is; playing amateur psychiatrist ...

Praising evaluatively: Making a positive judgment of the other person, her actions, or attitudes ... (Many people find it difficult to believe that some of the barriers like praise are high-risk responses ... [but] I believe repeated use of these responses can be detrimental to relationships.)*

Ordering: Commanding the other person to do what you want to have done ...

Threatening: Trying to control the other's actions by warning of negative consequences that you will instigate ...

Moralizing: Telling another person what she should do. 'Preaching' at the other ...

Excessive/Inappropriate questioning: Closed-ended questions are often barriers in a relationship: these are those that can usually be answered in a few words – often with a simple yes or no ...

Advising: Giving the other person a solution to her problems ...

Diverting: Pushing the other's problems aside through distraction ...

Giving the logical argument: Attempting to convince the other with an appeal to facts or logic, usually without consideration of the emotional factors involved ...

Reassuring: Trying to stop the other person from feeling the negative emotions she is experiencing.

Bolton 1986 pp15–16 (abridged)

*Bolton later explains (p20) that in his experience praise is often used to manipulate, and makes people defensive.

Activity

- Can you recall an occasion when you have been on the receiving end of any of the 'communication spoilers' listed above?
- How could the person you were speaking to have expressed himself/herself differently on that occasion, and avoided the disabling effect of his/her words?
- Are you surprised to see any of the spoilers listed?
- Are there any that you feel you use quite often when you are listening?
- Can responses which are spoilers in one context be helpful in another context?

---

4 The skills of good listening

What are the skills of active listening? The analysis that follows is summarized in our own words from the much more detailed account in Robert Bolton's book *People Skills* (pp33–61). Bolton identifies clusters of skills which can be practised one at a time. These are *attending skills*, *following skills* and *reflecting skills*.

Attending skills

'Attending' means paying full and careful attention to the person who is speaking. The posture and body language you adopt, and the environment in which the interaction takes place, can significantly influence the speaker's perception of whether or not you are interested and involved in what he or she is telling you. Bolton gives advice on the following factors in effective attending:

1 **A posture of involvement** which is relaxed, open and alert. Positioning yourself squarely, at the same eye level and at a distance from the speaker which is appropriate to the culture is important.

2 **Appropriate body motion** which is neither too controlled or rigid, nor full of distracting gestures or movement.

3 **Eye contact.** A softly focused gaze on the face, shifting occasionally to other parts of the body, is preferable to staring or repeated looking away, especially when the speaker looks at you, as it helps the speaker figure out how receptive you are and how safe he or she is with you.

4 **Non-distracting environment.** This could involve unplugging the phone, turning off machines, moving away from barriers such as desks, and hanging up a 'Do not disturb' sign, so that you can give the speaker your undivided attention.

Following skills

'Following' means 'staying out of the other's way' by restricting what you say and do to minimal interventions which simply let the speaker know you are listening. It involves:

1 **Opening doors.** A non-coercive invitation can help a person you sense wants to speak, but needs encouragement.

2 **Minimal encouragers.** These imply neither agreement nor disagreement but show that the speaker has been heard and the listener will try to follow his meaning. Repeating the speaker's words or making non-distracting encouraging sounds in an appropriate tone and at an appropriate pace and time are often effective. *'Mm-hmm.' 'Tell me more.' 'And then?' 'Go on.' 'Really?'*

3 **Infrequent questions.** As a general rule it is not a good idea to ask questions as they can often focus on the concerns of the listener. It is not necessary to have the whole picture, as the speaker knows what is going on for him, and your listening will be most useful if you avoid seeking more information than is offered. Any questions that are asked are best kept as tentative and open as possible.

4 **Attentive silence.** Silence gives the speaker time to think, go deeper into himself and control the pace. If the listener feels tempted to shatter the quiet with questions, advice or any other sound to end the discomfort, the focus of the attention is on the listener's own disquiet. During the pauses in an interaction, a good listener attends to the speaker, observes him and thinks about what he is communicating. If you are doing all these things, you do not have time to be anxious.

Reflecting skills

'Reflecting' means that:

> the listener restates the feelings and/or content of what the speaker has communicated and does so in a way that demonstrates understanding and acceptance.
>
> *Bolton 1986 p50*

Quite often we do not hear people clearly because our perceptions are distorted by our own preconceived expectation of what they are going to say. We filter other people's messages through our own prejudices, worries and fears. Reflective responses effectively check and correct any misunderstandings that may have occurred as we listen. Reflecting back to the speaker what you understand him to have said gives him an opportunity to correct any inaccuracy in your interpretation and to clarify the message he wants to convey.

> Listening in dialogue is listening more to meanings than to words ... The words bear a different connotation for you than they do for me. Consequently, I can never tell you *what you said*, but only *what I heard*. I will have to ... check it out with you to make sure that what left your mind and heart arrived in my mind and heart *intact* and without distortion.
>
> *John Powell, quoted in Bolton 1986 p49*

Bolton identifies four kinds of reflective response: *paraphrasing, reflecting feelings, reflecting meanings* and *summative reflections.*

1. **Paraphrasing.** This form of response involves using your own words to restate the essence of the speaker's content and cut out details, to mirror the heart of the matter.
2. **Reflecting feelings.** The reflecting of feelings (*'You seem to be quite annoyed.' 'I notice some confusion in you.'*) helps the speaker understand his feelings and move toward a solution.
3. **Reflecting meanings.** This means making explicit the connection between a feeling and the cause of that feeling. Feelings are often triggered by specific events which are linked in the speaker's account of what is happening for her. A common formula for reflecting meaning is *'You feel [emotion] because [event or content associated with feeling].' 'You feel happy because things are going well for you in your new job.' 'You seem to feel pressured by the number of people making demands on you.'*
4. **Summative reflections.** A summative response recaps on the main themes and feelings expressed by the speaker during a longer period than would be covered by any of the other reflective skills. It can be useful when a speaker seems to have exhausted everything she has to say on a topic. It helps the speaker feel that, as she has explored herself, she has moved on and made progress in understanding herself a bit better. Even though there is no new material in it, it may seem new to the speaker as he is hearing it put together for the first time.

5 Exercises to develop better listening

This set of exercises is adapted from a number of workshops on listening that I (Pauline) have attended. The first is an exercise to help increase your awareness of how you normally listen.

Activity

You will need at least 20 minutes for this activity.

Work with a partner. One of you will listen while the other speaks. Decide which role you will take first. You will swop roles later.

1 The speaker chooses a topic that he or she can talk about for about five minutes. The topic can be anything you like, and doesn't have to be related to teaching. Examples of appropriate topics are: 'The best thing that's happened to me this week', 'A student I particularly remember', 'What I'd do if I won the lottery'.
2 The listener listens and joins in as seems appropriate, while the speaker talks. (It is helpful if the listener can also keep an eye on the time.)
3 After about five minutes you swop roles and repeat the exercise. The new speaker can choose any topic he or she likes.
4 When both partners have taken their turn at being the listener, reflect silently and individually for a few minutes on whether, as listener, you were tending to lead or to follow in the interaction. Is this true of the way you listen generally?
5 Then discuss with your partner whether listener and speaker perceived each of the interactions in the same way.

Learning how to listen more effectively

The five exercises which follow are designed to improve your listening skills. They may be done in a pair (speaker and listener) or in a group of three (with one person observing). The exercises will have more effect on the way you listen if you can space them out over a period of time, rather than rushing through them in a single sitting.

As these are *exercises* it may at first feel somewhat 'unnatural' or artificial to listen in the ways suggested. But the intention is to help you focus on the vital ingredients or skills which are needed for good, active listening. By identifying the components that make the difference, you can get insights into how you normally listen and how you can listen better.

In each exercise, the speaker chooses a subject (or is given a subject) and speaks about it for anything between 5 and 15 minutes. (As you do more of these exercises, you will find that a longer time is more beneficial, and you will find it less difficult than you thought to keep going!) The length of time given for speaking should be agreed beforehand and strictly controlled. In a pair, the listener is responsible for time-keeping; in a group of three, the observer can do it. Each exercise will be followed by a reflective stage (time also to be agreed), in which the participants express feelings and thoughts about the interaction. It is usually best if the reflection proceeds in the following order:

- How did you feel as the speaker?
- How did you feel as the listener?

and if there is an observer:

- What did you observe?

Be as detailed and accurate as you can be, and provide as much 'objective' data about the interaction between speaker and listener as possible, describing rather than interpreting what went on between you.

This framework can be used after all the exercises which follow, or you can use the more specific questions suggested after each one, while still keeping to the order given above.

Activity

Listen silently

Listen with your full attention and in complete silence, while the speaker talks.

Reflection:

Speaker: How did you feel?
Would you have liked anything more from the listener?
At what points?

Listener: How did you feel?
Would you have liked to do or say something?
At what points?
What did you gain/lose by not intervening?

Observer: Describe what you saw in the interaction.

Activity

Listen with body language

Listen with your full attention, and use body language to convey your attentiveness to the speaker by making encouraging noises, gestures, facial expression, etc which let the speaker know that he or she is being listened to.

Reflection:

Speaker: How did you feel?
Which gestures, expressions, noises, etc helped you?
Were any of the listener's 'messages' distracting?

Listener: How did you feel?
Did you hear more than you usually do?

Observer: Describe what you saw in the interaction.

Activity

Listen and lead

Listen and interrupt with your own questions and comments about what the speaker is telling you, in order to lead the topic on in the direction that you want it to go.

Reflection:

Speaker: Did you feel 'heard'?
Did you find that you wanted to 'follow' the listener?
Did you feel that what you were trying to say was 'kidnapped'?

Listener: How did you feel?
Were you aware of any resistance from the speaker when you intervened?
At what points?

Observer: Describe what you saw in the interaction.

Activity

Listen and follow

Listen and give your full attention to what the speaker is telling you, trying to follow what is being said by empathizing as deeply as you can with the experience that he or she is describing.

Reflection:

Speaker: Was there a difference?
What was it?
Would you have liked more direction? When?

Listener: Did you learn any more/less about the listener?
What strategies helped you to really follow the speaker?

Observer: Describe what you saw in the interaction.

Activity

Listen and re-tell

Listen to the speaker with your full attention. When the speaker has finished, tell back to the speaker as much as you can of what he or she told you, using the first person 'I' as if you were taking the place of the original speaker.

Reflection:

Speaker: Did you feel that the listener accurately represented what you said?
How did you feel at points where the listener 'got it wrong'?

Listener: How easy or difficult was the re-telling for you?
If you 'lost' or misrepresented particular parts of the original, why do you think this was?
Do you feel that re-telling the story in the first person helped you to gain empathy with the first speaker?

Observer: Describe what you saw in the interaction.

These last five activities invite you to pay attention to some of the subtle but significant effects which your behaviour as a listener can have on the way that other people are able to interact with you. As teachers, we pay a price for failing to pay systematic attention to how we can improve the learning and helping relationship with our students by developing our own ability to listen. Bringing to light the choices that are available by practising the skills suggested above, enables you to begin to make them part of your conscious repertoire and vary them to suit the moment.

6 Six Category Intervention Analysis

As you begin to develop better listening skills, as you become more able to pay attention to others when they speak, to reduce the amount of judgement and interpretation and to understand what they are saying with greater accuracy, so you will begin to feel the need for more skilful ways of intervening, of guiding, of eliciting, of giving feedback; in short, of being a more skilled helper.

Six Category Intervention Analysis is an interpersonal skills training model. It is designed for professional people whose job requires them to listen, support, guide and give feedback in ways that are honest, direct and supportive. It proposes six broad categories of intervention:

Authoritative	**Facilitative**
Prescriptive (giving advice)	Cathartic (learning from feelings)
Informative (giving information)	Catalytic (self-discovery talk)
Challenging (confronting supportively)	Supportive (raising self-esteem)

The strength of the model is that:

1. It enables you to make 'visible' and 'tangible' your previously 'invisible' and 'intangible' ways of communicating.
2. On the basis of that, you develop a new repertoire of intervening and facilitating skills.
3. It focuses not only on listening, understanding and respecting the other, but also on guiding, telling, advising and challenging. Thus the model is suited to all aspects of education and training.
4. At all times the focus is on the personal presence of the helper: you can only make effective and creative choices of intervention to the extent that you are really present to what is happening.

Having both attended training workshops, we (Katie and Pauline) both find that the Six Category model has proved particularly useful as a reference framework. I (Katie) find that students (not necessarily from my own class) often come to me with worries about their progress in learning, or about personal relationships, or about fitting in with the culture and lifestyle of their English host family. Before I had learned to work with the Six Category model, I felt quite unsure of my role in these conversations, which often seemed to require answers that I could not provide, or reassurance that I was unable to give. Training showed me that attention and understanding, even if I have no immediate solution, are often better than an unhelpful intervention, and provided me with a 'toolkit' of words and phrases which, while not prescriptive in any way, enabled me to intervene in more helpful ways. I often use the model to reflect afterwards on conversations with students and colleagues who have shared problems and anxieties with me, particularly if I feel that I have not 'helped' as well as I might have.

John Heron, who developed the Six Category model for the Human Potential Research Group at the University of Surrey, provides a full account of it in his book *Helping the Client*. While the skills he describes can really only be effectively learned through attending a workshop with a trained facilitator, we feel that it is important for you to know about the model, which has influenced many teachers (including ourselves) who have worked with it. A contact address for more information is given in the Appendix.

Activity

Six Category Intervention Analysis is based on the idea that our intention determines the quality of our help, and that we can become more effective helpers as we become more aware of our hidden, half-hidden and conscious intention within any helping situation. Once we are clear about our intention, it is much easier to choose words, gestures and behaviour that accurately convey that intention.

- Can you recall an occasion at work when you have wanted to talk to someone about a problem, and their response has seemed less than helpful?
- Can you say what the other person did to give you this feeling? For example, did she talk more than you? Did she shift the focus away from you and onto herself or someone else? Did she offer solutions which didn't fit? Did her body language give you the message that she wasn't listening or wasn't believing what you were saying?
- When a student comes to you for advice, do you think that you normally give it in an authoritative or a facilitative manner? If you decided that you would like to try using a different style of helping from the one you normally use, what would this involve for you?
- Is there one category that you tend to avoid? Can you think of possible reasons for this?

---

7 Effective helping

Heron defines 'helping' as 'supporting and enabling the well-being of another person' (1990 p11). Although in his view all people have what he calls 'inner grace' which is the primary source of effective helping behaviour, he argues that attempts to help are often obscured or distorted by professional training, socialization and cultural influence.

> One of the primary aspects of character needed for effective helping is ... 'emotional competence'. For helpers, this means that their own anxiety and distress ... does not drive and distort their attempts to help ...

> There are three levels of emotional competence. The first is zero level when a person's helping is always contaminated by hidden, distorted emotion and has an oppressive, interfering and inappropriate quality. The second ... is when a person does help in an emotionally clean way at some times, but also slips over at other times into compulsive, intrusive 'helping' *without realising that he or she has done so*. The third level of emotional competence is when a person makes this kind of slip much less often, knows when it has happened, and can correct it ... In my experience, the second of these levels is widespread in our culture. So there is a lot of misshapen compulsive helping around, among the tutored and the untutored, the professionals and the laity. Hence, the main preparation for helping ... is the widespread dissemination of emotional competence ...
>
> Much of this preparation, certainly among adults, can be done through the training of peer self-help groups, in which people learn to prompt and support each other's self-direction in emotional house-clearing ...
>
> *Heron 1990 pp11–13*

Activity

- Can you recall an occasion when somebody seemed to be offering you the wrong kind of help? Or you may have observed this happening between other people, for example a teacher trying to help a student. Does Heron's analysis help you to understand what might have been going on?
- Are you aware of 'a compulsion to help' in your own dealings with people at work?
- Where would you place yourself on the three levels of emotional competence that Heron identifies?

---

8 Cooperative Development

In the previous reading John Heron drew attention to the potential of self-help peer groups in developing interpersonal helping skills. The 'Cooperative Development' model proposed by Julian Edge is designed to facilitate interaction between two people for the purpose of helping one of the pair to develop their own ideas and plans supported by the other listening and attending in a facilitative manner. Julian Edge has used the model with language teachers in many parts of the world who are interested in working collaboratively on their own development. Here he explains the rationale underlying it:

> I want to investigate and assess my own teaching. I can't do that without understanding it better, and I can't understand it on my own ... I need someone to work with, but I don't need someone who wants to change me and make me more like the way they think I ought to be. I need someone who will help me see myself clearly. To make this possible, we need a distinct style of working together so that each person's development remains in the

person's own hands. This type of interaction will involve learning some new rules for speaking, for listening and for responding in order to cooperate in a disciplined way. This mixture of awareness-raising and disciplined cooperation is what I have called *Cooperative Development.*

Edge 1992a pp3–4

The framework for this model of Cooperative Development consists of one teacher being the Speaker and the other being the Understander.

By making every effort to understand the Speaker, the Understander assists the Speaker's development. The role of the Understander in Cooperative Development is to help the Speaker develop the Speaker's own ideas as the Speaker clarifies them and discovers where they lead ... Cooperative Development is carried out in the roles of Speaker and Understander, for a pre-arranged period of time, or until the participants agree to stop. On another occasion, of course, these roles can be exchanged.

Edge 1992b pp62–3

If you would like to read a full account with exercises which demonstrate how Cooperative Development operates, you need to get hold of Julian Edge's book (1992a) and work through it. We cannot provide such a detailed account ourselves. Our purpose in referring to the approach here is that it proposes a well-defined structure for teachers to put into practice the listening skills described in earlier sections. The role of the Understander is to listen and respond in just such ways, enabling the Speaker to explore his or her own beliefs and feelings about being a teacher.

The following account by a teacher in Turkey of how she and her colleagues have used Cooperative Development to prepare for peer observation, provides an example of its effectiveness.

A group of colleagues in my institution and I found a very effective means to teacher development. Through the idea of *Cooperative Development* (Edge 1992), which offers an accessible but rather disciplined framework that teachers can use to draw on their own experience and understanding of their own situation, we all became aware of the most important thing in teacher development: that is self development. What attracted us in *Cooperative Development* was the idea that *your development is in your own hands and this can be best achieved by co-operating with your colleagues.* Working together with colleagues in order to develop ourselves *to become a better teacher* in our own way, we discovered the importance of listening to each other ...

In 15 hours, we carried out the tasks in the book, in the roles of Speaker, Understander and Observer, which helped us develop certain techniques or abilities that we needed. There are nine such abilities grouped into three blocks of three. They are:

Exploration	**Discovery**	**Action**
Attending	Thematising	Goal-setting
Reflecting	Challenging	Trialling
Focusing	Disclosing	Planning

At the final stage, *Planning*, we discussed how to proceed with observation. We decided on which class would be observed and talked about the focus of the observer. Most of us observed each other in class and then held feedback meetings.

Before starting such a co-operative project in our school we used to have observations only for evaluation, which really made us feel nervous and anxious while we were being observed. However, when we had our colleagues watching us teaching in class, all of us ... felt so relaxed and confident because we knew why our colleague was there and that we would not be judged but would get feedback after the lesson ... I prefer *Cooperative Development* as a starting point because ... '*the aim is not to change each other but to make each other be aware of their opinions and ideas'.*

Kiratli 1993 pp7–9

9 Giving feedback in groups

As we saw at the start of Chapter 3, one characteristic of successful learning groups is that the members listen to each other. Once members are able to listen with respect and trust, they are able to move on and use the group to give each other personal feedback.

The Johari Window

The Johari Window is a feedback model used in group counselling. It takes its name from the psychologists who first developed it, Joseph Luft and Harry Ingham. It provides a simple and useful framework for understanding the limits of our present self-awareness and the possibilities of developing this through exploring different sections of the window.

“

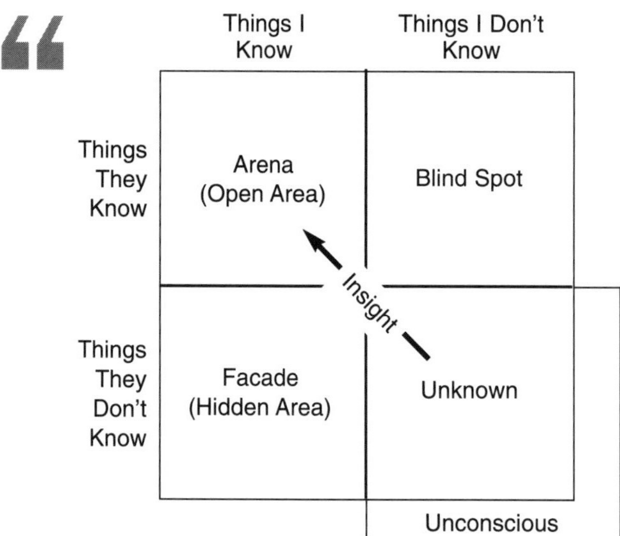

Luft 1984 From: *Group Processes: An Introduction to Group Dynamics, Third Ed by Joseph Luft*

Gertrude Moskowitz, who trains language teachers in the use of humanistic techniques in the classroom, finds the Johari Window helpful as a way of understanding the process by which groups of people, including students in a class, can become closer and more accepting of each other. In this excerpt she describes how the model works:

> The model is viewed as a communication window through which information is given and received about oneself and others. It works this way. There are four areas in the window. The Open or Public Area contains information which I know about myself and you also know; it is therefore public knowledge. The Blind Spot consists of those things you know about me but that I am unaware of. The Facade or Hidden Area is just the reverse, those things about me that I keep to myself, that I do not want you to know. Perhaps I need to trust you more to reveal these things, or I may feel that you will think less of me if I let you know these parts of myself. The Unknown Area has data about me that neither you nor I am aware of. Some may be at the unconscious level.
>
> Now how does the model work? Ideally, the largest area should be the Open Area in which you and I know a good many things about me, while the other areas should be quite small. The way this can come about is through sharing and feedback. That is, the more I let you know about me, the smaller my Hidden Area will be and the larger the Open Area will grow. My Blind Spot will decrease if you give me feedback related to the things I may not yet realize about myself.
>
> As I share things about myself with you and give you feedback, I may develop some insights into myself that are in the Unknown Area. If I then share these insights with you, they revert to the Open Area. Therefore, through sharing and feedback the Public or Open Area increases, while the other three areas decrease. Humanistic techniques ... aim at increasing the Open Area for everyone and, through the process of giving and receiving information about ourselves and each other, warmth and closeness develop ...
>
> *Moskowitz 1978 pp17–18*

Activity

The following activity allows group members to disclose as much personal feedback to others as they feel comfortable with.

For this activity you need a set of blank cards and some pens. Either the group leader alone, or everyone in the group, can write on the cards.

Stage 1

On each card you write down something that would be a reason for communicating to another member of the group some information about the way they appear to you. For example:

Tell someone why you would like them to teach one of your classes.	Tell someone why you would like to know more about them.	Tell someone why you would like to share a desert island with them.
Tell someone why you would not like to be with them in an emergency.	Tell someone why you would not like to go on holiday with them.	Tell someone why you would like them to help you cope with a personal problem.
Tell someone about how you see the contribution they make to the group.	Tell someone what leadership qualities you think they have.	Tell someone why you find them difficult to work with.

The idea behind the activity is to let individuals know what personal qualities they are manifesting in the group.

The group leader, or each person in the group, can write as many cards as they like. The cards are placed face down in a pile.

Stage 2

Each person in turn follows this procedure:

1 They pick up a card from the pile and read it.

2 They decide whether or not they can do the activity on the card.

3 They *either* do it *or* pass the card to somebody else in the group who they think *could* do it.

4 If they decide to respond to the card themselves, they speak directly to the person concerned.

5 If they decide to pass the card on, they tell the person they give it to why they are giving it to them. This person can choose either to respond to what is on the card or to pass it on again.

6 In a follow-up discussion, the group leader invites members of the group to express any feelings or ideas that have been highlighted by the activity. These are discussed in the context of developing awareness of how groups work.

I (Pauline) learned this activity at a workshop on groupwork skills given by 'Feedback Communications', an organization which teaches counselling and groupwork skills in the UK.

In this activity, feedback happens in many ways. Firstly, at the stage of writing the card the writer feeds into the group a concern that he has identified and would like feedback to be given on. Secondly, at the stage of deciding whether he can do the activity suggested, the person who picked up the card acknowledges both to himself and to the group something about his ability and readiness to cope with certain types of feedback. Thirdly, if he decides to hand the card to another person in the group, he is giving that person feedback about how his behaviour and group contribution is viewed. And fourthly, he receives feedback from the person using the card.

10 Language that builds up trust

The manner in which people address each other in a group is crucial. It can either build or destroy trust; enable or disable learning. In order to establish trust, it is important for group members to be open with each other and to communicate directly, while avoiding strategies which may cause hurt or damage. In their writing about student-centred learning, Donna Brandes and Paul Ginnis draw particular attention to the ways in which language can make a difference to the way that people relate to each other in a group.

1 Avoiding sarcasm

Sarcasm is one of the all-time great destroyers of trust. It is indirect communication. It often says the opposite of what it means, and people on the receiving end are often confused as to what is intended. It is argued that sarcasm is harmless amongst friends ... But we contend that there is always a risk involved; you can never really know whether the other person has been hurt or not, because we have been trained and conditioned to be 'good sports', to laugh whether we feel like it or not, and to join in the repartee.

Brandes and Ginnis 1986 p49

2 'Owning' your statements

... people tend to disown a statement by saying, 'One often finds ...' This generalises a personal feeling, which saddles the rest of the population with an idea which perhaps does not apply to them, and also allows the person making the statement to evade his ownership of the problem. Another way of hiding is to say 'You know how it is; you often feel ...'; not only does this transfer responsibility, but also it makes it more difficult for the listener to have and express his own feelings if they are not the same as the speaker's. A third evasion is to say 'We all feel ...' without consulting the rest of the people in the group. Such a statement puts pressure on the rest of the group to agree ... and so again blocks direct communication.

ibid p52

When we talk either to colleagues in a teacher development group, or to students in the classroom, we need to pay attention to the words we are using, to ensure that the language is clear, that we say what we mean and that we mean what we say. While expressing what is essentially a personal opinion, are we claiming to represent a more generally held view than is actually the case? While paying lip service to learner independence and student responsibility in class, are we using language that persuades or coerces the learners into doing what we want? Powerful messages from our own past, or accepted cultural norms, often lead us into habits of using language in ways that are more authoritarian than we are aware of. As soon as you begin to notice this in other people, you will probably realize that it is equally true of yourself.

3 Not 'rescuing' people

Many people find silence difficult. Whenever there is a gap in the discussion, they feel compelled to jump in. The particular person whose turn it is to speak knows that if they wait long enough someone is eventually bound to come to their rescue. This is where many of the listening skills described above come in handy. Allowing silence, using it in a positive way and supporting the other person with our attention and positive regard will ultimately help them much more than diving in and 'rescuing' them.

Handing over responsibility to students requires them to be confident enough to accept it. In order to build this confidence, the teacher will need to avoid rescuing them every time the going gets a bit rough. For example, we have seen the following exchange taking place on many occasions:

Teacher: Right, we need a volunteer for the next exercise.
Students: *(stony silence)*
Teacher: Come on ... who's going to volunteer?
Students: *(looking at floor; no answer)*
Teacher: Right then, Clare. We'll start with you.

In most cases, the teacher intervenes in this way because he cannot stand the silence; the students are very aware of this, and they know that if they wait long enough they will be rescued eventually, so why should they bother to take the risk and volunteer? We suggest an alternative interchange:

Teacher: Right, we need a volunteer for the next exercise.
Students: *(stony silence)*
Teacher: *(Waits patiently, feeling confident that the students want to get going as he does.)*
Students: *(looking at the floor; no answer)*
Teacher: Well, I see that no-one wants to be the first to volunteer. Shall we move on to something else, or what do you recommend we could do about it?

In this way the teacher indicates that he is there to support the students in accomplishing the task in hand, and that he is not there to rescue them or relieve them of their responsibility.

ibid pp54–5

4 Use of touch

There are many cultures around the world where touching is a normal part of interaction between people. Sometimes in groups a relationship develops between the members in which it feels natural and desirable for people to include touching among the ways that they communicate. A positive view of the role of physical touching between group members is that:

> ... touching can break down barriers and build trust within the group. If you allow a [person] to touch you, you are indicating your acceptance of him as a person; if you actively resist being touched, you may be sending a message which says 'You and I have to be separate; you must keep your distance.'
>
> *ibid pp56–7*

Touching can be unhelpful and set up resistances, however, unless it is a natural and comfortable empathic response between people. Individual needs and preferences need to be respected by the group.

11 Other techniques for effective communication

A central principle of groupwork is that each person's contribution is valued equally. Four techniques which encourage sharing and active participation by everyone in the group are *circles*, *brainstorming*, *rounds* and the use of *games*. They are described below.

1 Circles

There are a number of advantages to sitting in a circle to do groupwork:
- You can all see each other, and hear each other.
- You can all make eye contact.
- You are all equal.
- The facilitator or leader, if there is one, is a member of the group.
- It's easier to concentrate and listen to each other.
- There are no barriers between you.
- You feel like a group.
- You can speak to each other more easily.

However, the circle arrangement can feel very unsafe at first. People feel exposed and overly self-conscious. This is natural, but it can be overcome. The aim is for the circle quickly to become a safe place, where people can speak freely, express their opinions, share their feelings and contribute *or not* without fear of ridicule. Using the good listening and communication techniques we have described in this chapter will help this to happen.

It helps to have comfortable chairs and no extraneous furniture obstructing the circle.

2 Brainstorming

Brainstorming involves the whole group and is a very effective way of generating a large number of ideas quickly. It also encourages creativity and lateral thinking, which are necessary for personal development.

Donna Brandes and Paul Ginnis have the following advice if you are facilitating a brainstorming activity:

It is important to get across to the group that you are going to take seriously whatever it is that they say. We feel that the best way to do this is to write down absolutely everything they say, and censor nothing, even if it is silly …

Underlying all the purposes of brainstorming, there is one fundamental aim: the enhancement of self-concept. It is not magical, it is not a panacea, but it *is* a very subtle and effective method. The fact that all contributions are accepted and anonymous, that no one is excluded or evaluated, that most of the time the [facilitator] cannot even notice who is participating, all add up to a positive feeling in the group.

Brandes and Ginnis 1986 p37

3 Rounds

A round is an activity in which each person in the circle has an opportunity to make a statement about whatever subject is agreed by the group. One person starts, and the turns move round the circle. There are two rules. First, no one may comment on what anyone else says; second, anyone can say 'I pass' when it is their turn.

The aim of the round is to provide a structure within which everyone has a chance to say something, but is not forced to do so. All ideas and opinions are valued equally. The freedom *not* to participate is extremely important in establishing trust. It is also important that no-one is interrupted, and that no-one comments, positively or negatively, on anyone else's contribution while a round is in progress.

The round can be used at any point where there needs to be an expression of opinion, or feedback, or planning, or evaluation. It can be a good way of starting a group session and re-establishing a feeling of safety within the group members.

Bonnie Tangalos has regularly used the technique of rounds to start off teacher development sessions. She describes here how the teachers responded to this kind of activity.

We began all of our 2-hour sessions by going round the circle with each person relating one good thing that had happened to them during the past week. These incidents, or 'goods' as we called them, had preferably taken place in the classroom, but could have come from our personal lives as well. At first many participants had difficulty finding something good, as they all admitted to focusing more often on the negative as opposed to the positive. This slowly began to change over the course of our sessions.

Tangalos 1990

Generally speaking it is a good idea to 'accentuate the positive', as Bonnie did, by choosing a topic which leaves people feeling better about themselves at the end than they did at the beginning. Teachers often arrive at the group feeling tired and pressurized. Starting with something positive is a great energy-raiser, as well as focusing people's attention on the group and on the here and now.

Rosie Tanner suggests two activities (below) which both take the form of 'Rounds'.

Rosie has used these activities with teachers' groups, but the ideas can be used with any group wanting to work on building up the self-esteem of its members.

Activity

Things I do badly *(adapted from Brandes 1982 p112)*

This activity works best with a group of 8 to 10 people.

Step 1

- The group sits in a circle so that everyone has eye contact. The following sentence stem is written on the board:
  'I'm very bad at ...'
- Each group member takes a turn at saying something they believe they do very badly as a teacher or trainer.

Step 2

- A second sentence stem is put up:
  'People say I'm very good at ...'
- Group disclosure as above. Keep the theme of teaching going: each person should talk about an aspect of teaching/training that other people *say* they are good at.

Step 3

- A third sentence stem is written up:
  'I am very good at ...'
- The group members reveal in turn what they are good at as a teacher (compared with step 2, where they say what other people believe about them).

Rosie comments:

This third step is the most important. People can often talk for hours about aspects of themselves which they are unhappy about, but sometimes find it difficult to be positive about themselves. In the third step, to stimulate more positive thinking and speaking, the group leader can invite elaboration, by encouraging participants to ask questions about why the speaker feels s/he is good at something, or in which ways.

Tanner 1992

Activity

You are wonderful *(adapted from Moskowitz 1978 pp80–1)*

The group again sits in a circle.

Step 1

Each participant looks at everyone in their group and decides what each person's most outstanding quality is. They list everyone's names and make brief notes, including themselves in the list. If the participants don't know each other, they imagine what the others' greatest qualities are.

Step 2

The group focuses on one person at a time. Everyone else in the group reveals what they believe that person's most outstanding quality to be, beginning their sentence with that person's name:
'Tino, I think your most outstanding quality is your ability to include everyone. For example ...'

Rosie comments:

This can produce much amusement and a sense of release; and the using of first names reinforces the message. The person focused upon can react in whatever way they choose. If the group doesn't know each other, it is an effective activity to discover what positive images we project in the presence of strangers.

In many cultures, including the British culture, it is often taboo to voice praise for others or to speak about your own strengths. If you feel awkward about running such a personal growth activity in your own culture, one way around the 'Yes, buts' is to air this problem. Discuss why self-valuing and the valuing of others is difficult in your own cultural context. Be explicit about the reasons for trying to raise self-esteem: teachers often feel under-valued, people need praise and feel better for receiving it, trust building and support between colleagues improves the working atmosphere ... You can no doubt think of more reasons.

Both of the activities described above assume that a group leader or facilitator is present. As facilitator, you can choose one of two roles: you can either participate in one small group, and stay with it, or you can remain apart, guiding participants through the steps but otherwise not interfering. Too much monitoring of this kind of personal growth activity, eavesdropping on each group, can break the 'magic' of interaction between participants, which can be quite personal. An outsider entering a group, albeit a friendly facilitator, can break the special dynamic which occurs. The disadvantage of being the aloof facilitator is that you, unfortunately, miss out on the magic.

ibid

4 Using games

Games have many uses in groupwork. They help people to relax and they stimulate communication. Brandes and Ginnis find them particularly valuable in the early stages of a group, when ground rules are being established and trust is being built. Apart from this, they can 'lift' a session which is floundering or becoming over-serious. Brandes and Ginnis (1977) and Brandes (1982) have lots of good ideas for games that can be played in adult groups. They suggest that games can:

- provide a structure to lean on
- initiate group work skills

- defuse tension
- build trust and sensitivity
- enhance self-esteem
- provide opportunity for everyone to participate (or not)
- enhance academic achievement
- break down teacher/student and student/student barriers
- promote good communication
- improve group functioning
- increase self-disclosure
- increase concentration
- encourage creativity and lateral thinking

Brandes and Ginnis 1986 p43

Activity

- How do you understand the term 'games'?
- What games do you use when you are teaching?
- What is your aim in using them?
- Do you use them for some of the reasons above?
- Which of the games you use in class could be adapted and used in a teacher development group, and what adaptations would be necessary?

Several of the group activities we have already suggested in this chapter might be construed as 'games'. In addition, here are three more ideas for games that have worked well for us:

Activity

'All Change'

1 Arrange chairs in a circle with one less chair than the number of people in the group. The person without a seat stands in the middle of the circle.

2 The person who is standing gives an instruction starting with 'Change places if ...' which requires certain members of the group to change places. For example: 'Change places if you're wearing black shoes.' All the people wearing black shoes must respond as quickly as possible.

3 As the group members get up and move to new places, the person who gave the instruction grabs a seat, leaving someone else standing in the middle of the circle. This person must give the next instruction.

4 The game continues in this way for as long as seems appropriate.

If you are playing with a group of students, you can use the game to practise a particular grammar point such as use of the present continuous tense. If you are playing with a group of teachers, you might choose to focus on aspects of teaching;

for example 'Change places if you often use games in the classroom.' 'Change places if you think you talked too much in class today.' 'Change places if you thought the staff meeting was a waste of time.'

I (Katie) used to play a version of this game with my family at Christmas parties, but it was Katie Plumb who first gave me the idea of using it in the classroom. Davis and Rinvolucri describe a similar activity in 'The Confidence Book' (1990 p50) under the title 'Fruit Salad'.

Activity

'Pass the Object'

There is no speaking in this game. Everything is done in mime.

1 Group members sit in a circle.

2 The first person holds an imaginary object, and mimes using it for its normal purpose. He then passes it on to the person sitting on his left, who 'uses' it and then erases it by making a rubbing out motion with his hands.

3 This person now creates a new imaginary object, mimes using it in the same way as before, then passes it on to the person on her left.

4 The game continues round the circle until everyone has had a turn, and the final 'object' is handed on to the person who began the game.

I (Katie) learned this game some years ago in a teacher development workshop at the IATEFL Conference, and more recently came across it in 'The Gamesters' Handbook' by Brandes and Ginnis (1977 p96).

Activity

'Quick on the Draw'

This game works best as a competition between groups, so a larger group needs to divide into smaller groups of not less than three people. Each group needs a large piece of paper (or several smaller pieces) and a felt pen.

1 The leader stands at some distance from the groups, and has a 'secret' list of subjects.

2 When everyone is ready to begin, one person from each group runs to the leader, who tells them the first subject on the list.

3 The runner returns to his or her group and draws the subject on the paper for the rest of his group to guess. The runner is not allowed to speak, or to write any words.

4 As soon as someone in the group guesses what the subject is, that person runs to the leader, confirms the answer, and is told the next subject.

5 The game continues until one group has correctly guessed all the subjects on the leader's list.

This game is described by Brandes and Ginnis in 'A Guide to Student-Centred Learning' (1986 p259). The subjects on the leader's list can be chosen to suit the group playing the game: language learners could, for example, be given common colloquial expressions to draw, such as 'Pleased to meet you' or 'It's a pity he's out.' A group of teachers might have fun with ELT jargon such as 'autonomous learner', 'phrasal verb', or 'Silent Way'.

Some adults have an in-built resistance to any activity which is introduced as a 'game'. Yet just as medicine doesn't have to taste vile in order to do you good, so activities don't have to be intellectual to have a serious learning purpose to them. On the contrary, people learn best when they are relaxed and energized. If games are introduced in the right way, people resist them less and often discover that they have a wealth of creative talent. A group which keeps bursting into laughter while applying itself to the task in hand is unhindered by inhibition or embarrassment and free to explore every possibility.

12 Conclusion

Many teachers find, as they become more experienced in teaching their subject, that they want to know more about the way that groups work and to become more skilled in facilitating them. This chapter has looked at some of the skills and techniques associated with effective communication in groups. They can be useful in working with any kind of group, whether in the classroom, the staffroom, or a group you are involved in outside the workplace. In the next chapter we focus on some of the issues involved in setting up and running groups, with particular reference to teacher development groups.

Chapter 5 Starting and running teacher development groups

1 Introduction

As we use the term in this book, a *teacher development group* can be any form of co-operative and ongoing arrangement between two or more teachers to work together on their own personal and professional development. We begin this chapter with five personal accounts by teachers of development groups in which they have participated, or which they have facilitated. Their stories reflect the variety and richness of the ways in which teachers are working together on their development, as this concept is interpreted in different contexts, cultures and countries.

In the remainder of the chapter we look at some of the important issues that affect the life of groups. We have in mind particularly the kind of group which is formed for the purpose of mutual support and collaborative development (see section 3 below), and, because we know that many teachers are interested in starting or joining a teacher development group, our comments and activities refer frequently to such groups. But whatever kind of group you are or would like to be involved in, you are likely to face similar issues. We hope that this material will help you to deal with them.

2 Five 'own stories' of teacher development groups

These five accounts from the IATEFL Teacher Development Group Newsletter describe how teacher development groups have functioned in different parts of the world. As you read them, you may like to think about these questions:

- What features of this group made it effective?
- Is there anything I can draw from this account that will help me to see the opportunities for teacher development in my place of work?

'When you get lemons ...' (Greece)

Bonnie Tangalos facilitated a number of teacher development group meetings at the Hellenic-American Union in Athens, Greece. She sensed a growing need for the teachers to have a forum where they could release feelings of overwork and extreme pressure, from both their personal and professional lives; and where they could discuss attitudes towards their teaching. She also wanted to provide the teachers with some tools for self-analysis which they could use to reflect on their classroom behaviour and to make changes if they wanted to. Participation in the groups was voluntary, but a large number of teachers chose to attend the two-hour sessions.

... At one group meeting, I distributed a hand-out which summarized research on effective classroom teaching, entitled 'What the experts say about teacher effectiveness'. We then shared how this made us feel and we began talking about what makes us feel good, 'empowered', in the classroom. How do we know when we are effective? What are our own criteria for effectiveness? What limits our effectiveness in the classroom was next discussed, and we began listing situations which make us feel angry in the classroom. From there, we tried to figure out why these things make us so angry. Discussion then centred around how to better cope with those feelings to encourage greater effectiveness as teachers.

Other topics included our feelings about English teaching and the English language, our perceptions of ourselves and how others perceive us, and how we manage our time. The notion of time management arose because the participants found themselves continually saying that they never seemed to have enough time to do what they wanted to do. We used a questionnaire format to begin the discussion and the group took off ...

An activity to think or write about at home was distributed at the end of each session. The most provocative asked the participants to complete one of two tasks: to write either an advertisement about themselves as a teacher or a portrait of themselves. Many of the participants were very uncomfortable with the advertisement and this in itself brought up important feelings. The portraits were wonderful, with teachers writing original poems or quoting poems that they felt represented them. Some participants used collages to illustrate the various parts of their personalities ...

What outcomes, planned or unplanned, resulted from the sessions? All the teachers felt that they had grown closer to their colleagues and some of the groups were able to coalesce to a startling degree ... All said they felt less alone with their problems. All felt more relaxed and able to carry on with their responsibilities after a session.

Many participants exclaimed over a new-found understanding of their classroom behaviour and felt that this knowledge was an invaluable tool. All believed that the process of being in a group, sharing feelings and looking at values, spilled over into their personal lives ... Everyone felt that they were more able to look at the positive side and one of our favourite expressions was: 'When you get lemons, make lemonade!'

Tangalos 1990 pp10–12

'Caring and sharing at work' (UK)

Sue Greenland facilitated a group at a UK language school which met for two terms to look at 'counselling and self-assessment'.

... From a background of 2 years co-counselling and group dynamics experience, I have come to appreciate and recognise the importance of the personal development that counselling offers. It has been exciting to 'own' that the expression of needs and emotions is natural and professional in the right setting both inside and outside school.

As facilitator of the group consisting of 6 members, I took it upon myself to set out the following aims as I saw them:

- to become better listeners
- to develop counselling skills
- to create a safe space for the group to share our thoughts and feelings about our work as teachers and colleagues.

At the first meeting, two other considerations were drawn to the attention of the group: confidentiality, in that everything which was said in the group was confidential and not to be discussed or referred to outside the group without consultation; and time-keeping and attendance. With only 45 minutes once a week, the commitment to the group and to each other was very important.

... we met for two terms and looked at basic counselling theory, indulged in games and exercises to improve our listening skills and developed and practised our counselling skills. Though time was at a premium, we were able to achieve much more than we had set out to do. It is these achievements which I feel are particularly significant and which have had implications for our teaching.

- We have learned the importance of listening with attention to identify potential areas and patterns of distress, with a view to guiding the person talking to explore their feelings and the sources of distress.
- We have increased our own self-awareness and understanding in exploring our reactions to situations in the classroom.
- We have a greater awareness and understanding of the complexities which

can be beneath behaviour and attitudes displayed in the classroom which seem inexplicable, straightforward or superficial.
- We recognise the crucial importance of not drawing conclusions about a situation without seeking further knowledge of what may be behind a behavioural or educational problem.
- We have realised that learning/behavioural problems can be a direct result of past learning experiences and that exploring such experiences can affect and change present experiences.
- We have been able to establish closer relationships within the group and our classes (without creating emotional dependence) and remove barriers which hinder meaningful communication.
- We have much greater awareness of group dynamics and how individuals can affect group behaviour.
- We have been able to begin to reassess our role as teachers and our responsibilities to our students.

As human beings we are all, at times, counsellors. What has been important for us is that [we] recover these important, innate counselling skills and put them to a practical purpose in our work as teachers.

Greenland 1986 p2

'One year on' (UK)

A group of teachers in Cambridge decided to meet informally once a week after school, to discuss and try out humanistic techniques and provide a support system to give encouragement to each other. After it had been running for a year, Katie Plumb listed some of the topics the group had worked with, and reflected on why the group continued to flourish as it did.

A few of us found that we were gathering together after school to talk about our classes and new ideas or good lessons. We agreed to meet once a week ... About eight teachers started this group on a very informal and voluntary basis. The sessions were completely practical and any new idea was tried out so that we could experience it rather than just talk about it. These are some of the topics that we worked with:

- Humanistic techniques: these were basically ideas from [teacher's resource books] which had been tried out or adapted. These sessions sparked off ideas of our own ...
- Co-counselling: how it can be used in the classroom and for ourselves as teachers
- Pronunciation
- First week of a course activities
- Checklist of awareness points
- Assertiveness and positiveness, in and out of class
- Classroom comfort: walls, furniture, etc

I think one of the main reasons that the group is such a success is that it was totally voluntary ..., organised by teachers, for teachers ... Many of the ideas developed from one session to the next. An atmosphere was created where everything we did had a positive element and everyone felt they could listen to and respect others ... A lot of the ideas we tried out in these sessions have now become part of our teaching and there is always encouragement and enthusiasm to try out something new.

Plumb 1987 p11

'Is there time for much teacher development?' (Brazil)

At a branch of the Cultura Inglesa in Brazil, the teachers decided to formalize the ongoing exchange of ideas that takes place in the staff room during breaks between lessons. They recognized that there were other ways of satisfying their need to keep up with new developments in language teaching than to spend many hours reading and taking outside courses, and that in addition the exchange with colleagues would help each individual to develop themselves.

... It is not always possible to take courses or to read much considering the hectic sort of life some of us have to lead. For those who are overburdened with a large number of classes, with piles of students' written work to check and a family to look after, the only way is to rely on constant exchange of ideas with colleagues ...

... We teachers decided to add a little more to this exchange, feeling the need for activities that would help each individual to develop him/herself. We have started monthly academic meetings, the aim of which is to discuss topics of professional interest. These are planned and coordinated by groups of three or four teachers in turn, with the rest of the staff participating as a motivated audience.

After choosing the topic of their preference, each member of the group in charge reads extensively about it. This is followed by a discussion about what was read, and they then decide which aspect of the topic each one would like to be in charge of. There is usually a third 'get-together' for a final discussion before the meeting itself ...

For the first meeting the three teachers in charge got together and agreed that 'Teaching grammar creatively' would be a relevant theme. We decided to start mentioning the important role of grammar in our English classroom. That was followed by an account of our personal experiences as students of English facing grammar in class some years ago, and our views on the teaching of grammar nowadays. To round it all off, some successful techniques were demonstrated, as a more practical contribution to the event.

The second meeting was about 'Writing', another crucial issue in Brazil. The results have been rewarding ... Ideas are being exchanged, and suggestions are being made, everything in a most friendly atmosphere. Discussions have led to reflection, which has contributed significantly to our development not only as professionals but also as human beings.

Parreiras 1991 pp8–9

'Recharging our language batteries' (China)

Cheng He, a teacher in Xi'an, China, writes about the priority for foreign language teachers in her country to keep up their language proficiency, in order to improve their chances of promotion and to be respected by their learners. She explains that in China the traditional view of teachers is still very pervasive, and that teachers are judged on the extent of their 'knowledge' and ability to answer students' questions.

Groups of teachers have found that by meeting together they can help each other to improve their English. By identifying their own needs and setting their own agenda for self-improvement, these teachers are engaging in teacher development.

In our institute, we have done some experiments to find a proper method which could give us an easier way to 'recharge' ourselves ... In the last half year we tried another method, the main aim of which was to improve our English. We three teachers met every week to work as a group. Instead of discussing teaching methods each time, we met to discuss a story we had chosen last time and had prepared for this meeting.

As all of us had read for the meeting carefully, we had worked out what we individually understood and what we had not understood, what expressions were new to us or which we thought were used beautifully in the story. We sometimes also discussed whether an expression could be replaced by other expressions and what the difference was if it were replaced. We also picked out some words which were difficult for us. Because of the lack of new authentic materials, the stories we chose were usually stories we had read long ago. At first, we were all startled that we had lost so much English. The stories were unfamiliar to us though we had read them before. There were a lot of new words. Some expressions appeared to be hard to comprehend. The authors seemed to be strangers. We all said we had spent much time looking up words which had not been new to us. For each story, we chose one member to introduce the author to the others. Little by little, we picked up the English language and literature we had forgotten. And now we all believe that we have made great progress, for during the discussion each of us had the opportunity to reach a better conclusion by speaking our minds and determining each other's opinions.

Cheng He 1989 p4

3 How groups can help

There are a number of reasons why groups can be more effective than individuals, both in initiating change for themselves and in managing change imposed from outside.

Firstly, other people's views are a primary resource for enabling individuals to increase their self-awareness. In a caring and supportive environment, learning from other people how they see you as a colleague and teacher can also be an important way of building up self-esteem and feeling positive about the possibilities for development.

Secondly, a group of people who meet together regularly and are free to decide their own agenda tend to develop strong interpersonal bonds which can support an individual member in any decision that they might be making about their own development. You may be thinking about applying for another job, undertaking some further academic study or practical training, taking on a project such as learning another language or doing some research into your learners' backgrounds, or trying your hand at a new skill such as writing for publication or using a new piece of equipment. Perhaps you have an idea for changing something in your school, or perhaps change is happening anyway and you need to find ways of coping. The group provides a safe environment in which to explore your thoughts and feelings about development issues like these.

Thirdly, a group of people with similar ideas and objectives can exert a powerful collective influence on the culture of institutions. In the context of organizational change, people do well to combine their efforts in managing the change process, and to make it their business to get the best they can for themselves.

4 What kind of group?

There are various models for the kind of teachers' group we have in mind. We have drawn for information and ideas on several sources from the 'feeder fields' of counselling and groupwork skills, as well as on personal accounts of successful teachers' groups. It goes without saying that some of the ideas we look at in relation to peer support groups also have relevance to groups of learners working together in the classroom. Some of our source material was in fact originally written with classrooms and learning groups in mind.

Adrian Underhill, the founder of the IATEFL Teacher Development Group, explains why he believes that groups offer such a powerful way of working:

> My experience is that the psychological climate that facilitates teacher development is characterized by interpersonal caring, understanding, and trust, along with a shared commitment to the process of intentional development. Such an atmosphere may help participants to feel secure enough to be more honest with themselves and with others, to have less need to pretend or play games in their responses, and to be willing to reciprocate in supporting the developmental efforts of others. This supportive and genuine atmosphere can help them to take the risks and make the efforts required in trying to extend and deepen their awareness, and to do so with curiosity and excitement rather than with defensiveness and anxiety. This facilitative climate can assist the development of self-awareness through making it safer to be more open to learning from primary experience ('what I can tell myself'), and to be more open to secondary experience ('what others can tell me').
>
> Reduction of judgement of others is one hallmark of such a group, and this in turn makes it easier to open up to one's real experience, and to accept what one finds ... My personality, and how it affects my teaching, becomes visible to me through relating to others. Feedback from other colleagues offers me opportunities to experience myself.
>
> *Underhill 1992 pp77–8*

Activity

Adrian Underhill describes the psychological climate that can characterize a teachers' group that is working well and in some depth on the issues that matter to its participants. The description can also apply to a learner group that has formed and is functioning well. One of the key variables seems to be the degree to which individuals feel the need to judge each other or themselves.

- Of the groups you have been a member of at any time in your life, which have had similar qualities to those described above?
- How does the atmosphere in a group affect your participation?
- What role do you typically take in a group? For example are you very active? Do you tend to be a leader? Do you like listening and observing the others? Are you the 'joker in the pack'?

Many people instinctively fear situations which may require them to reveal more of themselves than they are comfortable with. This is why it is so important, in any group, to respect the principle of self-direction and to allow each person to use the group in whatever way is safe and appropriate for them.

5 Starting a group

Starting a teacher development group involves identifying one or more other people who might be interested, talking through your ideas, fixing a time and place for a first meeting, and then issuing an invitation to other teachers to come and join in. Gaie Houston, who has long experience of facilitating groups, suggests that a subtle approach works best. The skill is to make other people think it was all their idea to start the group; if you do all the organizing yourself, people will see it as 'your' group and are likely to resist joining it.

> In Zen there is a tradition of the Whispered Transmission. One explanation of this is that people will listen if they want to hear. If you tell someone receptive about the advantages of a small group, and then a little later have someone else ask you if you will join or run one, then the whispered transmission has worked. If you put out your message two or three times, and hear no more, then it is possible that nobody is interested, and you had better look elsewhere, or take up a different hobby.
>
> Before you do any whispering, or any other kind of advertising, be sure that you know what the potential group is for. Begin ... with several conversations about this, with people you hope will enrich your thinking.
>
> *Houston 1990 p12*

EFL teachers Katie Plumb and Ian Jasper have successfully established teachers' groups in several countries where they have worked as English teachers. The groups consist of a core of individuals who meet to discuss and try out ideas on a very informal basis. It is taken for granted that everyone is a fully competent teacher who has a lot to offer other members of the group, and that by sharing ideas within the group, each member is able to grow personally and professionally. Katie suggests the following list of steps for teachers who are interested in trying to organize a development group.

1. Determine who is interested in exchanging ideas and information as well as sharing the socialization aspect of the group.
2. Arrange a suitable time.
3. Start the first meeting by introducing a new game or light activity to 'break the ice'.
4. Encourage the group to think of new ideas and issues they'd like to discuss or something they'd like to learn about. Begin with the most popular suggestion.
5. Choose a group member for starting the next meeting with discussions or a game.
6. End each meeting on a positive note with a fun activity.
7. When enough time has been spent on one topic, agree on the next topic and determine who will be responsible for getting that discussion started. This could simply mean photocopying an article for the group members.
8. After a few sessions decide what the next area of discussion will be.
9. The group will vary in size from meeting to meeting, and change its focus and style. Don't give up during the less active periods.
10. It's important that more than one individual have responsibility for starting a session and contributing ideas in case of absence.

Plumb 1994 pp2–3

Activity

Suppose that you decide to get together a small and informal teacher development group in your school or local area. Make some notes on the following questions concerning its organization. If you already have experience of teacher development groups, you can use this experience to inform your answers.

- What do you want to get out of it?
- How will you talk to others about your idea?
- What will you do at the first meeting?

As the group becomes more established, there are other questions to consider.

- When and where will the group meet?
- How often will it meet, and for how long?
- Who will come?
- How will you attract people?
- Is there anyone you will exclude from the group (for example, teachers in promoted positions, course leaders, Directors of Studies)?
- Will there be a group leader or co-ordinator? Why?/Why not?
- If not, how will you deal with issues of responsibility in the group?

- Is there any need for people outside the group to know what is happening? If so, how will you supply this information?
- Will you plan your programme in advance, or will you 'go with the flow' as Katie Plumb suggests above?

These questions aim to start you thinking about some of the practical issues involved in starting a teacher development group. However informal you try to keep it, there is always a need for some kind of formal agreement as to how it will be run. Remember a support group doesn't have to have a large membership. If two or three people are keen, it might be good to start from there with a look at the purpose, composition and format of the group. Then you could invite others to join and there will be a sense of what it is that they're joining.

6 Establishing ground rules

In any group it is important to agree a set of ground rules near the beginning. The ground rules form a contract between the members of the group, and constitute the method of control. One set of ground rules is suggested below as an example, but it is important that your group makes its own and that the rules are negotiated by all the group members.

- We listen to each other.
- We respect each other's ideas and values.
- We take responsibility for ourselves.
- We avoid punishment.
- Participation is optional.
- It is OK to make mistakes; they are valuable learning points.
- We keep our agreements.
- We avoid hurting each other, verbally or physically.

Brandes and Ginnis 1986 pp40–1

It is best to maintain as informal an approach as possible in deciding on the rules that will apply in your group, and to rely on the inner cohesiveness of the group and the members' own sense of belonging. A group which does not have at least some of the following characteristics, identified by David Jaques, is unlikely to be successful.

A group can be said to exist as more than a collection of people when it possesses the following qualities:

1 Collective perception: members are collectively conscious of their existence as a group.
2 Needs: members join a group because they believe it will satisfy some needs or give them some rewards.
3 Shared aims: members hold common aims or ideals which to some extent

bind them together. The achievement of aims is presumably one of the rewards.

4 Interdependence: members are interdependent inasmuch as they are affected by and respond to any event that affects any of the group's members.
5 Social organisation: a group can be seen as a social unit with norms, roles, statuses, power and emotional relationships.
6 Interaction: members influence and respond to each other in the process of communicating, whether they are face-to-face or otherwise deployed. The sense of 'group' exists even when members are not collected in the same place.
7 Cohesiveness: members want to remain in the group, to contribute to its wellbeing and aims, and to join in its activities.
8 Membership: two or more people interacting for longer than a few minutes constitute a group.

None of these characteristics by itself defines a group, but each indicates important aspects.

Jaques 1984 pp1–2

The rules can be negotiated at the start of the group and reviewed periodically so that they don't become too rigid and constraining. Too many rules can set too many boundaries and create expectations around what the group is going to do. It is often better to encourage a flexible approach to roles and expectations within the group, and to establish just a few basic principles which everyone can agree on. The kind of teacher development group that Katie Plumb has started in different places (see earlier in this chapter) operates with a minimum of control and depends on its members to be actively responsible for seeing that it fulfils everyone's needs and expectations.

7 Dealing with feelings in the group

Human beings are capable of a vast range of emotions; yet some societies, especially in the west, seem geared to limiting emotional expression to a narrow, safe and comfortable band of acceptable, 'mature' feelings and behaviours. We want to argue that it is not dangerous to allow people to experience their feelings by bringing them to the surface and expressing them; and that, on the contrary, it is important that teachers learn to understand their own and other people's emotions, in order to become better able to deal with them. It can be good to spend time exploring our feelings. The group provides a safe environment in which this can happen.

Sheila Levy and Sue Leather decided to lead a staff development session on stress at the UK language school where they were both teaching. Here is their account of what happened.

A staff development session on stress

We started by asking those present to make a note of the situations which they found particularly stressful. Here are a few of the comments:

'Having to appear more cheerful in class than I really feel!'

'Feeling that you're expected to be more than human, never lose your temper, etc.'

'Trying to separate home and work.'

'Setting up a discussion and finding nobody says anything.'

'Trying to find innovative ways of teaching and keep up with the latest EFL jargon and methods.'

'Having a new set of people every ten weeks and being faced with new students in the middle of term.'

Next we asked our colleagues to jot down what they saw as the symptoms of stress. These were surprisingly varied, ranging from the fairly common (eg sleeplessness, fatigue, irritability, dreaming about work, headaches, stomach complaints) to the less expected symptoms (eg mild paranoia, poor memory, manic behaviour, lack of perspective and judgement, and even reduced sex-drive).

Following this we asked our colleagues to consider what strategies they use to cope with the symptoms of stress. The answers varied greatly from person to person. Some found that falling into the routine of domestic life was sufficient while others felt that a change of environment was necessary [such as] taking the dog for a walk, [or] browsing round a bookshop ...

Several people said that when they found the emotional pressures of dealing with people all day got them down, they turned to activities requiring logical thought only, such as computer games or crosswords.

Most of us agreed that we found physical exercise beneficial whether it was a gentle stroll or a challenging game of squash, but several people recommended yoga or meditation as their most effective strategy for coping with stress.

Other ways of counteracting the effects of stress included reading, having a bath, watching TV and losing one's temper but we decided that the latter could create more tension than it dispelled because of its effect on others!

So how successful was this as a teacher development session?

Well, we didn't suddenly discover how to avoid stress altogether but it gave us the opportunity to speak honestly about ourselves and recognise that we all suffer from similar stresses particular to our profession. As one teacher put it: 'We're forced to keep up this veneer of professionalism and it does us good to discuss our vulnerability from time to time.'

Levy 1988 p8

Activity

This activity is based on a brainstorming idea suggested by Gaie Houston, which she calls 'Naughty Talk'. The idea is to let out all your pent-up feelings about the people and problems that put you under pressure at work, by imagining what you would really like to do with them if there was nothing to stop you. Brainstorms are most effective when they are not constrained by considerations of reality. The activity is undoubtedly more fun if you do it in a group, and if the group is ready for some not-too-serious adventuring into the realms of fantasy.

You need a large piece of paper and some coloured pens.

1 In as large a group as possible, brainstorm all the people and situations that you would like to exterminate from your workplace.

2 Break into smaller groups and write or draw a set of 'ultimate solutions' that would rid you of them permanently. Let your imagination run riot!

3 Share your ideas and see if you can agree on the most effective and dramatic solutions to your problems.

The serious point to this activity is that it gives people permission to develop creative solutions as a response to real pressures which, when acknowledged, are seen to arouse great extremes of feeling and intent. In discovering the power of their own creativity, most people are instantly energized and uplifted. Of course there is no question of acting on the actual ideas that emerge! Yet letting off steam in a way that is both outrageous and humorous can be a way of putting problems in perspective. And through voicing these impossible solutions, people can sometimes find their way towards a more realistic and achievable strategy for coping.

8 Defining leadership roles

Groups can be led in various ways. Self-help groups often don't have a formal leader, yet there is still a need for forward planning and decision making. Some form of leadership pattern generally emerges, although it may rotate among the members (see Katie Plumb's model above).

The fact that any group owes its existence, and perhaps its inspiration, to a particular founder member, is likely to mean that that person takes on some kind of leadership role, at least in the early days. But, as David Jaques indicates, the choice of leadership styles is wide ranging and there is advantage in being able to move between them and select the one that is most appropriate on a given occasion. The following list follows Jaques' classification, although we have used our own words to expand on what each style of leadership involves.

Leader/Instructor. This is the 'directive leader' who takes full charge of the process and content of the meeting. The danger of this role is that it develops dependency in the group members.

Neutral chairman. The 'neutral chairman' style of leader supervises procedure at the meeting but does not determine content. This means that the group has control of the agenda.

Facilitator. The 'facilitator' role involves careful listening and eliciting of other people's ideas and knowledge, rather than imposing your own.

Counsellor. The role of 'counsellor' is appropriate in an intimate group where the leader's intention is to draw out emotional issues on the grounds that sharing them in the group is beneficial.

Commentator. The 'commentator' sits outside the group and comments from time to time on the group dynamic or on the things that the group members are saying. In this way he or she avoids being used as a reference point or focus of attention.

Wandering minstrel. The 'wandering minstrel' circulates between pairs or small groups, monitoring and helping as required.

Absent friend. Most groups have occasions when the leader is unable to attend. The 'absent friend' is the leader who trusts the group to function effectively without the need for him or her always to be physically present.

Classification from Jaques 1984 pp147–9

Activity

- Consider groups in which you have been a participant. How would you characterize the group leader's style of leadership, using David Jaques' headings?
- Are there other types of leader who don't fit any of these categories? What new category or categories would you add to the above headings?
- Which heading fits you? How do you know?

The categories suggested by David Jaques are not mutually exclusive. An effective leader is able to move between them as the group develops and changes, and as different needs arise. Nevertheless most of us are more comfortable in one or perhaps two of these leadership modes than in the others. While considering your options it is useful to recognize what mode of leadership suits you, as well as what might suit the group, and to try to reconcile the two.

9 Modes of facilitation

John Heron is founder and former director of the Human Potential Research Group of the University of Surrey, England, which trains group leaders from many different professional backgrounds to become skilled facilitators. He prefers to use the term 'facilitator' rather than 'leader' to describe the person formally appointed as responsible for helping participants learn in a group, and recognized by the group members as having that role. Heron distinguishes three modes of facilitation which suit different kinds of group situation.

1 The hierarchical mode. Here you, the facilitator, direct the learning process, exercise your power over it, and do things *for* the group: you lead from the front by thinking and acting on behalf of the group. You decide on the objectives and the programme, interpret and give meaning, challenge resistances, manage group feelings, provide structures for learning and honour the claims of authentic behaviour in the group. You take full responsibility, in charge of all major decisions on all dimensions of the learning process.

2 The co-operative mode. Here you share your power over the learning process and manage the different dimensions *with* the group: you enable and guide the group to become more self-directing in the various forms of learning by conferring with them. You prompt and help group members to decide on the group programme, to give meaning to experiences, to do their own confrontation, and so on. In this process, you share your own view which, though influential, is not final but one among many. Outcomes are always negotiated. You collaborate with the members of the group in devising the learning process: your facilitation is co-operative.

3 The autonomous mode. Here you respect the total autonomy of the group: you do not do things for them, or with them, but give them freedom to find their *own way*, exercising their own judgement without any intervention on your part. Without any reminders, guidance or assistance, they evolve their programme, give meaning to what is going on, find ways of confronting their avoidances, and so on. The bedrock of learning is unprompted, self-directed practice, and here you give space for it. This does not mean the abdication of responsibility. It is the subtle art of creating conditions within which people can exercise full self-determination in their learning.

Heron 1989 pp16–17

None of these three modes is more valid than the other, but each could be used appropriately or inappropriately, and well or badly. The aim of the facilitator, according to John Heron, is to be able to move easily between the modes as the occasion requires, and to be equally comfortable in all three.

Activity

- Which of these modes is most typical of your way of leading a group? (Remember that your class of learners is also a group.) Do you identify with one of the modes more than the other two?
- Is that your conscious choice – or is it due to the way you were taught at school, or brought up, or trained as a teacher?

If in a group there are people who would like to try leading a session, but who are not very confident about taking on a leadership role, you might like to use the following activity, which was created by members of an international group of teachers attending a five-day workshop on 'Dimensions of Facilitator Style' at International House, Hastings.

Activity

Stage 1

Working alone, complete the following sentence stems.

1 The steps I could take towards facilitating a group session are:

Before the session ....

During the session ....

After the session ....

2 The area in which I would particularly like to improve my facilitation skills is

....

3 The worst possible scenario that could happen when I facilitate is

....

4 I would feel comfortable facilitating in the following situation(s):

....

....

Stage 2

Working in a pair, tell your partner what you have discovered in this exercise.

(It is suggested that while the speaker is speaking, the listener listens with full attention and without interrupting the speaker. See the section on developing listening skills in Chapter 4.)

In a teacher development (or other) group people sometimes feel hesitant about taking on the facilitator's role. The above activity helps you to look at these feelings and can help to overcome anxiety.

10 The first meeting

Getting acquainted

People who have not met before will very likely want to begin with introductions. Here is one highly participatory way of organizing this.

> Ask people to pair up and take turns interviewing each other for 3 minutes. Two pairs then meet, to make a foursome, and each person introduces his/her pair to the other. The fours then come back to the whole group, and each person makes a one-sentence introduction of one of the other pair in his/her foursome.
>
> *Houston 1990 p15*

Most people arrive at a first meeting with their heads full of questions and anxieties. 'What am I letting myself in for here?' 'Do I have to do anything, or can I just listen?' 'I hate the way people use sessions like this to have a good moan.' So it can be a good idea to kick off the meeting with an activity which gives people a chance to focus on something positive about themselves and each other. What they choose to say in an activity like this is also very revealing about the kinds of interests and priorities they have, and this can be useful information to build on.

Here are some ideas for topics which accentuate the positive:

1 Participants talk about one pleasant thing that has been in their thoughts a lot in the last few days.
2 Participants say one thing that they hope to change in their lives within the coming year.
3 Participants say one thing they have done in the last 24 hours that makes them feel pleased with themselves.
4 Participants say what they are feeling at the present moment, and what image goes with that feeling.

adapted from Houston 1990 p16

Expectations and fears

Sometimes it is useful to take some time in the first session to allow people to express their expectations and worries about the group. One way of doing this is for people to discuss the following questions in pairs:

- How would I like the members of this group to treat each other?
- How would I like to be treated?
- What would I like to get out of attending the group?

Following this discussion time, people can be invited to share with the whole group anything useful that has come up. This can be conducted as a brainstorm, with someone listing the points on a board or flipchart. If a flipchart is used, the list can be kept for reference later on in the group's life, when feelings may have changed and comparisons are interesting.

Aims and objectives

The next stage is to identify, using the list as a basis, some aims and objectives which are immediate and realistic. These can also be written down.

After this, it may be appropriate to assess the amount of time and energy people want to devote to each topic. One way is to ask people to work in small groups to produce pie charts which they can then negotiate with the other groups.

The following is an example of what we mean by a pie chart. The available space is divided up in proportion to the amount of time that the group would like to spend on each type of activity.

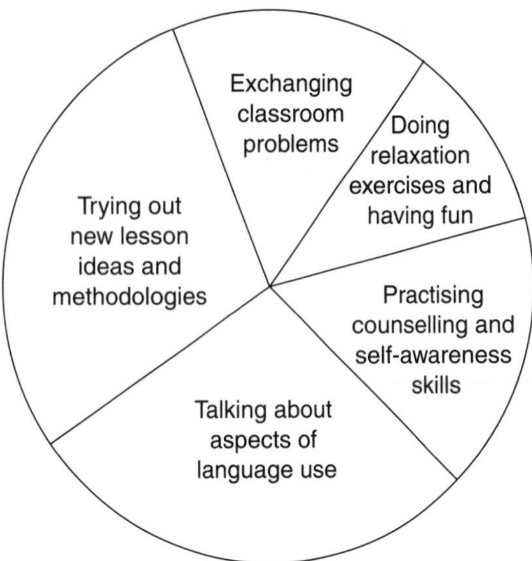

At this point differences may well emerge which result in responsibility being dumped back onto the facilitator of this first session. Gaie Houston describes this as the 'restaurant patron' approach. The participants have made their choices from the menu, and now hand the waiter their orders. They expect the facilitator to give them what they want. So it is helpful to introduce some discussion of how individual needs and preferences can be catered for within the group, and perhaps to define an agenda, at least for the next two or three meetings, to which everyone can agree. This can include some clarification of the facilitator's role, and of how responsibility for running individual sessions might be delegated. At the same time, Gaie Houston suggests, people need to be reminded that ultimately each individual is responsible for seeing that they get what they want from the sessions, and for keeping up an ongoing debate as to the direction that the group is taking, while also considering how the interests of the whole group may best be served.

The list of wants and hopes could also serve to lead in to a discussion of some ground rules for the group.

Using questions as discussion-starters

In a teacher development group, one aim of a first meeting is likely to be to decide what the participants think teacher development is. Chapter 1 of this book contains some activities which could be used to open up such a discussion. Here are some more questions suggested by Martyn Ellis.

Activity

- What is a 'good' lesson?
- What is a 'bad' lesson?
- How do you feel about late-comers or poor attenders in your class?

- How do you occupy yourself while students are carrying out learner-centred activities?
- How do you feel about your coursebook?
- Do you feel the need to defend what you are doing to your students and colleagues?
- Do you have any absolute rules in your professional and personal life?
- Do you get tired? How do you channel your energy?
- What annoys or frustrates you most about your profession?
- What do you like/dislike most about the work you do?

Ellis 1987 p44

A group of English teachers from several different schools in Bologna, Italy, formed a teacher development group and decided to base their second meeting on Martyn Ellis's article. They found that discussion of the questions and issues he raised led beyond moans and groans to an identification of the real problem in the kinds of English language schools where they worked.

We feel that it is the structure of ELT schools, more than anything else, which lies behind the frustration felt by teachers like ourselves ... ELT schools are places where individuals go into a building to have, or to give, 'group private lessons', rather than places where people work together, sharing their problems, successes, failures, achievements ... We feel, however, that the formation and continuing success of our TD group has removed that sense of isolation and resulted in a feeling of fellowship among the teachers in our city.

Bologna Teachers' Development Group 1988

Maria Silvia Andreau, a teacher in Argentina, also used a questionnaire when teachers met together for the first time to start thinking about their own development.

We're a group of eight teachers working together in a private English Institute in Tierra del Fuego (Argentina). We've been working hard and seriously from the very beginning, when we were only two teachers, but although we thought we were doing things right, we also felt things could be done better. We wanted to grow and develop ourselves both as teachers and as individuals. We wanted to get in touch with the latest trends in methodology and the newest techniques. However, the 3000 km that separate us from Buenos Aires made us feel 'professionally isolated'. Congresses, conferences, lectures and talks were held so far away, so how could we develop here in the 'far south'? ...

We wrote a questionnaire and asked our colleagues to answer the questions as truthfully as possible. The questions were these:

1 How did you get into English language teaching as a career?
2 What makes you feel good about your teaching and what frustrates you?
3 How much of the contents of seminars do you apply to your actual classroom situations?

4 Can you suggest ways of improving your teaching in your present working conditions?
5 Have the meetings with your colleagues at the Institute helped you in any way?
6 Have you found that planning your lessons helped you improve the quality of your teaching?
7 Can you share with us some teaching experiences which have proved to be 'special' in one way or another?
8 What's your opinion about being observed by your principal?

The answers allowed us to learn lots of things from one another. We learned for example that although each of us had different reasons for becoming a teacher of English (vocation, tradition, economic reasons, or just simply by chance) we were all conscious of our responsibility as educators. We learned that we all felt happy with more or less the same things: our students' progress or satisfactory exam results. Yet, there was one thing that made us feel great and that was when our students show their love and care for us. We, too, need to be loved and appreciated! We also learned that we all had the same problems (What a relief! They too have problems in their classrooms!) and immediately afterwards we started sharing experiences and solutions to this or that problem.

Finally we realised that we were a group of teachers who had been working together for some time and knew very little about each other. We discovered that the solutions to our problems could be found not only in conferences but also in the person rubbing shoulders with us in the teachers' room.

Andreau 1993 p16

11 Stages in the life of a group

Successful groups take on a life of their own, and experience distinct stages in their development. These stages have been described in various ways, and we find two models particularly illuminating. Tuckman's model, explained below, and Heron's, which follows, both help us to see deeper into the dynamic we have experienced as members of groups, including teacher development groups.

Tuckman's model

Tuckman's study of stages in the evolution of groups is described here by Tony Wright in a training manual written for language teachers.

What individuals contribute to the group amounts to a set of expectations about how others will act and what roles they will adopt. These expectations will initially influence what actually happens in the group. Initial expectations and behaviour will be modified according to the duration and quality of the group's activities ...

Tuckman (1965) established that a small group went through four stages from its formation ...

> **Stage 1 Forming:** In the group, there is some anxiety. There is a great deal of dependence on the leader ... and a great deal of behaviour directed towards finding out the nature of the situation and also what behaviour is acceptable.
>
> **Stage 2 Storming:** There is now conflict between sub-groups and also rebellion against the leader. Opinions are extreme and there is resistance to group control. Role relations are not agreed upon. All of this behaviour is a resistance to the demands of the group.
>
> **Stage 3 Norming:** The group develops cohesion: norms of behaviour emerge and participants begin to accept group control. Conflicts are forgotten and members begin to support each other. At this stage co-operation is the rule and there is open exchange of views and feelings about the task and each other.
>
> **Stage 4 Performing:** All individuals' problems are resolved and there is a great deal of interpersonal activity. Members' roles in the group now lose their rigidity and become more functional. At this stage solutions to the problems of the task are found and all efforts are devoted to completing the task ...
>
> *Wright 1987 pp11, 36–7*

In one account of Tuckman's model that we have come across, a fifth stage has been added: that of **Mourning** the ending of the group. We feel that this is a helpful addition to the first four, and a very important stage which must be attended to.

Activity

Tony Wright says that Tuckman's model is also valid for understanding how classes function as groups.

- Using a current or recent experience of either a group of teachers you are/have been involved in, or a class you have taught, see if you can trace its life through Tuckman's four stages.
- If you are thinking of a current group, what stage do you think it is experiencing at present?

One group to which we (the authors) both belonged reached the 'storming stage', and succeeded in releasing a lot of the tension when the facilitator introduced an activity in which each member thought of a metaphor for the group at that stage of its life. We then went round the group, with each person describing their metaphor. These were some of the images that emerged:

- rays of different coloured light, meeting at a central point
- a chameleon shedding its skin while still clinging tightly to the branches
- waves rippling outwards on a pond
- the dark cold waters of the Atlantic
- an ox stuck in the mud
- circles of different colours, bright, overlapping, and rotating like wheels at different speeds.

Heron's model

John Heron also sees four distinct phases in the development of the dynamic of a group. He compares the shift from negative to more positive forms with the cycle of the seasons in a year.

The stage of defensiveness. This is usually at the outset of a group. Trust is low, anxiety is high ... Wintertime: the ground may be frozen, and the weather stormy.

The stage of working through defensiveness. The group is now under way, trust is building, anxiety is reducing ... A fresh culture is being created. Springtime: new life starts to break through the surface crust.

The stage of authentic behaviour. The group is deep into its real destiny. Trust is high, and anxiety is a spur to growth and change. There is openness to self and others, risk-taking, working, caring and sharing ... Leadership is shared, with a good balance of hierarchy, co-operation and autonomy ... Summertime: there is an abundance of growth, and the sun is high.

Closure. As the group draws to a close, the members gather in and review the fruit of their learning, and prepare to transfer it to life in the wider world outside. At some point in this process separation anxiety will loom up – the distress at parting after such trust and depth of interaction. It can slip the group back into defensiveness unless dealt with awarely – firstly by accepting that the end is nigh, secondly by dealing with any unfinished business, thirdly by celebrating each other and what has gone on, fourthly by saying a warm, friendly farewell in the group and one-to-one. Autumn: the fruit is harvested and stored, the harvesters give thanks and go their way.

Heron 1989 pp26–7

12 The natural life of a group

Like individuals, groups have their ups and downs, their good times and their low times. People will inevitably want to join or leave the group, and on each occasion there needs to be some adjustment to cope with the change. Individuals often tend to become cast in particular roles – the organizer, the carer, the joker, the one who never listens or the one who never speaks. Somebody may try to take the group over or mount a challenge to established routines of organization and leadership. There may be times when is it hard to hold the group together, when difficult relationships develop between members, attendance is erratic, or people begin to break up into splinter groups. These experiences are all natural and normal within the life of any group of people. In a group which is focused on the development of its members, it is important to talk about what is going on and how people are feeling. All these issues have to do with the group process, or the group dynamic. They are the issues around which change may be needed to move the group on in a developmental way.

Gaie Houston's *Red Book of Groups* is full of ideas for helping people to work successfully in groups, and to deal with the kinds of problems that can arise at different stages in the life of the group.

We like this quote from John Heider's *Tao of Leadership* which challenges traditional notions of responsibility and control in groups.

> Group process evolves naturally. It is self-regulating. Do not interfere. It will work itself out.
>
> Efforts to control process usually fail. Either they block process or make it chaotic.
>
> Learn to trust what is happening. If there is silence, let it grow; something will emerge. If there is a storm, let it rage; it will resolve into calm.
>
> Is the group discontented? You can't make it happy. Even if you could, your efforts might well deprive the group of a very creative struggle.
>
> *Heider 1985 p115*

13 Closing the group

Some groups know from the start that they will exist for a limited period. Others may continue to meet indefinitely, experiencing the natural ebb and flow of interest, enthusiasm and participation, until ultimately the natural time will come to end the group in its present form. In either case, this time is best prepared for gradually and people need to make decisions about whether to go in new directions with the same group or to close the group.

Here are three rather different ideas for 'closing' activities which can be used with groups of all kinds – classes of learners, teachers' groups, and others – which celebrate the life of the group and the contribution of each member.

Activity

The sun wheel

For this activity you need a piece of paper, size A4 or larger, for each member of the group. These instructions assume that you are sitting in a circle, although this is not essential.

1 Look at the example overleaf. Draw a circle, about 4 cm across, in the middle of each piece of paper, and then draw lines extending outwards from the circle to the edge of the paper (like the rays of the sun) so that the spaces between them represent the number of people in the group.

2 Give a paper to each person in the group.

3 Each person turns to the person on their *right* and writes the name of that person in the circle in the centre of their paper. Then they write, in one of the 'rays' of the 'sun', a message to that person – it can be anything at all, anonymous or signed, and *positive* for the person to keep.

4 Then each person passes the paper to the person sitting on their *left*, who writes

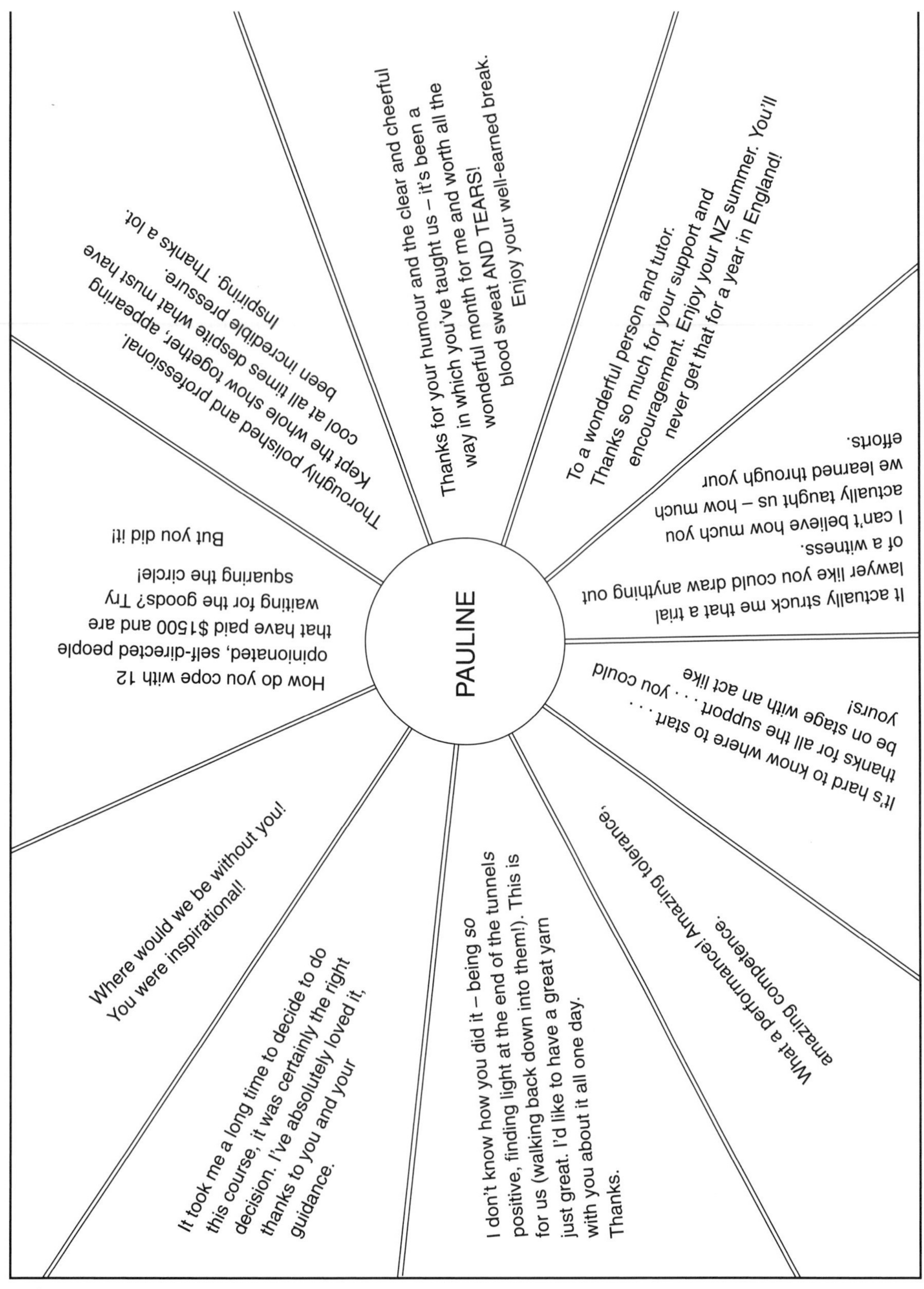
PAULINE
Thanks for your humour and the clear and cheerful way in which you've taught us – it's been a wonderful month for me and worth all the blood sweat AND TEARS! Enjoy your well-earned break.
To a wonderful person and tutor. Thanks so much for your support and encouragement. Enjoy your NZ summer. You'll never get that for a year in England!
I can't believe how much you actually taught us – how much we learned through your efforts.
It actually struck me that a trial lawyer like you could draw anything out of a witness.
It's hard to know where to start . . . thanks for all the support . . . You could be on stage with an act like yours!
What a performance! Amazing tolerance, amazing competence.
I don't know how you did it – being so positive, finding light at the end of the tunnels for us (walking back down into them!). This is just great. I'd like to have a great yarn with you about it all one day.
Thanks.
It took me a long time to decide to do this course, it was certainly the right decision. I've absolutely loved it, thanks to you and your guidance.
Where would we be without you! You were inspirational!
How do you cope with 12 opinionated, self-directed people that have paid $1500 and are waiting for the goods? Try squaring the circle!
But you did it!
Thoroughly polished and professional. Kept the whole show together, appearing cool at all times despite what must have been incredible pressure. Inspiring. Thanks a lot.

in another 'ray' of the 'sun' their own message to the person whose name is in the circle.

5 The papers pass round the whole circle until they reach the person whose name is in the centre of the paper.

6 When you receive the paper with your own name in the centre, there should be one space left for you to write a message to yourself!

I (Pauline) use this activity with classes of language learners and with groups of trainee teachers. They can take away a lovely reminder of the people who were with them in the group.

Activity

This activity is an adaptation of the 'Find someone who ...' idea. Each person finds someone they want to thank for something that they have contributed. The worksheet could either be prepared by someone beforehand, or compiled as a group activity.

Find someone you would like to thank for ...

... making you laugh
... being encouraging
... listening
... giving you a good idea
... helping you cope
etc.

adapted from an idea in Hadfield 1986 p165

It can often be difficult to tell people what it is about them that we appreciate, and this activity provides a framework for doing this.

A group that has worked well and had fun together may like to try the following activity, which we learned from Angela Faulkner, a participant with us in a five-day workshop on 'dimensions of facilitator style'. It assumes considerable intimacy and trust between the group members, but we found it a very effective and enjoyable way of ending a group that we both participated in.

Activity

You need plenty of space and a clean carpeted floor for this activity. The instructions should be given one at a time, by one group member. The others should not know in advance what is going to happen, otherwise the activity won't work.

1 Clear a large space on the floor.

2 Everyone lies down on their back, in such a way that their head is resting gently on someone else's stomach.

3 With your eyes closed, recall the series of events that the group has shared together. Run them through your mind.

4 Gradually focus on one particular event which you find funny, and let yourself start laughing.

During our workshop there had been a good mixture of frustration and frivolity, and the effect as one person after another began to shake with laughter at the memories that came back to them was unforgettable!

---

14 Action planning

As well as being a time for looking back, ending the group experience can be a time for looking forward individually to what lies ahead and for making action plans. Action planning builds a vital bridge between the short-lived freedom enjoyed in the group and the long-term constraints of the workplace and home to which you are returning. It creates the framework for transferring and integrating the new insights that have emerged from working in the group.

Activity

Here is a series of steps you can use for action planning at the end of a group.

1. What have you learned in this group that you want to take away with you?
2. Can you identify one piece of learning that you would like to put into action back in your workplace?
3. What steps can you take to put this into practice? It is important to be concrete and practical in your thinking about this.
4. What will prevent you, and how will you deal with this?
5. When will you start?

Work alone on these five questions, then share your answers with others in the group. You may find encouragement and inspiration in the answers that other group members give to these questions.

---

15 Conclusion

We know, from our experience of co-ordinating the IATEFL Teacher Development Group, that there are a lot of teachers around the world who are already working on their own development and are interested in ways of setting up teachers' groups in their school or local area. One of the ongoing requests from members has been for a 'starter pack' with practical tips on forming a group and planning activities for meetings. We hope that this chapter will have encouraged you to get involved in a group, answered some of your questions about how it can be run and given you confidence if you would like to begin one.

In the end, however, teacher development groups are but one of the many kinds of group in which you may be or want to be involved. Your own class of learners is perhaps the most significant group of people in relation to whom these ideas, and the activities we propose, may prove useful.

Chapter 6 Supporting yourself

1 Introduction

In earlier chapters we have looked at the skills and attitudes needed in a teacher who hopes to promote learning that is meaningful and appropriate to the needs of his/her students. Person-centred teaching requires us to relate to our learners as whole people (by which we mean people with feelings, experiences, anxieties, hopes, secrets, thoughts, learning styles, spiritual dimensions, etc, who are here at least partly because they want to learn something). Relating in this way asks of the teachers and learners an ability and willingness to embrace change and qualities such as genuineness, courage and honesty. It also requires fitness, because, while keeping up with your learners' interests and needs can be immensely enriching, it also demands energy and commitment from you. Fortunately, there are many effective ways to develop these qualities and to care for yourself and keep yourself in good shape so that you can enjoy your work and maintain an open, interested and relaxed relationship with students and others. In this chapter we will look at some of these ways.

2 Looking to other fields beyond teaching

Many teachers have used knowledge and skills from other fields to help promote their own personal and professional development. This has often been prompted by a particular feeling of being stuck, burnt out or stale; or when a specific problem has arisen in their teaching. When looking for sources of support and inspiration, they have found that ideas from other fields – counselling and interpersonal skills, yoga and voice training, to name just a few – have helpfully influenced their growth and their teaching persona. These other fields have provided them with practical techniques and skills and helped them acquire the attitudes needed both to promote learning and to maintain energy, enthusiasm and openness to further change. A number of the readings in this chapter are taken from teachers' accounts of their experience of such influences.

Activity

Sources of support

- Make a list of the sources that you draw on for support, motivation, energy and when confronting a problem. Sources might include:
  - articles in magazines or books on self-help
  - leisure activities
  - friends
  - other teachers, including your past teachers
  - music
  - psychology
  - spiritual practices
  - courses
- How much do these sources influence the way you teach?
- Are there further ways in which you could use what you know from these sources in your teaching? Take each item on your list of sources and write down as many ways as possible that you can draw on these sources both to support yourself as a teacher and to help your learners. For example, I (Pauline) do Yoga exercises to increase my own stamina and help me relax. I also use it to help my students relax while they learn.
- If you find yourself saying, 'I could never use this particular influence', don't give up. Take a little time to try to prove yourself wrong. Be as absurd as you like, but think of several potential connections that could provide a link between the source and your teaching.

We have noticed ourselves that while we have found some of the above sources of influence helpful in our personal lives, we haven't always recognized the possibility of drawing on them for support in our working lives.

3 Essential learning

It is possible for a person's skills and knowledge to lack balance; for example, if your training has focused on academic solutions rather than practical, experiential and emotional ones. As the following Sufi tale demonstrates, this can have serious consequences, particularly in a profession where people are experiencing new and increasing pressures. Bringing other influences to bear can help create a better balance.

Nasrudin is ferrying a professor across a stretch of rough water and says something ungrammatical to him. 'Have you never studied grammar?' the professor asks.
'No,' Nasrudin replies.
'Then half your life has been wasted.'
A few minutes later, the storm grew fiercer.
Nasrudin turns to his passenger to speak. 'Have you ever learned to swim?'
'No,' says the professor.
'Then all of your life has been wasted, for we are sinking!'

Quoted in Jensen 1988 p34

4 Giving attention to the things that matter

While recognizing that personal qualities and attitudes, rapport and atmosphere are what makes the difference between a class where significant and lasting learning takes place and one where it does not, trainers have often felt that these could not, or should not, be taught within teacher training programmes. Alan Maley does not share this view. In the following article he looks at the physical and psychological pre-conditions of teaching, recommending that teacher education programmes should take account of these and make teachers aware of what they can do to take care of themselves physically and psychologically. His article signposts some directions which this chapter will take, as we go on to look in more detail at various factors affecting teachers' physical and psychological well-being, and at strategies for supporting yourself.

Alan Maley writes about 'finding the centre' which balances mind, body and spirit so that teachers are fully supported and able to function at every level. This understanding is based on insights from other fields. In this chapter we will suggest many ways of training yourself in techniques which help to achieve this balance.

Finding the centre

Physical pre-conditions

Undoubtedly, a significant part of the effect teachers have derives from their physical presence. Our body and what we do with it is our prime teaching resource. And, because it is observable, we can relatively easily both raise trainees' awareness of physical factors and train them to make the best of them.

The main physical components are: posture, breathing, voice, gesture/expression, dress/appearance. Of these the inter-related trio of posture/breathing/voice are in my view both the most important and the most amenable to training. And I would strongly contend that some sort of 'physical' training (not in the sense of physical jerks!) should form an integral part of training programmes.

Psychological pre-conditions

These are more difficult to define. They can be regarded both as a preventive protection against negative factors such as excessive stress and as a positive basis for further development.

Teachers are not unique in being subject to high levels of job related stress, which saps their effectiveness, but they must be among those most open to occupational stress. Among other things, they tend to develop high levels of guilt about not doing more for their learners, they feel insecurity about peer-comparison and criticism from students and anxiety connected with self-esteem. If they are to perform effectively over long periods, they need to develop the ability to distance themselves from such preoccupations – to find a calm and balanced centre.

The same is true if they are to sustain an interest in their professional life and to continue to develop both as individuals and as professionals.

The problem for trainers is precisely how to train/develop this 'centring' process so that trainees can operate with 'effortless effort', the way a seagull uses the air to achieve apparently effortless, graceful movement; the way a skilled carpenter enters into the grain of the wood and uses it for his purposes; the way a cook makes a perfect soufflé. We can recognise this harmony between forces, where we cannot 'tell the dancer from the dance' – but to produce it is more problematical. But I would argue again that we need to make the effort to provide some formal training in this area too.

Maley 1993 pp14–15

Activity

- Which of the physical factors mentioned by Alan Maley do you pay attention to?
- Do you tend to find yourself caught up in feelings of guilt, stress or low self-esteem, or are you able to detach yourself from them?
- Is there anything that you do, or could do, to find a calm and balanced centre in your teaching life?

---

5 The challenges that we face

Often your behaviour can be so habitual that you don't pay much attention to it. As a result you can be driven by old patterns rather than make conscious choices about the way you act. For example, I (Pauline) often tried to offer solutions to people who told me about problems until I learned how unhelpful it was to them and to me. Once you begin to pay attention to your ways of behaving and reacting to external pressures, you can then notice what it is you are able to cope with, and at which point the challenges you face become problems.

Denis Postle (1988) makes the point that, while it is important for people to be flexible and able to adapt, there is danger in believing you should be able to cope with everything, because if you then find that you can't, you tend to take the blame personally, without noticing that some of the demands made on you are unreasonable or overwhelming.

Postle identifies four areas of challenge: *responsibility without power*; *relying on people*, *difficult people* and *time pressures*. The following activities invite you to explore these areas of your own experience.

Activity

Responsibility without power

Teachers sometimes find themselves responsible for the outcome of a situation, but without the power to influence it.

- Can you identify situations like this in your teaching life?
- Is it one situation that you feel quite often, or does it happen in a number of different situations?
- And how does it affect you?

Activity

Relying on other people

In your work you may find yourself having to rely on other people for the success of something that is important to you, or that you have invested time and energy in. When one stage relies upon the success of another it creates a state of suspense. Examples could include:

- preparing a classroom
- publicizing a room change
- contacting parents
- ordering new equipment or materials
- technicians supplying equipment
- other teachers teaching your students
- educational visits
- outside speakers
- project work
- attracting funding
- timetables
- choice of coursebook

- Can you identify times when this happens in your teaching life?
- Is this something you find happening frequently or occasionally?
- Can you describe the effect this has on you?

Activity

People who make our lives difficult

Many teachers mention the stress of working with 'difficult' people. These could include people who seem to be:

- undermining
- malicious or wounding
- blaming
- abusive
- manipulative
- incompetent
- insensitive
- uncooperative
- deceitful
- racist
- sexist
- negative

– capricious and contradictory in their demands
– harassing and unwilling to take 'no' for an answer
– unable or unwilling to give straight answers
– giving double messages

- Can you identify any people like these in your teaching life?
- Do you work closely with them, or do you only deal with them occasionally?
- What is it about them that particularly makes them difficult for you?
- Do they remind you of figures from your past?
- Do you notice any patterns in the way you deal with them?
- Does anyone find you difficult? From their perspective, can you understand why?
- Is it easier to name your difficult people or to name what is difficult in you?

Activity

Time pressures

If your life seems to be getting fuller and your job more and more demanding, it can be helpful to analyse precisely how your time is being taken up. Once this is done, you can begin to see where change is necessary or desirable, not necessarily so that you can 'do more' but so that you have more awareness and control over how your time is used. Meg Bond suggests the following activity to help with this.

The time available in any period – a day, a week, a month – can be broken down according to how we use it. There is some overlap, but it could be categorized as:

Self-maintenance: The time you spend doing what is necessary to care properly for yourself: sleeping, shopping, cooking, eating, washing and so on.

Sold time: The time you spend doing the things you have to do besides looking after yourself. These could be job related: travelling to work, teaching, planning and marking, and would also include your other responsibilities such as looking after other family members.

Free choice: The time you spend on other activities of your own choice. You may feel that at present this time is well used or not well used, and you can decide to make changes; but it is important that it exists in your time schedule, and that there is enough of it.

1 Write down all the activities you do in a typical working day. Beside each activity write a very approximate amount of time you devote to it.
2 Now, write down as headings the three categories above: self-maintenance, sold time and free choice.
3 Under each heading, write the activities from your list that belong in that category.
4 Add up the approximate amount of time spent on each category.
5 Now repeat the same steps to look at a typical working week.
6 Look at the two pie charts below. One represents a typical day when you are working, and the other a week during which you are working. Perhaps using different colours, plot in the approximate percentage of time dedicated to what

could be described as 'self-maintenance', 'sold time' and 'free choice' activities, as described above, so that the time in the day and week is divided up amongst those categories. For example, in a day, if you spend 5 hours at work and 3 hours on top marking and preparing, and 1 hour travelling to and from work, on average 9 hours of your time is 'sold' so you would mark in 9 hours as sold on the 24 hour chart. You need to allow plenty of time to do this – but it is time well worth spending!

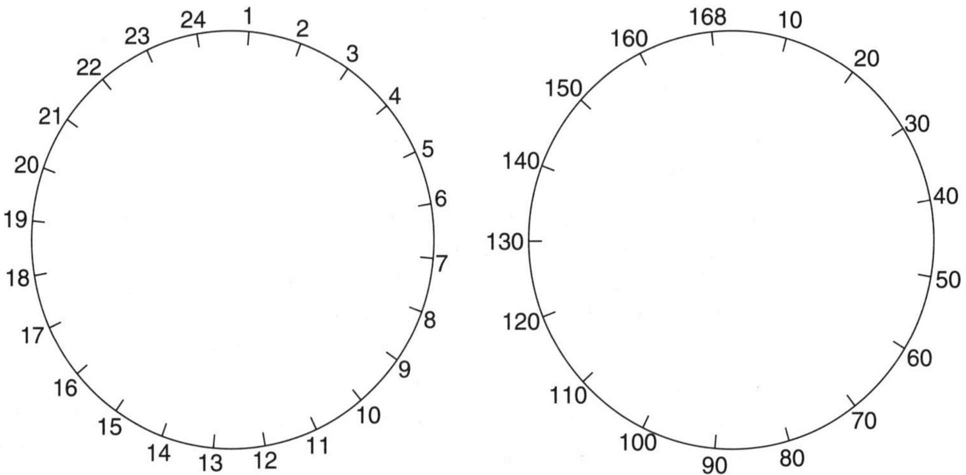

7 Look at the diagram and answer the following questions:
   – Are you using your time as you want to?
   – Do you feel obliged and without choice?
   – Can you change obligations into choices?
   – Do you plan your time?

8 Write down a list of your 'time robbers'. For example, personal disorganization, overcommitment, intrusions, meetings, custom and practice and travel and waiting.

Adapted from a workshop led by Meg Bond and an activity in Humphrey and Humphrey 1990 pp27–8

Some of the challenges you are facing at the moment may be out of your control, but there will be other areas that you can do something about if you choose to make changes.

6 Improving your ability to cope with challenge

Denis Postle writes:

Coping is a complex human phenomenon in which inner resources, such as ingenuity, a sense of humour, stamina and fitness are mobilised in response to outside demands. If your ability to cope collapses or is threatened, the [body's] state of arousal is affected. When faced with a challenge, the [body] responds by mobilising your energy reserves. Adrenalin is released into the bloodstream, digestion shuts down, the heart rate increases and breathing quickens. The result is a heightened state of arousal. Coping well depends on you managing your arousal well. Under poor management, you can become stuck in high arousal – when you feel restless, excited, elated, sleepless, anxious or hyper-active. Alternatively, you may become stuck in low arousal – often as a result of insufficient challenge – and feel depressed, lethargic and despairing. Both limit your freedom of choice. In sustained high arousal, calm, quiet consideration becomes difficult or impossible. With sustained low arousal, opportunities slip by, attention is unfocussed, and everything 'seems to be too much trouble'.

Postle 1988 p55

Activity

- A first step towards improving your ability to cope is to become more aware of just how much pressure you feel comfortable with. If you have become used to a certain level of pressure, try adjusting the level either up or down so that you can notice any differences in the way you function, and check whether the present level of pressure is indeed a comfortable level for you.
- The next step is to become proactive rather than reactive, and learn how to manage the demands made on you so that you can maintain the reasonable level of pressure that allows you to function most effectively. Here are some strategies for doing this:
  - Plan your time and include quiet times.
  - Be clear about when you are (and are not) available.
  - Get and give support so that you build a network of good relationships.
  - Be consistent.
  - Communicate effectively and assertively.
  - Have a positive attitude.
  - Learn how to relax.
  - Balance and pace yourself.
  - Monitor yourself and your body for fitness and diet.
  - Do something you enjoy every day.
- Referring back to the four areas of challenge that Postle identified earlier, how would you apply some of these strategies to the challenges you have identified?

Several of the strategies we have listed here are looked at in more detail elsewhere in this chapter. In addition, you will find in the Bibliography some books we have found helpful, which will take you further into many of these areas. Addresses of organizations that can provide information about particular disciplines and techniques are listed in the Appendix.

7 Identifying burnout

Burnout is something which is experienced by many people who have spent years in so-called 'caring professions' such as teaching, when the constant demands made on them seem to drain them of creativity and make it impossible to 'switch off' and relax.

In a review of Christina Maslach's book on burnout among carers, Susan Barduhn defines the syndrome and its effect on teachers.

> Burnout is a syndrome of emotional exhaustion, depersonalisation, and a reduced sense of personal accomplishment. It culminates in a build-up of negative feelings about our students, colleagues and administration. As motivation decreases and frustration increases, we lose the desire and energy to be creative, developing teachers. Physical and emotional stress play on our self-esteem as we lose the sense of being in charge of our lives.
>
> The three sources of burnout are involvement with people, the particular job and its environment, and the personal characteristics of those who choose the helping professions. The burnout syndrome appears to be a response to chronic, everyday stress, rather than to everyday crises.
>
> *Barduhn 1989 pp2–3*

Activity

The above text identifies three sources of burnout: working with people, the job and its environment, and the personal characteristics of those who choose to work in a helping profession. This activity invites you to look at your own work environment and make some connections.

a Working with people

There is a value in learning both objective detachment and sensitive concern.

- At the moment, how easy is it for you to remain both objectively detached and sensitively concerned when at work?
- Do you sometimes feel trapped or crushed by the demands that other people make on you?
- Who is the particular person, or group of people, who has this effect on you?

b The particular job and its environment

- What institutional regulations, for example financial constraints, make your workplace an uncomfortable environment?
- How comfortable is it for you to speak to those in authority whose decisions could affect your future?
- Are your colleagues seen as rivals, or as a source of support and a valuable resource for growth?
- Do you feel that you are trapped in one undeveloping job for life, and that no other jobs are available?
- Is there any possibility of dividing up the work differently? For example, course directors and class teachers could have an opportunity to share each other's jobs.
- Are you given time off to attend workshops, conferences and training days?

c Your own personal characteristics

- Can you identify times in your working life when you take on too much because of the need for approval or because of high expectations of yourself or others?

- Do you feel personally responsible when your students don't appear to be making progress?
- How does this affect your teaching?
- How do you make the mental transition between work and home each day?

Susan Barduhn summarizes Maslach's constructive approach to coping with, and preventing, burnout as follows:

Ms. Maslach's basic advice is to work smarter instead of working harder. Her suggestions include setting specific, realistic goals rather than noble, abstract ones; doing the same thing differently, while changing what can be changed; breaking away, including honouring hourly breaks as time to refresh oneself; taking things less personally; accentuating the positive; 'knowing thyself' (she offers the vehicle of a Daily Stress and Tension Log); rest and relaxation techniques; making the transition between work and home each day; a life of one's own; and, when necessary, changing jobs.

Barduhn 1989 p3 quoting Maslach1982

A teacher's experience of burnout

Judy Winn-Bell Olsen speaks of her personal experience of burnout and offers practical insights on how to deal with it.

Most of us are in education because of a commitment to growth, to finding and realising potential. This commitment is not just to our students, but to ourselves as well. As we enable others to develop, we should also be developing ourselves. The state we call 'burnout' can happen when our development is blocked for too long (stagnation) or pushed to its limits for too long (overextension).

When stagnating we may feel that nothing 'works' any more because the delight of shared discovery is gone. We feel that we can't teach that same lesson one more time, answer the same old questions once more, or attend one more meeting with the all-too familiar personalities on our faculty. The terrain has become too predictable for the journey to be personally meaningful (actually, we may be performing quite competently, but we are turned off by our own teaching because the routine has become too ... well, routine).

When overextending, all we see is the mountain of work, not the achievement at the top. We've taken on more and more and more, first because we've sought it out, later because people know we can do it (or think we can) and each challenge brings new insights, new creative tasks, and more time-consuming work with head, paper and people. Each project promises more rewards, but eventually demands more than we can give, until finally we feel we cannot spend one more iota of attention, intellect, or energy on our work, much as we have loved it in the past; much as we have sought the challenges which now face us.

How much can we handle at once? We don't know until we try. New and different projects give us an expanded sense of ourselves ... what our strengths are, what our hidden talents might be. And pushing our limits helps to extend them. But occasionally, unavoidably, we push too far for too long, and we find ourselves in burnout.

It is ironic that the reward for doing things well can be to receive so many interesting choices that we can't possibly do them all well ... but how do we select (and schedule) the right ones? When do we say 'no, enough' and when do we push ourselves that little bit harder? A sign of the overextender's burnout is the despair when something really interesting comes along, but there's nothing left in us to give, much as we have sought out such opportunities (we wouldn't be where we were if we hadn't).

Whatever the cause, I don't believe that burnout should be viewed as a sign that one's development is at an end. I believe that for most of us, it is inevitable ... more like another stage in our development (hopefully a brief one). It should be respected as a clear signal that change is needed. For both stagnators and overextenders, it's a sign that it's time to reflect on where we are, then shift gear, or lighten up, or just let go.

Olsen 1989 p1

Activity

Burnout has been identified as happening when we are stagnating or overextending. You may be able to identify points in your teaching life when you have felt yourself tending towards one or other of these states.

In this activity we invite you to draw a time–events line similar to the one we invited you to draw in the first activity in Chapter 1, but this time the focus is different, as you will see. You may be able to use the first time line in this activity.

- Draw a time–events line which includes significant events in your teaching career. You can divide up the time into chunks meaningful to you, for example months or years, and plot along the lines the events that show your career in a way that will help you identify patterns and become aware of tendencies towards certain states, or even cycles of growth and/or rest.
- Now do a more detailed line of a period you have identified from the first line, of a time when you appear to have experienced burnout. Notice when it occurred (at what stage in your life, career, the school year and so on) and what you did, or could have done, to deal with the state.

Working with burnout

In the next part of her article, Judy Winn-Bell Olsen suggests strategies to help both the stagnators and overextenders mentioned above and puts forward a positive view of burnout.

... Stagnators should probably think about redirection: are there other duties in our workplace we could try for a while? Can we work with administration or testing or some other aspect of our programme, instead of what we are doing now? If we can't do so immediately, is that a possibility we can plan for? Merely the act of planning for something new can sometimes get us 'unstuck' and out of the doldrums.

If not, perhaps it's time for redevelopment: taking courses in related areas we haven't explored, or haven't explored lately: have we kept up with current trends in sociolinguistics, psycholinguistics or classroom anthropology?

Overextenders, on the other hand, may already be active explorers – so active that our explorations may be contributing to burnout overload. Generally, overextenders need to pull back for a while; take on fewer challenges rather than more, and generally be kinder to ourselves ...

Reflection. Time to think. We encourage it for others, and probably deny ourselves enough of it. But a burnout phase is a particularly important time to take our own bearings. Keeping a journal is one way ...

But what if we can't let go of any of our commitments? ... Well, for one thing, we can remind ourselves of the good times, our achievements and successes with our students. Have you saved those photos, notes and cards from your students? Start a scrapbook if you haven't already. It's too easy to forget our successes when we're constantly looking ahead to our next have-to-do, and the memorabilia from our workplace can, for many of us, be a meaningful reminder of happy events and accomplishments. I think it's also important to remember that there is something to be gained from burnout, that it enhances our perspective on who we are individually and collectively, and adds another dimension to being a professional.

For burnout builds compassion. When in high professional 'supergear', it's easy to consider others who are achieving less as less talented or less committed. But when 'out of gear' – when nothing meshes right in our professional lives – we can develop empathy for colleagues who themselves have been struggling. The experience can help us become better team members or leaders on our faculties, which is good for our schools and good for our own professional development ...

And if we continue to push our limits in our own professional growth, burnout should be expected as a recurring phase. (Hopefully, though, it will be easier to get through the next time around.)

... By recognising the reality of burnout, we can name the dragon as we chart our own personal maps. We can see it more clearly as another stage in a developmental process we are all part of ...

ibid pp1–2

8 Caring for your body

As teachers we work with our minds a good deal of the time. In order to achieve balance in ourselves and in our lives, and so ensure that we can cope with the demands and stresses of our job, we need to make sure we maintain and exercise our bodies. There are as many ways of caring for the body as there are types of people, so it is important to find the type that suits you. In the following sections we explore a number of different approaches to dealing with the physical manifestations of stress.

9 Breathing

Although it is often impossible to do a full set of exercises when we are very busy, just taking the time to breathe deeply and fully has a calming effect and increases the energy and stamina needed for clear thinking. Focusing on slow, full breathing is a very simple and effective way of relaxing the physical tension that can precede, for example, a demanding class or a difficult meeting.

Activity

Some tips for full breathing:

- When you first start, do just one or two of the full breaths described in the following steps and then relax your breathing. You can try another round of two breaths and relax your breathing, and so on. Don't do too many rounds. Six rounds will probably be enough. Always do what is comfortable.
- Breathe in through your nose and out through your mouth.
- Always start with an out breath.
- Think of your ribcage as doors on hinges opening outwards to the side so that your whole chest expands. Keep your shoulders down and relaxed.

Now try this round:

1. Keeping your shoulders down, breathe out through your mouth, pushing the air completely out of your lungs by pulling your abdomen in. You'll hear the air pushing out through the back of your throat.
2. Breathe in through your nose. Keeping your shoulders down, feel your abdomen expanding and your ribcage opening out sideways. Keep breathing in as you fill the bottom, then middle, and then top of your lungs. Pause a little, and then breathe out through your mouth.
3. Relax your breathing into a normal rhythm until you feel ready to start again. Six rounds is probably enough at first.

---

10 Progressive relaxation

We should never be too busy to find the time to relax! Learning how to relax is as essential for the mind as food is for the body.

Jane Cranwell-Ward suggests the following straightforward approach to relaxation. It is designed to reduce tension by helping you to control your breathing and relax your muscles.

Activity

Procedure

1 Sit in a comfortable position.
2 Close your eyes.
3 Starting with the muscles in your face, clench the muscles then relax them.
4 Relax all your muscles, from head to toes, in turn. Keep the muscles relaxed.
5 Become aware of your breathing. Count as you breathe in and out: breathe in, 'one, two, three', breathe out, 'one, two, three'. Breathe easily and naturally.
6 Continue for ten to twenty minutes. At the end of that time open your eyes and get up after a few minutes.

Conditions

1 Practise the technique once or twice a day, but not for at least two hours after a meal. The digestive process seems to interfere with the relaxation response.
2 A quiet environment should be chosen with as few distractions as possible.
3 Try to adopt a passive attitude. Don't worry about how well you are relaxing. To avoid distractions and maintain a passive attitude keep repeating a word or visualise an object. This will stop your mind from wandering, which prevents the relaxation response.

Cranwell-Ward 1987 p146

When doing the last step, try using peaceful words or objects. A sound like 'Om' has no meaning to distract you and also works on a physical level to relax you.

11 Massage

Monika Struna and Connie Church remind us that massage is the earliest known form of healing. It improves muscle tone by getting rid of the aches and tensions that accumulate in our busy day-to-day lives. If you find it difficult to relax yourself, try letting someone give you a massage, or if this is too expensive or inhibiting, you can use these guidelines to do a self-massage of your head, neck and shoulders.

The first massage works by applying pressure and the second one involves stroking. It is best to listen to your body and only work for ten minutes, as you can always come back to it. Relax and avoid strain especially by breathing in a relaxed way and moving unhurriedly. Do not massage inflamed, painful or sensitive areas.

Activity

Head

Position Any, with curled fingers.

Application

1 Place your fingertips at the centre of the scalp, on the hairline, close to the forehead.

2 While slightly pulling your hands in opposite directions, apply moderate to deep amounts of pressure. Work your way, making a line, up and around your head to the base of the skull. Start again at the hairline, about a quarter to half an inch to the side of the previous starting point.

3 Repeat from front to back, each time starting approximately a quarter of an inch to the side of your previous position.

Helpful hints If you discover a sensitive point, hold it a little longer before moving onto the next point. Return to it often until sensitivity has passed.

Beneficial effects Good for headaches and sinus membrane congestion. Increases circulation.

Neck and shoulders

Position Any, using one or two hands.

Application

1 Begin just under the head on either side of the spinal column. Keeping four fingers straight, pressure is applied through balls of fingertips. Elbows are pointing up.

2 Stroke forward with pressure going deep into the muscle.

3 Upon exhalation let the *head fall back* into the fingers as the elbows descend, pulling the *hands forward.*

4 With a gliding motion separate individual muscle fibers.

5 Travel the length of the back side of the neck and outward along the superior border of the shoulder blade.

6 This can be done with both hands simultaneously on both sides.

Helpful hints The work is in the upper portions of the fingers, keeping arms and shoulders relaxed.

Apply movement over clothes to avoid burning or apply oil to skin first.

	Follow slow breathing patterns.
	If you are 'nervous', stroke slowly for a more calming effect.
	If you are 'tired', stroke vigorously for a stimulating effect.
Beneficial effects	Relieves excessive muscular tension.

Struna and Church 1983 pp44, 48

12 Yoga

This ancient discipline has helped many teachers to find a centre of calmness and harmony in their stressful lives. I (Pauline) am one of them. Here I describe what Yoga is and how I use it in my teaching life. The breathing exercises above are part of Yoga.

Yoga is an ancient system from India, and, in its most integrated forms, takes into account all of a person's nature. The word Yoga means 'union' or 'joining' and through postures, breathing and meditation brings all levels of a person's nature into harmony. It becomes a way of life and is very effective at allowing people to relax and let go. Therefore, it is recommended for people under stress, developing as it does concentration and flexibility, strength and openness in mind, body and spirit. It is very gentle and each person works at their own level and so avoids strain and competition. It also teaches people to listen to themselves and become aware at all levels of mind, body and spirit.

It has been used in many approaches to learning, such as Suggestopedia, where a relaxed state and silence help learning. I use it myself in teaching and teacher training in order to teach students a practical, effective means of relaxing, as students do learn more in a relaxed, alert and balanced state. I often incorporate it into a lesson in order to help change the energy. For example, I begin the lesson with a simple breathing or gentle stretching exercise and the students gradually learn to listen to their bodies and notice what they need. They can use this knowledge when they are studying at home. It also has the effect of either reducing adrenalin or allowing them to become more alert, depending on the stage of the lesson, the time of day and the kind of activity they are involved in. It has been suggested that logical work needs more alert states and creative activities benefit from more relaxed states. Various music, breathing and exercises can help students to get into these states.

I have often offered actual Yoga sessions in an option programme or before classes or at lunch time. On residential courses we start the day with these sessions before breakfast. In the class we notice we work more closely because of this. The calm feeling has a very good effect on the other activities on the course and has been particularly welcomed on teacher refresher courses, where participants have felt stress in their teaching.

When I do these exercises myself, I also find I teach in a calmer, more centred or less distracted way and I have more stamina. They help me to develop inner strength and focus, and these, combined with reading, help me to develop the qualities of compassion, openness, non-violence to myself or others (and this means not over-working!), non-attachment and the ability to let go. It now forms the central part of my approach to life and teaching.

Activity

When you are feeling tense or in need of waking up, try this invigorating exercise. Do Yoga before you eat and wear loose, comfortable clothing and no shoes or socks. Always listen to your body and work within a comfortable range of movement for you. Relax between each exercise and breathe naturally.

1 Stand with your legs hip-width apart and with the weight evenly on your feet, keeping the outside edges of your feet straight.
2 Breathe out through your mouth and take a deep breath in through your nose as you raise your arms above your head.
3 Bending your knees as you come down with your arms, release your breath with a 'Ha!' and push your arms in a chopping motion through your legs, bending at the waist.
4 Relax and breathe naturally and when you are ready, do another five rounds in your own rhythm, remembering to relax when you need to, and bend your knees to protect your back.

You can also use the above exercise if you need to unwind, or you could try the following gentle stretching exercise.

Activity

1 Kneel on the ground on all fours like a cat.
2 Slowly and gently, as you breathe out, lower your head and arch your back like a cat. Hold your breath for a short while.
3 Again slowly, as you breathe in, raise your head and hollow your back like a cat and hold it for only a short time.
4 Remember the graceful motions of a cat and do this cycle gently two or three times and then relax.

---

13 Tai Chi

Tai Chi, one of the 'soft' or 'internal' martial arts of China, is based on Taoist principles of harmony, simplicity, and naturalness. It is a gentle sequence of self-defence movements woven into a form which creates new levels of self-awareness and teaches you how your body relates to your mind and your inner being, creating a deep sense of their unity. The systematic programme of exercises invigorates the entire body with minimal strain and can heal injury and cure sickness.

Allan Bramall writes about his use of Makkoho stretches in teaching. These work on the same energy centres as Tai Chi :

I had been doing Makkoho stretches as part of a Shiatsu class which stopped and I wanted to continue doing the exercises. Knowing that I lacked the discipline to do it on my own I started a class at school and invited students to come along. The stretches are designed to stretch parts of the body that house the energy centres or meridians used in Chinese healing. The stretching is a prelude to the breathing and meditation, all of which is empowering and encourages letting go. So you can breathe out all the tension and negativity and feel good.

The class is very complementary to the learning programme as there is a spirit of companionship and co-operation and a greater intimacy, which is not necessarily exclusive. The ethos is nice and acceptable to most people. It gives a message of being interested in natural and spiritual things. Some people are frightened and sceptical about these things while many find them welcoming. More and more, it is becoming socially acceptable to be aware of yourself. There are very close links between noticing what is going on in yourself and being aware of what is going on in people. This is especially useful for students learning to teach, for example.

The benefits for me as a teacher are the stillness and calm, which is the effect of a regular routine of stretching and being calm for a bit. I can take advantage of it in moments in the classroom and these are often moments of choice or stress. I can notice what is going on in other people when they are getting stressed and suggest what they can do, or leave them alone, or do what I guess they might need.

There's a kind of general perception that these kind of oriental stretching exercises in large groups are not acceptable in, for example, England because they look mechanistic and seem to involve loss of identity, but group movement is very powerful and if the movement is designed to work on particular energies, so much the better.

Allan Bramall (specially written)

There are many books on Yoga, Tai Chi and similar approaches. They are powerful tools for developing self-awareness, and it is recommended that you find a teacher to guide you if you decide that you would like to learn more.

14 The Alexander Technique

The Alexander Technique is one of the more modern approaches to supporting your body. John Lofts, a teacher of the Alexander Technique, describes the technique.

The Alexander Technique is a simple, practical way of learning how to tackle those habits which interfere with our natural reflexes as we carry out such basic human activities as moving, breathing and speaking.

Frederick Matthias Alexander (1869–1955) was an Australian actor, who in the course of solving his own voice problems, discovered that we cannot function with maximum ease and efficiency unless we are free from any habits which interfere with the proper relationship between head, neck and back. Alexander found that by a process of conscious awareness he could not only restore this relationship within himself but could also, with the additional help of his hands, teach others to do the same.

Over the years we build habitual patterns of using ourselves badly. These rob us of our coordination and consume our energy. At one level they can produce, or contribute to, a wide range of clinical conditions, from 'bad back' to depression.

John Lofts, Alexander Technique Pamphlet

Tara Bucklow is both an EFL teacher and a teacher of the Alexander Technique. She recognizes that she applies her knowledge of Alexander to help her function better, whichever subject she is teaching.

A tip for teachers in general: The most obvious thing is that on a subconscious level, students are picking up from you how you're using your body, and you're sending them messages. So if you're somebody who slumps, or sits in a very twisted way, or collapses over on yourself, then you're sending a message of not being very enthusiastic, not very interested, lacking in confidence, certainty, direction or whatever; and if you're talking about pacing a lesson, then if you adopt certain postures which are more upright, more open, then you're giving the message that here is someone who is dynamic, someone who knows what they're doing, and someone that you pay attention to. The other thing is that if you are slumped in a chair in front of a class, you'll find that your students will slowly descend into a heap as well. They will tend to mimic your behaviour.

Bucklow 1992 p9 (abridged)

Activity

You can't learn the Alexander Technique from a book but Michael Gelb suggests here one procedure you can practise now. His suggestion is for preparation for giving presentations and this can equally apply to lessons. You need a carpeted floor space and a few paperback books.

The Balanced Resting State

- Begin by placing a few books on the floor.(Most people require a small pile of books 5–15cm in height. To approximate the right height for you: stand upright with your buttocks and shoulder blades against a wall and measure the distance from the wall to the back of your head, then add 1–2.5cm.) Stand your body's length away from the books with your feet shoulder-width apart. Let your hands rest gently at your sides. Facing away from the books, look straight ahead with a soft, alert focus. Pause for a few moments.
- Become aware of the contact of your feet on the floor and notice the distance from your feet to the top of your head. Keep your eyes open and alive, and listen to the sounds around you.

- Maintaining this expansive awareness, move lightly and quickly so that you are resting on one knee. Then roll yourself back so that you are supporting yourself with your hands behind you, feet in front and flat on the floor, knees bent. Avoid holding your breath.
- Let your head drop forward a tiny bit to ensure that you are not tightening your neck muscles and pulling your head back. Then gently roll your spine along the floor so that your head rests on the books. The books should be positioned so that they support your head at the place where your neck ends and your head begins. If your head is not well positioned, then pause, reach back with one hand and support your head while using the other hand to place the books in the proper position. Your feet remain flat on the floor, with your knees pointing up to the ceiling and your hands resting on the floor or loosely folded on your chest. Allow the weight of your body to be fully supported by the floor.
- Avoid fidgeting or wriggling around to 'get comfortable'. If you are uncomfortable then start over from the beginning. All you need to reap the benefit of this procedure is to rest in this position. As you rest, gravity will be lengthening your spine while 'undoing' unnecessary twists and tensions. Keep your eyes open to avoid dozing off. You may wish to bring your attention to the flow of your breathing (without trying to change it) and to the gentle pulsation of your whole body. Be aware of the ground supporting your back, allowing your shoulders to rest as your back widens. Let your neck be free as your whole body lengthens and expands.
- After you have rested for ten to twenty minutes, get up slowly, being careful to avoid stiffening or shortening your body as you return to a standing position. In order to achieve a smooth transition, decide when you are going to move and then gently roll over on to your front, maintaining your new integration and expansion. Ease your way into a crawling position and then on to one knee. With your head leading the movement upward, stand.
- Pause for a few moments ... listen ... eyes alive. Again, feel your feet on the floor, and notice the distance between your feet and the top of your head. You may be surprised to discover that the distance has expanded. As you move into the activities of your day, think about 'not doing' anything that interferes with this expansion, ease and overall buoyancy.

For best results, practise the Balanced Resting State when you wake up in the morning, when you come home from work and before retiring for the night. The procedure is especially valuable *prior* to giving a presentation or performance, engaging in a competition or meeting to resolve a conflict with a loved one or boss, or before any activity that may be stress-inducing.

Gelb 1994 pp162–3

---

15 The Feldenkrais Method

Moshe Feldenkrais, a physicist, engineer and Judo teacher, combined the knowledge from all of these disciplines to help him recover from a serious sports injury. He became interested in the physics inherent in movement generally and went on to develop his approach, first in Israel and then internationally.

There are two distinctive approaches: group lessons are called 'Awareness through Movement', and individual sessions are called 'Functional integration'.

In a one-to-one lesson, the practitioner guides students by gently doing movements for them. The students are then free to pay attention to their movements and can move more gracefully by taking away any unnecessary strain and effort. As the teacher proposes new ways in which students can move, they have more freedom and choice.

Chantal Kickx defines the group classes as follows:

In 'Awareness through Movement' classes, the student is invited to focus on sensory awareness. Movement is used for perfecting the brain. Mindfulness and acceptance are the means to realise how easy and graceful it can be to change habitual patterns which interfere with better functioning of mind and body. The student is guided verbally to move slowly and gently, mostly lying on the floor, sometimes sitting or standing. It is the quality of the attention of the student in the process of moving that is inviting freedom and transformation.

Chantal Kickx, Feldenkrais Pamphlet

Wilfrid van Dorp uses the Feldenkrais Method to inform his approach to teaching.

I find Feldenkrais useful in immersing me in the process of learning, and giving me methodical ways of using my faculties. Feldenkrais led me to explore how we connect ourselves in patterns. Each pattern learned is a choice made and carries with it restrictions and liabilities. One pattern will work in one situation and not in another. I become more accurate in making these distinctions, which gives me the means to make better decisions. The Feldenkrais Method generates more options and enables me to learn to overcome limitations brought on by stress, illness, misuse, tiredness, and accident. As a result I feel and perform better. By helping myself the results are not just remedial and I can shift out of old inappropriate habits into new useful ones.

Wilfred van Dorp (specially written)

16 Supporting your voice

Rowena Whitehead, a former EFL teacher who currently runs voice workshops for people interested in exploring their singing voices, offers some thoughts on the importance for teachers of caring for the voice.

The voice, 'the muscle of the soul', is our most personal musical instrument. As teachers, the voice is one of our most important tools. A well-modulated voice enhances communication and can make a great contribution to the students' experience of the classroom as a relaxed, calm learning environment.

In teaching students to communicate, it is important to model using the voice to maximum effect, in a relaxed, natural and unstrained way. Being able to do this is crucial if you wish to avoid vocal problems during your teaching career. The continuous use of the voice can impose a heavy toll on it and the development of student-centred learning has imposed more pressure as teachers interact one-to-one with students against a background noise of student talk and other activity.

It is interesting to note that over half of a trainee actor's or singer's timetable is allotted to vocal training and movement. On the other hand, it is rare for any time at all to be devoted to this area in the training of teachers despite the fact that arguably they experience more strain to their voices than stage performers. Some teachers have a natural ability to use and care for their voices effectively, but many teachers experience vocal tiredness at some point during their careers which could be avoided with greater awareness of how to look after their voices.

So what can be done to avoid problems? The key areas to be aware of are as follows:

Breathing and support

Breathing and support are all-important: each time we speak, we use our breath to expel the sound. The breath needs the support of our abdominal muscles to sustain our voice. The calmer, deeper and more regular the breath, the more chance we have of staying centred and communicating effectively.

Take a few minutes before classes start, and whilst students are otherwise engaged, to focus your concentration on posture and breath.

First, monitor your body for useless tension: are your shoulders relaxed, not forced back or slumped forward? Are your neck and jaw relaxed, your hands unclenched?

Is your spine flexible, not braced back or bent over towards the front of your body?

Are your knees relaxed, your feet untensed and comfortable? (When you communicate, you do so from the soles of the feet upwards!)

Next, allow your breath to fill your lungs, expanding your rib cage on all sides of your body, feeling your lower abdomen expand as you breathe in and contract as you exhale. Your shoulders and chest remain relaxed. Imagine you are breathing into the area just below your navel. When you speak, this area is the power base for your voice, from where it gets crucial support.

Lubrication of the voice

Coffee, coke, chocolate and cigarettes tend to dry out the throat, which can lead to vocal damage, and their consumption is better confined to the evenings. Water and herbal teas are recommended, as many as ten to twelve glasses a day; keeping a jug of water in the classroom can be helpful. Medicated lozenges also dry out the voice and should not be used for lubrication.

Vocal pitch

The volume of noise in the classroom may cause you to raise the pitch of your voice beyond its natural register, which will put stress on the larynx. Ground rules for controlling the amount of noise you have to compete with should be agreed with the students. Put more of your energy into articulation to help clarity.

Pain

In the event of pain, try to vocalise as little as possible through pain or discomfort in the throat; the pain is a warning that you are doing potential damage to your vocal mechanism. Never whisper to save your voice as this tires the vocal chords and can lead to further damage. In extreme cases of pain or loss of voice, you should give your voice a total rest – without speaking or whispering – for two to five days.

Rowena Whitehead (specially written)

As with all the other work on the body, caring for our voices impacts on other aspects of ourselves and our personal development. In Western countries, especially, many people have been told at a young age that they 'can't sing', and they carry this belief around with them. This often stops them feeling free to lead or join in singing in the classroom, and leads to a negative self-image and lack of self-confidence in this area, shutting them off from the enjoyment of singing with others. In cultures where everybody sings, particularly as an accompaniment to work, it is taken for granted that everyone has a natural ability to sing.

Voice workshops provide an opportunity to experience the liberation of discovering that you can sing, or that you can extend the range and confidence of your speaking or singing voices. They can release you from the tensions of your own and others' judgement of how you 'ought' to sound.

Finding a voice is important if you are to express your power. It is often included in assertiveness training where you learn that using the right tone to express your ideas and needs can be the key to real personal power.

Activity

Liberating your body and its voice

If you would like to free your voice and experience the happy feelings singing brings, try these exercises suggested by Alan Mars, an Alexander Teacher, NLP Practitioner and teacher at the Arts Educational Drama School. Before you begin, take a good look around the room you are in now, and notice your sensations. How big is it? How bright and friendly is it? How much personal space do you have in it?

Experiment 1:

Vocalising from restriction

Think of a time when you were feeling a bit pressured and restricted. Remember this as fully as possible ... what you were seeing around you, what you were hearing and also what you were feeling ... Stay fully in this state for a while longer.

Now take a look around the room you are in. Does it look any less bright or any less friendly than it did before? Now walk around the room. Do you feel taller or shorter? Do you feel wider or narrower? What size does your personal space seem to be (indicate with your hands)? Is your walking lighter or heavier? Vocalise an *aahh* sound. How easy or difficult was it to vocalise?

Experiment 2:

Vocalising from ease

Move around the room and stretch to dissipate the effects of the last experiment.

Remember a time when you felt 'on top of the world'. Recall and relive this experience ... what were you seeing, hearing and feeling ... stay fully in this state a while longer and allow yourself to take two or three easy, deep breaths with the emphasis on the out breath. Allow this feeling to spread through your entire body ...

Look around the room. Does it look any brighter or friendlier now? Walk around the room. Do you feel shorter or taller? Narrower or wider? How large is your 'personal space' now? Is your walking heavier or lighter?

Vocalise an *aahh* sound. Notice how your voice feels and sounds different from the first experiment. You have just taken the first step in tuning your instrument and liberating your voice.

Dealing with the critics

When someone has been criticised in the past about their singing a strange thing can happen. They become very self-critical and consequently knock themselves out of that state of easiness which will help them to develop their singing.

Instead of agreeing with the internal critic or fighting with it, try chuckling at it and humouring it. Even if it feels a bit false at first, try a few *ho hos, ha has* and *hee hees.*

Do a few vocalised *aahhs.* Play around with the volume – a bit softer, a bit louder (without pushing or straining). Play with the pitch – a bit higher and lower. Whatever note you make, fully enjoy it – even if it is not the note you expected to make! Soon enough you will find that the sounds you hear inside your head and the sounds you hear yourself actually making will come into a closer and closer correspondence.

Developing your internal coach

You can also develop your internal 'coach'. Your internal coach is absolutely lavish and extravagant in its praise and encouragement of your vocal and singing exploration. Your coach not only says the right things, it says them in a kind, enthusiastic and motivating tone of voice.

Practice

Set aside five to ten minutes a day to play around with these body and voice awareness experiments. Maintain a sense of your body as a whole and of letting go while you vocalise.

Do some vocalised *aahs*, and as you do, gently bring your lips together to make a humming sound. Allow your breath to return effortlessly between *aahs*. You may notice a subtle tingling or buzzing feeling spreading across your lips and face. This feeling may spread to other parts of your body – throat, chest, fingertips, etc. This tingling is associated with muscular release and increased peripheral blood flow. Sing a song. Sing several songs!

Carry on singing

There are many ways ... and remember the longest, and most fascinating, journey begins with the smallest step.

Mars 1993 pp27–8

The nice thing about these series of steps is that you can apply them to other things you want to learn, as I (Pauline) found when learning how to use a computer and how to play the violin.

17 Basic drama techniques

Many people working in the field of drama use Yoga and the Alexander Technique to work with their bodies. The loosening up, grounding and centring exercises can help teachers to use their bodies flexibly and skilfully in the same enlivening way.

Rowena Whitehead, a voice and singing teacher, suggests the following exercises as a beginning to work on presence, projection and flexibility. You can do these in a pair or group, or using a mirror if you're working alone.

Activity

1 To stretch the body, begin by reaching up with your arms one after the other as if you were climbing a rope ladder. Reach up on tiptoes and enjoy the feeling of stretch as you reach up higher. Work within your range of comfort and breathe naturally and easily. Keep centred and relaxed and aware of your body.

2 When you are fully stretched up with your hands outstretched and standing on tiptoes, tense up your muscles and make a star. Extend your tongue as far as it can go. Make eye contact with someone if you're working in a group or look at yourself in the mirror. Then flop down with your knees

slightly bent and relaxed, to protect your back. Feel the weight of your arms pulling down and allow your breathing to deepen. When you're ready, slowly uncurl your spine, keeping the relaxed feeling, and bring your head up last of all. Repeat this stretch and flop a couple of times, again working within your range of comfort.

3 Now, stand with the outside edge of your feet parallel, your legs hip-width apart so that your feet are directly under your hips. Rock on your feet gently between your toes and heels until you feel the weight is evenly distributed. Lift your shoulders up and back and as you breathe out let them relax down into a comfortable position. Imagine that a jet of water is shooting up your nice, straight spine and out of the top of your head, which is like a ping pong ball bobbing about loosely and gently on top of the water. Your shoulders are completely relaxed with your arms by your side. Imagine you are holding shopping bags in each hand so that your arms are weighted downwards in an unstrained way. Check out your body for any tension and breathe out as you release it. You feel centred and grounded and have released energy.

4 Allow your breath to flow in and out of your lungs which are like two balloons, filling up in the bottom, middle and top, your ribs expanding sideways as they do. Your shoulders remain down and relaxed. Breathe out through your mouth as you push the breath out with your ribs. Open your chest as you breathe in through your nose and sigh on an out breath through your mouth. Increase the range of your sigh as you start the sigh gradually higher and higher in pitch and finish deeper and deeper. Play with your voice and begin making the noises you hear around you every day. 'Hiya! Yaay! Hi! Yuck! Na!-Na!-Na!-Na!-Na! Brrmm! Brrmm!' Laugh in lots of different ways – 'Hee! Hee! Ho! Ho! Ha! Ha!' Imagine you are on a hillside calling out to someone. We usually attract attention in a relaxed and powerful way. Now extend your ways of calling.

5 Now with a partner or the mirror if you like, start a conversation using only noises and lively facial expressions to convey your meaning. You can decide beforehand what the conversation is about. For example, one of you can ask the other to do something and the other one can refuse.

6 With a partner start by standing a little way apart facing each other. Throw your voice so that you imagine your partner catching it. At this distance you will be working softly. Begin to move apart backwards, still facing each other. As you do, you and your partner can 'throw' your voices to each other on an out breath, using your voice as you would on a hillside, that is in an open, relaxed, unrestricted and powerful way. Support your voice with your relaxed body. When you have gone back as far as you want, start moving towards each other, gradually lowering the range of your voice.

7 Go back to the balanced standing posture you adopted in step 3 of this activity. When you feel balanced and ready, begin to walk around in a relaxed way, arms loose and shoulders down. Keep this poised balance and adjust your posture as you walk. Feel what this feeling of balance is like, and each time you want to come back to a centred state in the classroom, adopt this balanced way of walking. Experiment with different ways of walking and see if your mood changes. Think about what you convey to

your students from your posture in the classroom and how it affects the atmosphere and your own state of mind.

Rowena Whitehead (specially written)

18 Co-counselling

Co-counselling is a form of time-sharing. It involves agreeing to work with another person in a particular kind of counselling arrangement, where speaking and listening time is shared equally between the two. There is a set procedure for co-counselling, which is as follows:

- Two people agree to meet from time to time to listen and help each other sort out their thoughts and feelings about what they are doing.
- They meet in a place where they can talk freely and will not be interrupted.
- They decide how much time they have and allocate half the time to one and half to the other.
- The first person speaks and explores whatever he or she finds important or significant at the moment. The other listens helpfully, encouraging the speaker by paying attention, understanding what is being said, and showing that they understand by offering summaries, by checking that they have understood, and by asking questions or making statements which are carefully chosen to help the speaker to gain a new understanding of the situation. The listener does not offer advice. The listener is also careful not to take over by talking about his or her own concerns, or by interrogating the speaker, particularly to satisfy his or her curiosity.
- This continues for the time allotted, and then the pair stop and change roles.
- Afterwards you might – without referring to the content of what either of you said – talk about the process of doing it.
- Everything discussed remains strictly confidential between the two of you.

Susan Knight, Adult Learning Consultant in Sydney, extols the virtues of this sort of professional co-counselling:

The attraction of co-counselling was that it offered me the chance of learning to assist other people in personal exploration and to pursue my own in a continuing reciprocal process whereby I could meet as often as I liked with another co-counsellor and spend half the time giving them my attention and half the time using their attention for whatever I wanted to work on ... the particular technique which is relevant here is the simplest of all, that of placing all one's attention and awareness at the disposal of another person, listening with interest and appreciation without interrupting or discussion. This is known as giving free attention. It sounds like a very simple process, and it is, but it is also surprisingly powerful ...

Susan Knight quoted in Brandes and Ginnis 1990 p154

Peta Gray explains how skills learned in co-counselling colour her teaching.

There are many ways in which my co-counselling experience has been helpful to me as a classroom teacher ... If I am feeling bad and about to teach a class, I often use activities I've come across in co-counselling groups to pull my attention back into the here and now. It might entail focusing on a pleasant or amusing memory or on my immediate surroundings or eliciting from myself a list of things I've done well recently; anything that helps me to leave my emotional baggage firmly outside the classroom. These work well for students too and can be used as warmers or for lifting the atmosphere in the classroom when it is necessary. The balance between safety and challenge seems to be crucial in any learning situation. To facilitate that in a classroom is not easy, as so many people have had distressing experiences in classrooms, and sometimes the old feelings hang around and get in the way. Careful monitoring can alert me to try something to help the students free up their attention, as I would if I were counselling them.

I also find my counselling skills useful in getting students to listen to each other well, and for raising their awareness of their own learning strategies and of how their previous learning experiences colour their present expectations. I am better able to read body language and this gives me a basis for all sorts of spontaneous decisions that have to be made in the course of a lesson: whether to cut short an activity or not, when to give a student individual attention, when we need some humour. In short I find it opens up new channels for communication in the classroom, and in a language class this is invaluable as it eases the anxieties and frustrations that inevitably arise when people are struggling to express themselves in language.

Gray 1992 pp8–9

19 Keeping a diary

A teaching diary can be both a factual record of your teaching, and a means of reminding yourself of the highs and lows of the job. This too can be a useful source of personal support. Ruth, a third grade teacher in the USA, who took part in a research project during which she kept a diary for over a year and met weekly in a seminar group, writes about the significance for her.

Sometimes teaching is a lonely business – imagine saying that when you are so involved with people! Lonely in the sense of feelings – caring, frustrated ones maybe. You know that others must have felt the same frustrations you felt, but where are they? That's the beauty of a support group such as this. I think that if we did nothing further than this journal business – I would still write for the catharsis. Going back I remember and understand how I felt. And I feel a better person and teacher for the writing ...

Quoted in Holly 1989 p11

Sylvia Welyczko has come to regard her diary as a good and loyal friend. Here she explains how she started to write it, and why it has become such an invaluable support.

Last night, before I finally went to sleep, I took a solid-looking book out of a drawer and wrote an entry into what has become 'My Diary'. I was interested to see that it was about two months since I had written the last entry so I spent a while 'up-dating' my life for future reference.

We hear a lot about teacher development through the various magazines and periodicals which pass through our staffrooms, but I often think we forget how closely our professional development is tied up with our personal experiences of life ... This can easily lead to the situation in which we find ourselves reproaching ourselves for a lack of progress in our careers or a seeming deterioration in our teaching abilities simply because we seem to underestimate the effect of living in a strange culture (if we are working abroad) or teaching a sometimes unpredictable or unstimulating range of classes (depending on our luck or our situation).

It was in my second EFL job (after just over three months of teaching) that I was advised to keep a 'lesson diary'. I was told to buy myself a sturdy, well-bound book which I found pleasing to the eye ... After each lesson I began writing a short commentary about it.

Sometimes I would simply record a new idea I had had, sometimes I would comment on difficulties I was experiencing with a certain type of student, and sometimes I would record some pleasant incident. My diary was my professional confidante ... and the entries, although at first very regular, were usually fairly pithy ...

Time passed, I moved to different places and the entries continued, at times after long intervals of 'unrecorded time'. Gradually I noticed that I seemed to be 'getting to know' my diary, as one does a new friend, and I was revealing more of my true self in the entries ...

If I take a more objective view of keeping an 'EFL Diary', I could justify it in various ways:

a) It provides a record of teaching ideas and problems experienced. Admittedly it is a somewhat haphazard record and ideas are not easily 'retrieved' for future use, but I think the disadvantages of this are more than adequately counteracted by the fact that the very privacy of the diary (as opposed to the usual card index type of system) provides a completely safe and non-judgemental 'site' for the ideas themselves. There can be no fear that some other teacher will secretly mock an idea; no worry that it has not been recorded 'helpfully' enough (that is so that other teachers can understand and use it themselves); no feeling that it must be educationally sound. The diary simply acts as a sounding board.

b) When it is re-read after the passing of time, it acts as a reminder of progress made (either in professional or personal terms). Reading some entries reminds me that I would go through horrible phases when nothing seemed to go 'right' in the classroom, when the buzz of ideas in the staffroom would secretly embarrass me as I felt the barren expanses of my own mind heaving in resentment. Other entries remind me of good things which happened that I would otherwise have 'forgotten' in a seemingly subconscious attempt at modesty.

c) It also acts as a record of one's career. Over the years I have been writing entries I have recorded any significant moment or moves I have made ... a significant conversation about a possible transfer, an application for a job, my feelings about various dilemmas ... even compliments or criticisms I have received which later act as an uplifting reminder or a sobering comment about my limitations and weak spots.

In the entry I wrote last night, I not only recorded recent events in my professional life ... I also commented on my latest romantic aspirations, on my feelings about Singapore, on my beliefs, on my new year's resolutions and on my hopes and ideas for the future.

When I next pack the tatty, old suitcase, the diary will be there: a solid blue friend.

Welyczko 1989 p5

20 Neuro-Linguistic Programming

Many teachers are now using Neuro-Linguistic Programming (NLP), a set of learning tools which help a person achieve their full potential. It looks at how to find out about the way people process and retrieve information and how we can use this knowledge for effective learning, change and communication.

NLP was first created in 1975 by Richard Bandler, a psychologist, and John Grinder, a linguist, who noticed how top communicators have characteristics in common, in that they learn and think fast and they have internal strategies for thinking which suit their style of learning. The key to understanding these strategies lies in noticing their eye movements and their choice of language, including body language. Here are my (Pauline's) reactions to NLP.

When I did an NLP course I learned some effective techniques for my own personal development and for listening and communicating effectively in the classroom. I also learned a tremendous amount about learning and teaching.

I learned how to observe eye movements, voice tone, posture and choice of language as a way of understanding how someone uses their senses and brain to process information. I now use this information to communicate with learners in a language they understand and so gain greater rapport and plan lessons to take into account preferred learning styles. I can now teach students to notice which of the five senses they prefer when learning, and how they can also develop their other senses to learn even more efficiently. I can also ask successful learners what they do and use the same strategies for myself or teach them to my students. For example, good spellers make a visual image of a word and copy it. I can see they are doing this because they look up with their eyes to spell. I teach students to look up to store and retrieve words. We have used the same strategies to store lots of information – prepositions that follow verbs, words and their meaning, lists of points for essays in teachers' exams and so on. In the same way that I can notice their eye movements, I can notice how people perceive the world and the beliefs they hold by listening to the language they use, including the metaphors.

Using the same information about how our brains work, I can help myself and learners to set goals and know when they have achieved the outcome. We can also understand our beliefs and change them if we feel these beliefs are holding back our learning. Likewise, I can teach learners how to get into good states so that they use the resources they have inside them to help them in more difficult situations, for example when they are trying to learn things they have found difficult in the past. I use exactly the same strategies to keep myself in those resourceful states and to interview, give feedback to, and train teachers.

When I work in this way with students, they enjoy the fact that there are very concrete strategies they can use, the changes can be fast, easy and fun, and they don't have to reveal the content of their difficulties.

For a description of how to use some NLP techniques to help in the process of change see Chapter 7, section 9, *Modelling new behaviour.*

21 Assertiveness training

Powerlessness, whether real or merely perceived, is one of the major causes of stress. Everyone who writes on managing change effectively, whether for ourselves or for others, acknowledges that clear and assertive communication is one of the keys to 'finding a voice'. According to Meg Bond, who facilitated a teacher development workshop on assertiveness and time management, this means:

> ... letting other people know what your priorities, preferences, wants or needs are in a specific situation while allowing others to state theirs and while taking them into account. You state these or make your requests with an appropriate strength of feeling, which indicates the extent to which they are important to you. When your statement or request is not being acknowledged or acted on sufficiently and it is important to you, then you would persist.
>
> *Mulligan (ed.) 1988 p120*

Anne Dickson is a psychologist who facilitates assertiveness workshops for women. In her book *A Woman In Your Own Right* she shows how assertive behaviour respects both parties in a transaction. The following diagram compares four possible behaviour patterns and shows how three of them can be degenerate.

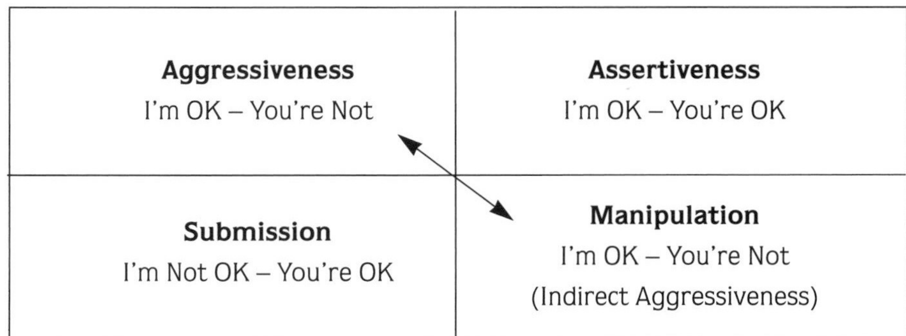

She also outlines some basic assertiveness skills. They are:

- making clear, specific requests
- learning how to say 'no'
- handling criticism – both on the receiving end and when you need to confront someone else
- learning about body language
- managing the expression of feelings, especially anger
- receiving compliments
- taking the initiative
- building self-esteem and improving your self-presentation.

Dickson 1982 p xvi

One of the things we need to be aware of when being assertive is the fact that everyone has rights. We must allow others the same rights that we assume for ourselves, and make sure that in asserting ourselves we are not taking away the rights of others.

On page 149 is a statement of personal rights and the rights of others, placed side by side on the page as a reminder that both are to be given equal consideration when we pursue our own personal development objectives.

Activity

This 'list of rights' has helped people to start making changes in their behaviour and has served as a useful reminder at difficult times. It can take some time for people to accept these rights for themselves or for others, so assertiveness teachers recommend you do all or some of the following:

1 Look at the list of rights. Is there one that is of particular significance to you – that 'jumps out' from the page? Why?

2 Are there any that you do not feel apply to you? Would you like to cross them off the list?

3 Are there any missing that you would like to add to the list?

4 Now that you have adapted the list, look at it and decide:

- Are there ways in which you don't accept the same rights for yourself as you do for others? For example, you may make excuses for others and even be too tolerant. 'You're only young once.' What are the things you say about yourself? Are they as tolerant and forgiving? For example, 'I'm 40! You'd think I'd have learned by now!'
- What responsibilities for the welfare of our family and colleagues, or for ourselves, does each right entail, remembering that others also have rights and responsibilities, and you have the responsibility of choice? For example, if you have the right to say 'no', so do others, and you don't always have to do so.

5 Try reading your own list aloud for yourself.

6 Read your list often, as this will help to reinforce it. Post it up on your mirror or carry it in your pocket.

7 You may wish to sign it.

Adapted from Beels, Hopson and Scally 1992 pp25–9

I have the right to state my own needs and set my own priorities as a person whatever other people expect of me because of my roles in life.	AND	You have the right to state your own needs and set your own priorities as a person whatever other people expect of you because of your roles in life.
I have the right to be treated with respect as an intelligent, capable and equal human being.	AND	You have the right to be treated with respect as an intelligent, capable and equal human being.
I have the right to express my feelings.	AND	You have the right to express your feelings.
I have the right to express my opinions and values.	AND	You have the right to express your opinions and values.
I have the right to say 'Yes' or 'No' for myself.	AND	You have the right to say 'Yes' or 'No' for yourself.
I have the right to make mistakes.	AND	You have the right to make mistakes.
I have the right to change my mind.	AND	You have the right to change your mind.
I have the right to say 'I don't understand'.	AND	You have the right to say 'I don't understand'.
I have the right to ask for what I want.	AND	You have the right to ask for what you want.
I have the right to decide for myself whether or not I am responsible for another person's problem.	AND	You have the right to decide for yourself whether or not you are responsible for another person's problem.
I have the right to deal with people without having to make them like or approve of me.	AND	You have the right to deal with other people without having to make them like or approve of you.

Adapted from Dickson 1982, in Bond 1986 p99

22 Conclusion

Teachers who are actively committed to their own process of development know that it requires personal energy and intention. However, the alternative may in the end turn out to be even more exhausting. In this chapter we have identified some of the various forms of care that teachers have found helpful to support their development. Attention to ourselves as whole people – not just mind, but also body and spirit – will keep us feeling fit and open to new possibilities. You may find it particularly helpful to have strategies for supporting yourself when you deal with change, which is the subject of the next chapter.

Chapter 7 Managing your own change

1 Introduction

Change happens within us and around us throughout our lives, whether we initiate it for ourselves or are faced with change imposed from elsewhere. People who decide to take control of their own development may be in a stronger position both to initiate the kind of change they would like for themselves, and to hold on to an inner sense of direction amid the pressures that external change forces upon them. In this chapter we look at ways of managing change and making sure that we get the best for ourselves from it.

Michael Fullan, whose work on educational change we referred to in Chapter 1, believes that the purpose of learning is to give people skills to deal with change. In the following extract, he outlines his view of why the change process should concern us so fundamentally:

> Society – for some time now, but increasingly more so as we head to the twenty-first century – expects its citizens to be capable of proactively dealing with change throughout life both individually as well as collaboratively in a context of dynamic, multicultural global transformation. Of all the institutions in society, education is the only one that potentially has the promise of fundamentally contributing to this goal. Yet education far from being a hotbed of teaching people to deal with change in basic ways is just the opposite. To break through this impasse, educators must see themselves and be seen as

experts in the dynamics of change. To become expert in the dynamics of change, educators – administrators and teachers alike – must become skilled change agents. If they do become skilled change agents with moral purpose, educators will make a difference in the lives of students from all backgrounds, and by so doing help produce greater capacity in society to cope with change.

This is not one of these goals that you can tinker with, that you can vaguely or obliquely expect to happen or that you can accomplish by playing it safe. The goal of greater change capacity must become explicit and its pursuit must become all out and sustained.

Fullan 1993 pp4–5

2 Uncovering hidden beliefs about change

One reason for beginning to look at change by setting out what you believe, think and do now is to bring to the surface the beliefs that shape your life and your work. These are for the most part deeply buried, but, as the following story illustrates, they are confirmed in a person's approach to everything he or she does.

A parable retold

Once upon a time an old man sat by the side of the road, smoking his pipe, and gazing off into the distance contemplating ... who-knows-what? Along came a stranger who stopped to pass the time of day, putting down his bundle and taking out a ham sandwich and a bottle of wine, which he forgot to share with the old man. In the course of the conversation, the stranger pointed to the village nestled in the valley below, and asked, 'What are the people like in the town down there? I'm just moving to that village, you know.'

The old man puffed a puff on his pipe, and threw the question back: 'What were they like in the town where you used to live, my friend?'

A thundercloud seemed to pass over the stranger's face: 'Oh, they were rogues and rascals of the worst sort. Liars, cheats, a pack of knaves they were. Never could get a kind word out of any of them.'

Smoke billowed from the old man's pipe, as he shook his head and spoke: 'Well then, that's what the people are like in that village down there, my son.'

The stranger heaved himself to his feet and walked sadly down the hill. The old man leaned back against the tree for his afternoon siesta.

Later, when he woke, he saw another stranger approaching. The newcomer smiled, and asked if he could share the shade of the old stately tree. The old man shifted over to make room for him, and gratefully accepted the stranger's offer of an apple and some cheese.

As they chatted, the stranger pointed to the hamlet in the valley: 'What are the people like in that village?' he asked, 'I'm thinking of moving there soon.'

A twinkle, unobserved, appeared in the old man's eye, as once again he parried the question. 'What were they like where you have just come from, my son?'

The stranger's face lit up. 'Oh, they're wonderful people, the salt of the earth, not a harsh word nor a dishonest act have I heard of these many years. I only wish I could stay, but it is time for me to move on.'

The old man hid his pleasure by lighting his pipe, as he responded, 'Well, I'm glad to say that that is exactly how you'll find those people in the village below.'

Brandes and Ginnis 1990 pp214–15

Activity

1 Read the story above, on your own or with others. Think about or discuss the meaning.

2 Write a moral for the story and relate it to a school context.

3 Write down an action you would condemn. Think of a situation in which that action might be interpreted positively, or have a positive function.

4 Do you see yourself as tending to be more like the first stranger in the story, or the second? Or do you think you see aspects of both in your reaction to different situations? What insights can you draw from this?

---

3 Starting with yourself

In his book *Awareness* Anthony de Mello reminds us of the fact that our perspective is always coloured by who we are, and as a consequence all change needs to start with ourselves.

Many people swing into action to get rid of negative feelings ... only to make things worse. They're not coming from love, they're coming from negative feelings. They're coming from guilt, anger, hate; from a sense of injustice or whatever. You've got to make sure of your 'being' before you swing into action. You have to make sure of who you are before you act ... *Then* you might decide to swing into action. You might or might not. You can't decide that until you are awake. Unfortunately, all the emphasis is concentrated on changing the world and very little emphasis is given to waking up.

Imagine that you are unwell and in a foul mood, and they're taking you through some lovely countryside. The landscape is beautiful but you're not in the mood to see anything. A few days later you pass the same spot and you say, 'Good heavens, where was I that I didn't notice all this?' Everything becomes beautiful when you change. Or you look at the trees and the mountains through windows that are wet with rain from a storm, and everything looks blurred and shapeless. You want to go right out there and change those trees, change those mountains. Wait a minute, let's examine your window. When the storm ceases and the rain stops, and you look out the window, you say, 'Well, how different everything looks.' We see people and things not as they are, but as we are ... When you are finally awake, you don't try to make good things happen; they just happen.

You understand suddenly that everything that happens to you is good ...

Put this programme into action, a thousand times: (a) identify the negative feelings in you; (b) understand that they are in you, not in the world, not in external reality; (c) do not see them as an essential part of 'I'; these things come and go; (d) understand that when you change, everything changes.

De Mello pp87–9

4 Processing your beliefs

One way of looking at your beliefs is to brainstorm them (see also Chapter 4). Brainstorming uncovers the various unconscious messages you have absorbed and the hidden beliefs you hold. It is a useful way of examining a new belief, particularly one you are finding difficult to adopt, but one which you feel you need or would like to explore further. The same can be true for ideas which are already part of your existing belief system and which you would like to examine again.

Gill Edwards explains the steps involved in brainstorming. In this method, you begin by choosing a topic around which you would like to examine your beliefs. This could be the topic of change, teaching in general, a particular area of teaching, or a new idea in one of those areas.

If you are a language teacher, you might want to look at a particular aspect of language teaching, such as:

- accuracy and fluency
- pronunciation
- use of dictionaries in class
- what constitutes 'correct' language
- teaching grammar
- speaking
- listening
- reading
- writing

Teachers of any subject could examine their beliefs around an area such as:

- lesson planning
- classroom management
- student–teacher interaction
- homework
- testing
- mistakes and correction
- grading
- punctuality
- learner strategies
- mixed abilities
- class size
- appropriate materials

Activity

Choose one of the topics above, then scribble down everything that comes into your head about it. (Don't just think about it.) Don't censor thoughts. Just brainstorm as many ideas as possible, including ideas which seem to *you* like obvious truths. You might fill a page or a dozen pages before you come to a standstill. Note any feelings that come up as you write ...

Then begin to sift through what you have written. What are your central beliefs and attitudes about this topic? Where have these beliefs come from?

What contradictions emerge from what you have written?

Do you hold other beliefs which might 'explain' the contradictions? (For example 'All teachers are creative' and 'I'm not creative' might be bridged by the belief (possibly unconscious till you looked at this) that 'I'm different from other people'.) Make a summary list of your beliefs about this topic – including the contradictions.

Don't dismiss any of your ideas by saying 'everyone believes that'. It is most unlikely that 'everyone' does – and in any case if *you* believe it, it is affecting your life, so you need to examine it. We all surround ourselves with people who share our beliefs so that we feel comfortable, so it's often the obvious truths that we most need to question.

Edwards 1991 pp61–2

Activity

- Write each statement below in the centre of a separate sheet of paper and write your beliefs about each statement around it in a mind map.
  1. My beliefs about creativity
  2. The advantages of being creative
  3. The advantages of not being creative
  4. What I will have to give up if I change
  5. What I will gain if I change
  6. What I am afraid of if I change
  7. What I am looking forward to if I change

Many of these statements are similar but sometimes yield different answers. As in the exercise above, keep going till you run out of ideas. You may want to do this over a longer period of time to make sure that all your beliefs come to the surface.

- Look at where your beliefs may have come from. Your family? Your teachers? Friends? Books? Films? TV programmes? Your partner? Perhaps you can't remember. You chose them though, and for a good reason at the time.
- Do you still need all of these beliefs? If not, acknowledge that the ones you don't want served you well in the past, but are no longer useful or necessary. Write them on a piece of paper and tear it up. The unconscious loves symbols!

---

5 Moving from disabling beliefs

In the course of teaching and life in general you are likely to have acquired a set of beliefs that strongly influence the way you teach and the way you feel about your teaching. Beliefs can become disabling after a time, in that they sometimes get in the way of change. Holding on to them can keep you stuck and contribute to feelings of stress, strain and burnout.

People are 'stuck' when they need to change in some way, but yet are unable to. They cannot find in themselves the resources to develop some of their potential that will 'unstick' them. In a curious way they may even resist their own development, somehow finding it easier, or safer, not to develop, and not even notice that they can and it is possible. Most of us go through this phase. The question is how aware we are of it, and how we deal with it.

Activity

1. Write down your own list of characteristics you associate with a 'stuck' teacher.
2. When you have done this, read the list below compiled by a group of EFL teachers who were brainstorming associations they made with the idea of a 'stuck' teacher, while attending a Teacher Development seminar at International House, Hastings. Compare your list with theirs.
   - stale, cynical
   - dwindling enthusiasm
   - lack of interest in students
   - finds work a grind
   - cruises through predictable routine
   - unwilling to take risks
   - hate their own lessons
   - getting older
   - uncooperative
   - uninquisitive
   - does not respond to opportunities
   - drag on others
   - mean, complaining, resentful, bitter
   - projecting blame onto others
   - 'I'll only do what I'm paid for'
   - closed to friendships
   - poorly prepared
   - lacklustre
   - unavailable
   - contagious discontent
   - us versus them
   - resentment at lack of promotion and low pay
   - resentment at bureaucracy
3. Add to your own list any from the list above that you find relevant.
4. Now, beside each 'stuck' characteristic in the list you have compiled, substitute its opposite. For example:
   Stale, cynical → Fresh, hopeful
   Finds work a grind → Finds work an adventure
5. Notice your response to each list of opposites.

Changing the words to their opposites can alter our perspective and renew our energy. This happens because we focus on words and ideas which have positive force. Of course, people who are really feeling stuck may not change instantly and dramatically by simply changing the words that describe their feelings, but what the activity shows is that looking at their opposites restores some balance to, and inspires some freshness in, the situation. And it can have a powerful effect.

6 Applying appropriate antidotes

One way of letting go of a disabling belief is to recall an experience which has actually contradicted the belief, and shown that it is not as true as it seemed to be. Responding to a newsletter article where the writer had identified a very common set of beliefs that keep teachers stuck, EFL teacher Sue Greenland came up with an antidote for each one which enabled her to move on.

BELIEFS	ANTIDOTES
1 It is a dire necessity for me to be liked and approved of by virtually everybody. Therefore I must do what I can to avoid being disliked, rejected, laughed at or criticised.	1 Remember a time or times when someone praised you or did a caring thing for you.
2 A worthwhile, mature adult can and should go through life without making mistakes. Therefore I must do what I can to avoid failing or being seen to fail.	2 Remember a time or times when you did something well.
3 Worthwhile people do not feel confused, uncertain or ignorant – and if they do they should feel ashamed. Therefore I must do what I can to appear knowledgeable and in control.	3 Remember a time or times when your thinking on something was very clear.
4 I am who I think I am – my image of myself is accurate and binding. Therefore I must not act out of character. (I'm not the sort of person who ... I could never ... It wouldn't be me ...)	4 Think about your strong points and what you like about yourself.
5 To feel and show fear – anxiety, nervousness, apprehension, insecurity, need, timidity – is a weakness. Therefore I must try to hide and deny my anxiety.	5 Remember a time or times when you overcame a fear.
6 Life ought to be easy. There is something wrong if my life contains problems to which I don't readily have solutions. Therefore I must appear to be problem-free.	6 Think about what is good in your life at the moment.

BELIEFS	ANTIDOTES
7 I am powerless. Life is unfair and insufferable because it simultaneously poses me hard problems and denies me access to the solutions. I am a victim. Therefore I must be resigned to my problems.	7 Remember a time or times when you asserted yourself in a positive way.
8 If I can do nothing, it is pointless (and frustrating) to think about what I might do. Therefore I must not plan or dream.	8 Think about or write down your goals and dreams for the future and decide on the first small step you can take towards achieving one of them.
9 I do not have the right to say what I see or think is wrong (with school) unless I have a clear vision of how it ought to be, and a well-worked-out and infallible means of achieving it. Therefore I must keep quiet about my thoughts and feelings.	9 Think about what you like about your workplace.
10 It is better not to pay attention to things that are upsetting. Therefore I must distract myself from such experiences, or deaden myself to them.	10 Remember a time or times when you have been able to face something you were afraid to face.
11 Stress is an inevitable consequence of a high level of pressure, demand and uncertainty. Therefore I must seek to blame or avoid the circumstances; not look at my part in the matter.	11 Remember a time or times when you have responded well under pressure.
12 To ask for help is a sign of weakness, for which other people will scorn me. Therefore I must appear self-sufficient.	12 Remember a time or times when you have asked for help or assistance and received it.

BELIEFS	ANTIDOTES
13 If I am responsible for something and it doesn't work, I am to blame. Responsibility carries the risk that I might feel bad about myself. Therefore I must not take on or invite responsibility. I will keep quiet about my schemes lest I be called to account for them.	13 Remember a time or times when you have taken on responsibility successfully.
14 If people let me down, I am released from all responsibility to respect them or keep my word. Therefore I may repay forgetfulness or indifference with forgetfulness or indifference.	14 Think about those people you respect and remember a time when you have forgiven people.
15 If we don't agree, one of us must be wrong. If it is me, that implies that I am bad, stupid, ignorant, inadequate ... so it can't be me. Therefore I must prove it is you to protect me from being the failure.	15 Remember a time or times when you have expressed your opinions well and been able to listen well to someone.
16 If you ask me to do something that I don't want to do, I have only two choices: to do it, and feel resentful; or not to do it, and feel guilty. Neither of these makes me feel good. Therefore I must try to avoid being asked for help or support, because I feel controlled.	16 Remember a time or times when you have helped and supported another person.
17 If you criticise me, I feel inadequate. If you praise me, you are either placating me or manipulating me. So you are either hostile or untrustworthy. Therefore I must avoid finding out what you think.	17 Think about those people you trust and can be yourself with.

Greenland 1986 p8

('Beliefs that keep you stuck' first appeared in the newsletter of the Education Network, January 1986.)

Sue Greenland suggests the following activity which we invite you to do. She suggests steps for working in a group, but the procedure can easily be adapted if you are working on your own.

Activity

1 With a partner, choose who is going to be speaker and who is going to listen.

2 As speaker, you select any point from the list of 'stuck' beliefs (or one of your own) that applies to you, and talk about it for about 3–5 minutes. The role of the listener is to listen with full attention, ie not interrupting or advising.

3 The listener says the antidote, maybe as many as two or three times, and you talk about any responses you have.

4 When you are ready, you say the antidote for yourself. The more times you say it, the more you may begin to feel it is your own.

5 Change places. You become listener while your partner speaks. Take strict turns.

If this activity seems a little alien to you, you may find it helpful to refer back to the sections on listening skills and co-counselling (Chapters 4 and 6).

7 Focusing on enabling beliefs

As we have seen, acknowledging the beliefs that habitually determine your attitudes and behaviour patterns is the first step towards changing those that are disabling you. You may find it helpful as a next step to list the set of beliefs that you would like to adopt, that would enable you to change and feel more effective as a teacher or teacher trainer.

Sue Mace, a teacher trainer responsible for setting up a teacher development programme in Bali, Indonesia, found this a useful strategy for establishing the principles that would guide her practice. In the following extract she describes these principles and the vision that accompanied them. Because the paper from which the extract has been taken was written jointly with another author, Sue is referred to in the third person.

She strongly believes she can do the job she has been entrusted with. Apart from the belief in herself she has some other very strong beliefs. These beliefs are the result of her past experience both in teaching and in life. She 'knows' these things at a very deep level and these beliefs will influence her behaviour when facilitating Staff Development.

1 Communicative language teaching is effective and enjoyable for both learners and teachers.

2 People develop best in an atmosphere full of positive suggestions and free from negative suggestions. In short people respond to love.

3 Each person is unique and can find their own unique way to develop.

4 People grow best when they take responsibility for their own development by planning it, being active in it and evaluating it, without being forced or threatened.

5 People learn more deeply and longlastingly from experience.

6 People in a state of perpetual professional change will be motivated and fresh and therefore motivating and refreshing. The positive qualities created by perpetual development are highly contagious.

7 People are innately perfect and have the capacity and desire to realise that perfection in their work and lives.

8 People have an essence which is the same. This provides a deep bond which makes team work possible.

9 Visualisation is a very powerful tool for personal and professional change.

10 Resource and institutional support are very important for ELT teachers to attain their full potential.

When Sue arrived in the Language Centre she had a vision, a picture in her mind's eye of how she wanted Staff Development to be after three years. It wasn't a detailed picture, she couldn't 'see' what each teacher would be doing but it was a deep sensing of the attitudes which would exist. It was a picture which sensed a commitment by all the teachers to be in a perpetual professional change because they knew from experience that this was a deeply satisfying and exciting state to be in. She didn't know exactly which strategies she would use to make this vision reality; she only knew she had to be sensitive to each current, changing situation. The vision was like a beacon towards which to move and the sensitivity to each current situation would ensure that the most appropriate strategy at each moment would be chosen to move closer and closer to that beacon.

Byomantara and Mace 1996

Activity

1 Read through Sue Mace's list of beliefs.

2 Read the last paragraph again. Sue started with a strong vision. If you wish to find, or look again, at your beliefs, try starting with a visualization. For the technique of visualizing, see Chapter 3, section 7. Then create a very full and vivid picture of a teaching situation that reflects what you really want. It may help to clarify some beliefs you have and help you with the next step, when you list your beliefs.

3 Make your own list of enabling beliefs. Adopt or adapt those you like from the list in the text and add your own.

4 Take each belief in turn and write down how this belief is, or could be, reflected in your own teaching.

5 Look at the list from time to time, and change it if you need to, especially when you feel in need of refreshment in your teaching.

---

8 Initiating change: using a problem-solving approach

Once you know where you are, and what you believe, you can set about initiating the change you desire. The use of a problem-solving cycle can clarify the issues and the steps by offering a strategy or systematic approach. Here is one possible cycle, suggested by John Mulligan, who has worked in the field of human relations. We have made small changes to some of his headings to clarify the stages in the cycle.

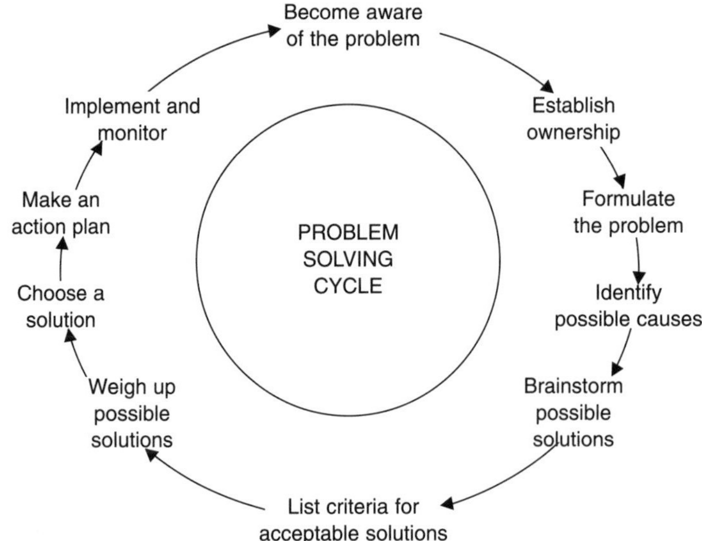

Become aware of the problem

You first need to list all the relevant details of the problem that you are aware of. This will include how you identify it as a problem, including the symptoms and effects.

Establish ownership

Once you have raised awareness of the nature and details of the problem, you need to find out whose problem it is. If it is not your problem it is not your business to solve it. However, if it is not yours, you may have a separate problem arising from the fact that it is not being sorted out by someone else. Solve your own problems not those of others. If it is a shared problem you need to work at it together.

Formulate the problem

The best way of formulating a problem is in the form of a question aimed at your anticipated goal. For example, 'How can I get this job done?' rather than 'I can't get him to do what he agreed'. It is important to formulate the problem to ensure that a successful conclusion is within your control rather than in someone else's hands.

Identify possible causes

Brainstorm if necessary, then limit your list to the most probable or potent causes. The causes may often indicate the best avenues to a solution, and the chosen solution will need to be checked to see if it addresses the causes.

Brainstorm possible solutions

Brainstorm a list of possible solutions. Do not evaluate or judge at this stage. No regard for feasibility should limit your suggestions.

List criteria for acceptable solutions

By setting out the hallmarks of a good solution at this stage you will know when you have succeeded in finding one. It will also help you to be clear about the basis on which you are making your final choice. These criteria will usually relate to the symptoms, effects and causes outlined above.

Weigh up possible solutions

This stage entails examining the pathway, the outcome and the implications or the consequences of the various solutions. You will look at the feasibility and the timing of each solution, and generally deliberate on their advantages and disadvantages. It is important not to dismiss options that may seem unrealistic. They may have elements of value which may be incorporated in the final choice.

Choose a solution

Choosing a solution means relinquishing other possibilities. More than one solution may be needed in sequence or simultaneously. When choosing your solution it is best to consider it from various angles, for example thinking, feeling, sensation and intuition. Does the solution fit in with your analysis of the problem? Does it fit with your gut reaction/ your values? Does it fit with the facts in your awareness? Is it practical? How does it compare with your hunch about what the right solution is?

Make an action plan

Your action plan will need to define the goal, that is the solution, and break it down into the stages or subtasks necessary to effect it. The plan will need to set target dates and indicate precisely how you intend to achieve your goal. It will also need to specify the materials and human resources required. Finally, it will need to indicate standards against which you will identify your level of success.

Implement and monitor

You now put your solution into action and monitor it according to the success criteria you have defined. You may need to adapt or compromise your solution in the light of information gained from monitoring. Sometimes the action planning is only useful if the situation is stable and predictable. If the situation is uncertain or unstable, then going into action may give rise to more information, which in turn results in a modification of the action. This process may be continued in an 'action, review, plan, action, review, plan' sequence until the solution is attained.

Mulligan (ed.) 1988 pp78–9

Activity

- Identify a problem you want to solve.
- Work through the steps outlined above, applying them to the problem.
- Evaluate the process of working through the steps.
- The last step involves applying a chosen plan to your life. Do this, and keep some kind of record of how you get on.

Using this kind of cycle can at first seem rather contrived. It is tempting to miss out stages or spend too little time establishing the nature of the problem before attempting to solve it. With practice you will find that the cycle will become familiar and that flexibility is not only possible but also necessary in its application. Sometimes you won't need to use all the steps, but it is important to make sure you are using the right heading for where you are in the process. The benefit of spending sufficient time on each stage is often in the change of perspective or the deepening of understanding that emerges. The problem may turn out not to be what you thought it was, or the solution could change as you go along. Sometimes consulting others to seek advice or support, or to share how far you have got, can help.

'Helpers' with change

John Mulligan sees people as having a number of internal 'helpers' and suggests that activating these helpers will help you put your ideas into action. Some of the useful internal colleagues that accompany you as you work with change include:

- The dreamer, who creates the vision or goal.
- The information processor, who collects together the data.
- The analyst, who breaks down the tasks into manageable steps and sequences.
- The planner, who decides who will do which tasks.
- The doer, who puts it into action.
- The reviewer, who helps boost performance by monitoring and giving constructive feedback.

ibid p113

Activity

- What role does each of these helpers play when you
  - plan and conduct your lessons?
  - solve a problem you face in the school?
- What other helpers do you have?

9 Modelling new behaviour

One way of bringing about a change in behaviour is to model that behaviour in someone who does it well. Modelling involves finding someone who does something really well – something that you would like to do as well as they do – and asking them questions until you find out what it is they do that makes them so successful.

We invite you to try these two activities described by Janet Olearski, who led a workshop on Neuro-Linguistic Programming at an IATEFL Conference. They are designed to help you model some behaviour you would like to adopt.

Activity

FIRST TASK :

Write two lists. *(Take a total of five minutes to complete this task.)*

List five skills that, in your role as a teacher, you can do very well. It could be, perhaps, something to do with classroom management, teaching listening, correcting written work, giving talks at conferences ... anything is valid.

1 ....

2 ....

3 ....

4 ....

5 ....

Write another list of five skills that you would like to be able to do better.

1 ....

2 ....

3 ....

4 ....

5 ....

SECOND TASK

(Take a minimum of fifteen minutes to complete this second task.)

Compare lists with your colleagues:

What would they like to do better that you can already do very well?

What would you like to be able to do better that they can already do well?

Focus on one 'skill' and find out how your colleague performs that skill. Take turns to ask questions to find out:

- the exact procedure your colleague follows to perform that skill (what they do first, second, third, etc.)
- what your colleague does to get good results

- how they know they're getting good results
- what they do to correct or improve their performance
- what they do that you don't do (what's the difference that makes the difference?)

Olearski 1993 pp5–7

To see the differences more clearly, a study of NLP can help measure the difference in very precise ways. It enables you to observe closely how the skilled person uses their brain to carry out the activity, as the brain activity can be observed in terms of eye movements, body language and choice of language, for example. (See Chapter 6 for a more detailed description of NLP.)

10 Adopting a new perspective

In his book *Breaking Rules* Fanselow encourages the reader to look at a set of practices which are the exact opposite of those most often followed in teacher education. In doing so he invites you

> not to judge, or if you do, to withhold your judgement, to substitute specific description for general prescriptions, and as a result to be free to generate alternatives unrelated to your preconceived notions of good and bad teaching, to serve as your own expert rather than to depend on those in authority, and to explore congruence between what you think you do, what you want to do, and what you actually do.
>
> *Fanselow 1987 p2*

As a way of illustrating how a change in perspective can help, Fanselow tells this story:

> I vividly remember one of the first times I realized how looking from a different perspective can make much we take for granted seem unimportant. I was 11 years old and was looking for a black washer that I had dropped on a black floor. As I was standing and looking down at the floor with intense concentration, seeing only black space and no washer, my uncle came in. He told me to lie down on the floor. I did, and in an instant, because of the different perspective, I saw the washer.
>
> *ibid p2*

Activity

- Can you recall any incident in your life that highlighted for you the importance of looking at something from a completely new perspective or point of view?
- Think of a time in the classroom when you have felt less than resourceful. It may be when a student is challenging you, for example. In order to get more perspectives on the situation it is useful to look at the situation from three

different perspectives; those of the two participants (positions A and B on the diagram), and that of the observer (position C).

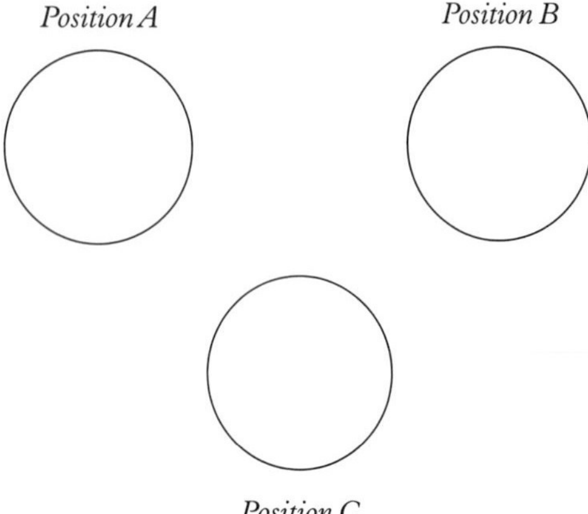

1 Imagine that the teacher is in position A. Sit or stand where he or she would stand and react as he or she would in the situation that you have just thought of. For example, imagine yourself talking to a student who is not doing the task set. Try to get completely into the feelings, body language and words you would use. When you feel you have experienced that situation, come out of it.
2 Imagine position B is where the student is in this situation. Go and sit or stand in that position. Feel what it is like to be in position B. Look at the teacher in position A. What does the teacher look like to you now, as you experience things in this position? What would it be helpful for A to do? What insights are you getting from this perspective? When you have experienced this fully, come out of this position.
3 Imagine point C as the position from which you can observe the interaction of A and B; the third point in a triangle. From this position observe the dynamics of the situation. What do you see is going on? Notice the body language, the position in relation to each other, facial expressions, gestures, tone of voice, words chosen and so on. Is there anything you would change to make the situation better? Be specific and pay attention to as many details as you can. What new insights are you getting? Then come out of it.
4 Now go back to position A. Replay the scene. Do you feel and act differently?

I learned this on an NLP course given by 'ChangeWorks'.

Having the ability to change perspective is often enough to effect change, if you can remember to keep applying it, particularly when you feel stuck or afraid to dare to strike out and break new ground. If, however, you can't change perspective easily, the physical movement into another position can help. Some people find it useful to change things around them, for example their living room, bedroom or classroom, or even just the things on one shelf, as a way of shaking themselves out of habitual action. Noticing how you habitually do everyday actions in a particular order, and then changing that, is also a useful way of ensuring that you are functioning in an alert way. All of these things help create the climate for observation, awareness and change.

11 Changing how you experience a situation

The next reading will take you through a process that can give you a strategy for changing the way you experience and face difficult situations.

> Think of a past experience that was very pleasant – perhaps one that you haven't thought about in a long time. Pause for a moment to go back to that memory, and be sure that you see what you saw at the time that pleasant event occurred. You can close your eyes if it makes it easier to do ...
>
> As you look at that pleasant memory, I want you to change the brightness of the image, and notice how your feelings change in response. First make it brighter and brighter ... Now make it dimmer and dimmer, until you can barely see it ... Now make it brighter again.
>
> How does that change the way you feel? There are always exceptions but for most of you, when you make the picture become brighter, your feelings will become stronger. Increasing brightness usually increases the intensity of feelings ...
>
> Brightness is only one of the many things you can vary.
>
> *Bandler1985 p21*

Activity

1 Take a pleasant memory. Experiment with the picture in the way Bandler suggested. If you find it difficult to see pictures, don't worry. If you want to develop this ability, just do it often and you'll get better at it. Also you can try using the other senses as suggested below.

2 Now go on to vary something in the picture: the colour, distance, depth, duration, clarity, contrast, scope, movement, speed, hue, transparency, tilt, foreground and background, or shape of the picture. It's fun to experiment and see what differences there are in your experiences as a result.

3 Now change the way your other senses experience the situation too; that is your hearing, smell, touch, taste and feelings. Each of these senses can in turn be varied in the same ways that the pictures were. For example, you could change the pitch, volume, tempo, rhythm of what you hear and so on.

4 When you are confident with pleasant memories use this method to work on an experience you would like to change. For example, you may want to give a workshop at school or a conference but be afraid of standing up and doing it. If turning up the experience makes it more intense, then turning it down can make it feel insignificant. So, imagine you visualize the audience as very small, or you turn down the volume of any criticism you fear or actually receive. In the same way, if you play very loud, rousing music, such as circus music, and turn it up, you could drown any negative internal voices and begin to feel confident. Don't stay in the bad feelings for long if it doesn't work. Just remember a good feeling and turn it up strong!

---

12 Understanding the change process

Change can be stressful, particularly if the change is imposed rather than chosen or initiated by you. Understanding the stages that you pass through on the way to successful change can help you to manage it better.

The stages of change and their relationship with performance are shown in the figure below.

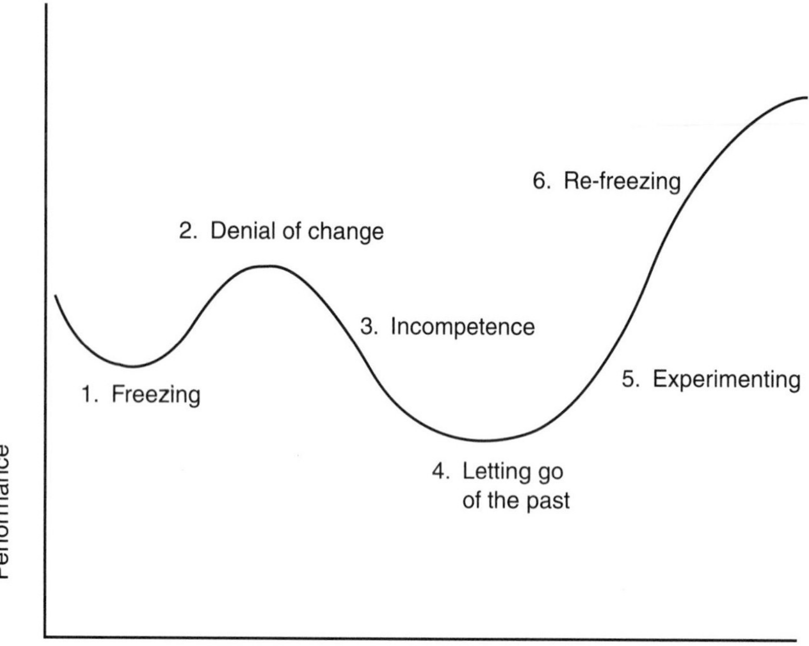

Stages of managing change

Stage 1: Freezing

At the time of change there is an initial period of shock, particularly if the change is for the worst. Work performance is low at this stage.

Stage 2: Denial of change

People often deny to themselves that any change has taken place. This is partly to protect themselves from fear of the unknown and to help them cope with the situation. For a short time performance improves but then it falls off and the person reaches Stage 3.

Stage 3: Incompetence

This is sometimes referred to as the 'Peter Principle'. The person is under-performing; unless he lets go of old ways of behaving and adapts to the change, performance is unlikely to improve.

Stage 4: Letting go of the past

At this stage the individual starts to come to terms with the change. This is sometimes referred to as 'unfreezing' and the person becomes more positive. He is more receptive to new ideas and new ways of behaving.

Stage 5: Experimenting

At this stage the person tries out the new behaviour. Performance starts to improve as the outdated ways of behaving are dropped.

Stage 6: Refreezing

This is the consolidation stage when the new ways of thinking and behaving become accepted by the individual.

Cranwell-Ward 1987 pp148–50

Activity

Jane Cranwell-Ward suggests the following activity which we invite you to try.

Next time you are facing imposed change in an area of your personal or working life, try working through the following checklist of points to manage the change process more effectively.

1 How can I be positive about the change?
2 How can I be more proactive, deciding what I want from the change and making it happen?
3 Do I know how to behave in the new situation?
4 What skills must I learn to cope with the new situation?
5 Who can give me emotional support and feedback, and advise and challenge me to assess myself and the situation?
6 What have I learned from previous situations that may help?
7 Do I know how to look after myself by positive talk, establishing some stability in my life and relaxing when possible?
8 Do I know how to establish priorities and set objectives?
9 Can I see positive opportunities?
10 Have I learned from the situation?

---

13 The emotions of change

The stages of change are always accompanied by emotions that influence our reaction at each stage. Doing what you have always done feels safe and secure. When we undertake any kind of change, the emotional journey can feel like a roller-coaster ride through stages of optimism and pessimism. Moving away from the familiar is always going to involve some sense of de-skilling and longing to be told what to do, before the change process is effected. Donna Brandes and Paul Ginnis recognize how this applies to teachers trying out new ideas:

Teachers trying a new style or method often go through a phase where they feel de-skilled. They have an initial experience with the new style, but are not yet fully competent in it; yet they are already dissatisfied with their old ways ... so for a while they feel they have nothing.

In the graph following we've adapted an idea from Pfeiffer and Jones:

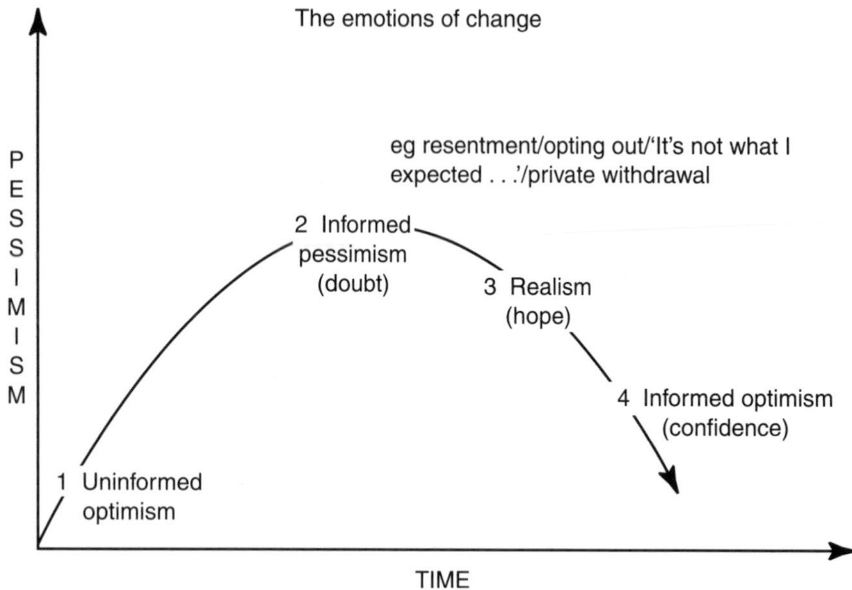

The emotions of change

People need to experience discomfort, frustration, longing to be rescued, wanting the theory explained, dying to be told what to do, experiencing impatience, anger, even some fear, before they take on responsibility for themselves.

Brandes and Ginnis 1990 p166

Activity

We suggest two activities here, one focusing on yourself as a developing teacher, and one which you can use to observe the changing emotions of your students over the period of a course.

For yourself

1 Choose a new idea from this book that you would like to incorporate into a development programme for yourself.

2 Monitor your progress over the next few weeks. You may find it helpful to keep a diary or other record of your feelings and reactions to the change.

3 Notice the extent to which your experience mirrors the 'emotions of change' graph above. What insights does this give you?

With your class

1 At an appropriate point in your course programme, introduce the 'emotions of change' graph to your students.

2 Discuss it with them. Ask them to identify where they think they are on the graph now.

3 Allow them to express the emotions that they feel around this point, and any they have felt along the way. Encourage them to talk about what they were actually doing at different stages of the course, and how their emotions coloured their experience of events.

I (Pauline) have found that the diagram has often helped me and my students make sense of what was happening in the group. Recognizing that the emotions they are experiencing are common and normal, and that there is a stage beyond pessimism to look forward to, brings immense relief and helps people to deal with negative feelings in themselves and each other.

14 How to really make a difference

As well as responding to change we can also be responsible for change all around us. As teachers we are in a unique position to influence a large number of people. In his book *Zen and the Art of Motorcycle Maintenance*, Robert Pirsig points out the paradox that we can have far-reaching effects by acting with quality and integrity within our own apparently small sphere of influence.

> I think that if we are going to reform the world and make it a better place to live in, the way to do it is not with talk about relationships of a political nature, which are inevitably dualistic, full of subjects and objects and their relationship to one another; or with programs full of things for other people to do. I think that kind of approach starts at the end and presumes the end is the beginning. Programs of a political nature are important *end products* of social quality that can be effective only if the underlying structure of social values is right. The social values are right only if the individual values are right. The place to improve the world is first in one's own heart and head and hands, and then work outward from there. Other people can talk about how to expand the destiny of mankind. I just want to talk about how to fix a motorcycle. I think that what I have to say has more lasting value.
>
> *Pirsig 1974 pp300–1*

Activity

- Does this extract by Robert Pirsig enable you to make a link between the simple act of teaching well, and your 'contribution' to education generally, or to the future?
- Think about the simple quality of what you do here and now, both at a moment in a lesson, and through the contribution you make by trying to develop your capacities and potential.

---

15 Working with change in a broader context

While we can initiate, cope with, and embrace change within ourselves, we also work within an institution, under a government and within a culture and society with its own values, history of change and present innovation. Teachers working within that culture, coping with a great deal of change, perhaps in the wake of a series of failed innovations, and faced with implementing yet more change under increasing pressure and expectations often without the necessary resources, may feel a sense of powerlessness. When I (Pauline) have worked with teachers looking at change, among the most frequently asked questions are: 'Is change by nature good?' What if change is imposed?' 'Do we just have to accept change even when we feel it is not useful or it goes against our values and what we perceive as our students' needs?' Michael Fullan and Andy Hargreaves, writers and researchers within the field of educational change, believe that change still demands an individual response and personal commitment to engagement with the change process.

One of the great mistakes over the last thirty years has been the naive assumption that involving *some* teachers on curriculum committees or in program development would facilitate implementation, because it would increase acceptance by other teachers ...

Change is a highly personal experience – each and every one of the teachers who will be affected by change must have the opportunity to work through this experience in a way in which the rewards at least equal the cost. The fact that those who advocate and develop changes get more rewards than costs, and those who are expected to implement them experience many more costs than rewards, goes a long way in explaining why the more things change, the more they remain the same. If the change works, the individual teacher gets little of the credit: if it doesn't, the teacher gets most of the blame.

Fullan 1991 p127

It is so easy to underestimate the complexities of the change process. There is in fact a lot of common sense in successful change processes. Looked at one day, in one setting, successful change seems so sensible and straightforward. But on another day, in another situation, or even the same situation on another day, improvement cannot be obtained with the most sophisticated efforts. Change is difficult because it is riddled with dilemmas, ambivalences and paradoxes. It combines steps that seemingly do not go together: to have a clear vision and be open-minded; to take initiative and empower others; to provide support and pressure; to start small and think big; to expect results and be patient and persistent; to have a plan and be flexible; to use top-down and bottom-up strategies; to experience uncertainty and satisfaction. Educational change is above all a personal experience in a social, but often impersonal, setting.

Coping with change effectively requires that we explicitly think and worry about the change process. We should constantly draw on knowledge about the factors and insights associated with successful change processes. But we must employ this knowledge in a non-mechanical manner along with intuition,

> experience, and assessment of the particular situation, each time adding to our store of common knowledge. Respecting the change process means seeking common patterns while being prepared for uniqueness. This amounts to being self-conscious about the change process as it affects us, and promoting collective self-consciousness about how the change process affects others.
>
> There are no short-cuts, and there is no substitute for directly engaging in improvement projects with others. Like most complex endeavours, in order to get better at change we have to practice it on purpose. What makes this guideline all the more important is that we can be assured that countless others around us will not be respecting the change process in their hurry to impose or avoid change.
>
> *ibid p350*

Their answer to the question 'Is change necessary?' is a resounding 'Yes' in the North American and UK primary schools they have studied, and since it is not only necessary, but also inevitable – 'change is inevitable, growth is optional' – they advocate that all change within schools begin with the teachers. They propose recognizing and developing 'total teachers' in 'total schools', that is looking at the teacher's purpose, person, the context in which they work, and the working relationships they have with their colleagues. They feel that concentrating on the personal growth of teachers while ignoring the society in which they teach is misguided. Paying attention to and taking charge of the change process with others could be a way of combatting the sense of powerlessness many feel in the face of the ever increasing changes being imposed in the form of educational reform and new conditions of service. Deciding what is worth fighting for and ensuring that we get the changes we want is within our own hands.

> Teachers are the key to unlocking the future ... they have been neglected and misunderstood in attempts at school reform.
>
> It is essential that those outside the school come to recognise the power of developing total teachers and total schools. But individual teachers should not wait for that to happen, because institutions do not change themselves. Local Education Authorities, governors, governments, universities, teacher unions, and other agencies will need to be pressured and persuaded to change.
>
> Many recent trends and developments are now providing the right kinds of conditions and pressures for these to occur, but it will require concerted actions to bring them to fruition. Among these trends are the changing multicultural populations of our schools; distressing signs of persistent and increasing disaffection with school as pupils proceed higher up the system; insensitive and inflexible reform strategies ... and associated in-service training; and renewal of large proportions of the teaching force as older staff move through and out of the system; and the emergence of alternative forms of leadership. Teachers themselves can add a lot to this pressure and persuasion. Favourable conditions already exist. Alone and together, teachers can ignite the spark that will set it alight. Conditions always have to be right for change, but conditions have scarcely been more 'combustible' than now.

> Teachers need to make the vital effort to exploit this opportunity. This is their individual and collective responsibility ...
>
> Across the world today, we see people profoundly dissatisfied with the institutions which dominate their lives, and teachers should be dissatisfied with their schools and their systems. It may take only a few timely sparks to create the momentum for radical change. What is needed is for teachers and their heads to show the courage and commitment to ignite those vital sparks and to make the individual changes that will set in motion and contribute to institutional change. There are enough examples of developments along these lines already in evidence to predict that individuals and small groups can soon intersect with like-minded others to create ever increasing pockets of power. Administrators should be looking for and supporting these kinds of positive pressure points in helping to bring about reforms in institutions ...
>
> Teachers and heads can start in their own schools. Educators at all stages of their careers have a responsibility to act – beginning teachers to add new ideas and energies to the profession, and to avoid succumbing to the stale breath of routine; mid-career teachers to get out of the doldrums; and experienced teachers to pass on wisdom instead of cynicism. All have a responsibility to shape the schools of the future so that they are more productive and satisfying places to have a career and be a student.
>
> *Fullan and Hargreaves 1992 pp136–8*

16 Conclusion

There are many different ways in which change happens and many different understandings of what change is. While change affects all of us, our responses to it are very varied and subjective. In this chapter we have explored some approaches to working with change which enable the individual to examine his or her beliefs and responses, and so to approach change with greater awareness and ability to take control of the process. Our knowledge about the way we can go about the process of change is growing. We now know that we have enormous capacities as human beings and there is great potential for change and growth. As we change we also change others, and we will be blocked or supported by the people and institutions around us. Educational change is a slow, social and never-ending process, not an event. Going through our own change may give us more understanding of change and how others experience it. This insight can help us more readily facilitate change in others. In the next chapter we look at appraising how far we have come and where we would like to go.

Chapter 8 Finding out where you are

1 Introduction

Most schools and colleges have some form of annual review or appraisal procedure for their teachers, in which an individual's performance over the past year is evaluated and objectives are set for the next twelve months. Teachers who are already working in a reflective, developmental way are well prepared for this kind of review and likely to value the opportunity for an evaluative appraisal, in which they can clarify their own personal and professional development agenda in terms of the institutional context in which they work.

In this chapter we look at a number of ways of creating opportunities to assess how well you are doing and what kind of changes you would like to make so that you can go on developing both personally and professionally. In deciding what you want for yourself it is worth spending time on setting clear objectives and ways of proceeding which can be reviewed from time to time, perhaps in consultation with others. This is an important part of the responsibility that you can take for your development.

2 Self and peer assessment

Self and peer assessment are indispensable to any developmental approach. They can be used as part of a formal appraisal, as a way of evaluating performance for grade or award giving, as a way of starting a feedback session following observation or team teaching, or as part of an ongoing teacher development programme in which they play an important role in raising awareness.

Some aims of self and peer assessment might be:

- To affirm the validity of the individual's subjective experience, no matter whether things have gone well or not, as the only starting point they have.
- To help the individual to make sense of his or her own experience, to stand back from it and to see it from the outside.
- To enhance the individual's capacity to become more self-aware and more self-directing.
- To create conditions which allow the supervisor or colleague to add their assessment by building it onto the individual's self-assessment.

Adrian Underhill proposes the following sequence of steps for conducting self and peer assessment:

1 Establish criteria – these are sometimes assumed or left implicit.
2 Give self-assessment against the (implicit) criteria, citing evidence* in support. This self-assessment should give equal weight to strengths and to points to work on.
3 Clarification by helper of any unclear points in the self-assessment.
4 Challenging (supportively) any possible oversights or inconsistencies.
5 Peer/supervisor gives his or her assessment which builds on the self-assessment.
6 Both parties stand back and review the process they have just been through, and how they (particularly the self-assessor) feel about it.

*Some sources for gathering this evidence:
1 Own observations, feelings, experiences
2 Own journals, letters
3 Video and audio recordings, photos
4 Observation by others and their feedback
5 Talking with colleagues and others
6 Feedback from learners, spoken and written
7 Self-assessment questionnaires
8 Performance in TD activities in groups. Feedback from group members.

Underhill 1995a

3 A framework for effective self-monitoring

Self-monitoring is a way of being systematic about observing how you teach, and what you would like to do differently. Jack Richards has wide experience of working on teacher development programmes with language teachers around the world. He reports that teachers who are accustomed to self-monitoring are able to improve their own understanding and management of teaching far more effectively than those who submit themselves only to external assessment. These are his guidelines for effective self-monitoring:

1 Decide what aspect of your teaching you are interested in learning more about or you wish to improve. What are your strong and weak points? Are there areas of your teaching that you would like to know more about? Find out where you are in your professional development by reflecting on problems you may be having with specific aspects of your teaching, by reviewing supervisors' comments and student evaluations, by inviting a colleague to view your teaching in order to offer suggestions, or by reviewing current issues in the literature and considering how they relate to your own teaching. You may discover that you are a poor classroom manager, that you make poor use of the blackboard, or that you spend too much class time on nonessentials. There are virtually no areas of teaching that cannot be improved through self-monitoring.

2 Narrow your choices to those that seem most important to you. In order to make effective use of self-monitoring techniques it is necessary to focus on one area at a time.

3 Develop a plan of action to address the specific problem area you have identified. Which of your teaching behaviours will you attempt to change? What effects will these changes in your behaviour have on student behaviours? ...

4 Draw up a time frame to carry out your goals. You may decide to give yourself a week or two to try out new approaches and then monitor yourself to discover the effectiveness of the strategies you have chosen. Decide on the self-monitoring procedures you will use. Check ... to see if you have been successful in modifying the behaviours you wanted to change.

Richards 1990 pp129–30

Activity

- From all your experiences of learning find one example where your learning was guided mainly by someone else's monitoring, and another where it was guided by your own self-monitoring.
- In what ways were the two kinds of monitoring similar and different?
- How did this affect your relationship to your learning?
- What stops you from monitoring yourself in the way Richards proposes?

---

4 Using video and audio recording

For self-assessment purposes, the most reliable way to record what actually happens during a lesson is to make a video or audio recording. Audio recording is much simpler to set up, in that it is simply a matter of placing a tape recorder in a position where it can capture the spoken interaction that occurs in class – a non-directional microphone on the teacher's desk seems to work well, especially if you are particularly interested in the nature of teacher–student exchanges. Even so, it is a good idea to make several recordings over one or two weeks, so that you can choose the best one for closer attention. Video has the advantage of recording non-verbal as well as verbal behaviour, and of revealing aspects of classroom activity which normally remain hidden to the teacher. Because both teacher and students often initially resist being video-recorded, it can be a good idea to explain to the students what the recording will be used for and who will see it. Perhaps you could even get them to help you make it, for example by asking a student to operate the camera.

In order to make use of the information provided by a video or audio recording, you need both to know what you are looking for and to keep an open mind about what the recording might show. Formulating the questions that interest or puzzle you before you watch or listen allows you to focus your reflection and discover the unexpected. You might, for example, want to enquire into one of the following areas, which are likely to contain elements that would puzzle any teacher:

- classroom management
- teacher–student interaction
- grouping
- structuring
- tasks
- teaching resources
- classroom interaction
- opportunities for speaking
- quality of input
- communicativeness
- questions
- feedback

Activity

- See if you can extend the above list by adding a few other areas that interest you about your own teaching.
- Now choose one item from the list and write down a few detailed questions that puzzle you.
- Make an audio or video recording of one of your classes, and review it using the questions you have prepared.
- What surprised you, and what did you learn about your teaching?
- And what did you learn about your questions?

Recorded lessons can't capture the full atmosphere of the class but they can provide a lot of objective data, and analysing even short segments of interaction can produce a lot of food for thought. It is sometimes interesting to check out your intuitive feelings about how a lesson went, against what the raw data reveals, and to see whether your assessment of the lesson changes as a result.

5 Criteria for self-assessment

As an alternative to making up your own set of points that you would like to monitor, it is possible and sometimes instructive to make use of checklists used by external award-giving authorities such as examining boards. These lists, designed for evaluative purposes, indicate how 'good' teaching is assessed for purposes of accreditation. They can provide a framework and some possible aims to guide your own development. The example which follows is adapted from a checklist used by the RSA (Royal Society of Arts) to examine teachers for the Diploma in TEFL. It is fairly typical of those used by trainees and supervisors in initial training, but could equally well be used for self-evaluation, to help you identify strengths and weaknesses both in pre-lesson planning and in the way that the lesson proceeded.

Classroom Observation Checklist
(adapted from an RSA Cambridge checklist)

Rate the following statements according to how accurately they reflect what went on [in the lesson].

Key: 1 Does not reflect at all what went on
2 Only marginally reflects what went on
3 Neutral
4 Describes rather well what went on
5 Is a totally accurate reflection of what went on

1	There were no cultural misunderstandings.	1 2 3 4 5
2	The class understood what was wanted at all times.	1 2 3 4 5
3	All instructions were clear.	1 2 3 4 5
4	Every student was involved at some point.	1 2 3 4 5
5	All students were interested in the lesson.	1 2 3 4 5
6	The teacher carried out comprehension checks.	1 2 3 4 5
7	Materials and learning activities were appropriate.	1 2 3 4 5
8	Student groupings and sub-groupings were appropriate.	1 2 3 4 5
9	Class atmosphere was positive.	1 2 3 4 5
10	The pacing of the lesson was appropriate.	1 2 3 4 5
11	There was enough variety in the lesson.	1 2 3 4 5
12	The teacher did not talk too much.	1 2 3 4 5
13	Error correction and feedback was appropriate.	1 2 3 4 5
14	There was genuine communication.	1 2 3 4 5
15	There was teacher skill in organising group work.	1 2 3 4 5
16	There was opportunity for controlled practice.	1 2 3 4 5
17	Students were enthusiastic.	1 2 3 4 5
18	General classroom management was good.	1 2 3 4 5

Nunan 1988 pp147–8

Checklists such as the one above can be used after the lesson by the teacher, recalling what happened either from memory or, perhaps better, with the help of a recording of the lesson. Alternatively, an observer could be invited in to take notes during the lesson itself, and to exchange feedback with the teacher (see Peer observation, later in this chapter). A checklist of this kind is likely to be most useful as a diagnostic tool, as it helps to identify a number of areas in which change and improvement are possible. Once this has been done, it is probably less helpful to repeat the exercise than to prioritize development targets and focus on just one or two areas for ongoing self-monitoring.

6 Mapping constraints to development

Sometimes we convince ourselves that there is nothing we can change. This can become an excuse for inactivity, and for making others responsible for our own lack of development. It is important to differentiate clearly between those factors that we really can't change, and those that in fact we can change, and have just convinced ourselves that we can't.

Activity

You can do this activity alone or in a group. If you are working alone, leave out the last two steps.

1 Visualize the constraints on your development. What are the things that prevent you from doing your job as well as you would like? List them at random as they occur to you.

2 Now classify the items on that list as originating either from inside you, or from outside you.

3 Divide those two groups into four by adding the dimension: 'Which of those things can I change or do something about?' and 'Which of those things can I not change or do anything about?'

The four groups you have now are:

Things outside me that I can influence	Things inside me that I can influence
Things outside me that I can't influence at all	Things inside me that I can't influence at all

4 Now describe your four groups to a partner who listens and helps to clarify, without any attempt to interpret or solve the problems.

5 Pool the findings in the big group.

We learned this activity from Adrian Underhill (1995b).

This approach allows you to start with your own perception of what constrains you, rather than other people's views of what the problem is (or isn't). If you are working alone, the recognition of what things you can and can't influence will help you perceive your situation more clearly and decide on a way forward. The value of a supportive listener is that they can help to deepen this perception, and guide you towards a more complete awareness of what is really going on.

7 Planning action

Action planning is the process of turning intentions for development into concrete and specific action steps after a period of learning. Here are Adrian Underhill's notes.

Intentional action planning

1 Only I can make my action plan, but I can be greatly assisted by the facilitation of another person.
2 An action plan should be treated with respect as a kind of personal contract.
3 The steps on it must be clear, practical and attainable. If not, then I am writing my own contract for failure.
4 The steps must take account of the problems that may arise and how to respond to them.
5 An action plan must be purged of wishful thinking.

Setting

It requires the planner to work on their own, following the sort of sequence given below. The plan may be drawn up at one sitting, usually after a period of learning, reviewing and reflection. Once it is drawn up in a provisional form another person can help with:

- supportive listening while the planner talks through her plan
- catalytic questions for clarification and understanding
- creative challenging, that is taking the role of devil's advocate to help reveal unrealistic steps that the planner may have overlooked or be unaware of.

The planner may then make revisions.

Example sequence: action planning after a period of learning

1 First ask 'What are the major learning points for me?' Make a short list.
2 Then choose just one of these learning points to work with, perhaps the clearest or most immediate.
3 Then list all the individual steps needed to put that point into action in your work. Check that each step is concrete, clear and attainable.
4 Then look at any problems you may encounter and how best to respond to them. Put this into your action plan.
5 The plan should also include any help you will need, where you will get it from, and how.
6 The next question is, 'How will I know if I am making progress?' which is the same as 'What are my criteria for success?' Put this in your plan.
7 Then put in the time span, and decide the time and day when you will start.
8 Decide how often you will review the plan, perhaps with the help of another person.

Underhill 1995c

8 Finding out what your students think

All teachers are legitimately concerned about how they appear to their students. Student feedback is therefore an important source of information about our effectiveness. But it is not easy to find out what students really think, partly because they are not used to being asked, and partly because we cannot be sure that what they tell us is actually true. And the students' reluctance to express their opinions directly to the teacher may be matched by an equal reluctance on the part of the teacher, because of her own defensiveness, to listen with full attention to what the students are saying.

Leslie Bobb Wolff has taught English in Spanish secondary schools for many years. She thinks it is important to ask students for feedback on your lessons.

> As teachers, our objective is to help our students to learn as much as possible and to help them learn how to learn. If we don't ask them and they don't tell us what, in their opinion, is working well and what is not, how can we possibly know how well we are succeeding?... In addition, if we define the foreign language classroom as a place where a group of people work together towards a common goal, learners should be able to acquire the ability to comprehend and express themselves with the least amount of stress in the target language. As teachers, we must constantly look for ways to reduce this stress. Asking students their opinion about the class and showing them that we take their answers seriously is one way to do so.
>
> *Bobb Wolff 1990 p19*

Her strategy for obtaining student feedback is to ask learners to comment on lessons in writing and anonymously, although they can include their name if they wish. She suggests that if the class is large, just two or three students can be asked for feedback on a particular lesson, and the task can be assigned at the end of the lesson. Depending on the level in a language class, students can use the first or second language when the class is monolingual.

> The daily class comment written by the students can consist of the following parts:
>
> 1 The date of the class commented on (not the date the comment is handed in) and the name of the class. This helps the teacher to remember the specific dates.
>
> 2 A brief summary of the activities done in that class (three to five sentences). This again helps the teacher to remember the specific class, lets the teacher know how a specific learner perceived what each activity was and requires the student to reflect on what happened in class.
>
> 3 A subjective opinion on the activities – not simply an 'I liked the class or didn't' but why. This gives the teacher a student's opinion of the activities, of how the class went. It also requires the student to think about the usefulness and enjoyment of that day's class.
>
> 4 After everyone has written one or two class comments the following two steps can be added or suggested as optional additions.

5 Suggestions for improvements of that day's class. This gives the teacher new ideas for that particular set of activities and requires the student to think about what didn't go well and how it could be improved.

6 General comments on the classes. The student writes an overall view of how he/she sees the class are at that point in time. This gives the teacher a student's vision of the class and requires the student to think about how the class is working out in a more general way.

ibid p19

Activity

- Adapt the framework above to suit yourself. Make it something that you could use.
- Then try it out with two or three of your classes.
- When you have gathered some written feedback, sort it into themes and identify comments you find particularly significant.
- Can you share some, even all, of this feedback with your class?
- Could you make a poster from them to display in the staff room, perhaps with another teacher who has tried the same thing? Leave space to encourage other teachers to add to it.
- Keep the comments that make you feel good, for when you are tired or stressed!

---

9 Involving students in forward planning

One way to encourage authentic student feedback is to involve them in the ongoing planning of their course programme. Sue Leather and Mario Rinvolucri introduced **student planning committees** (SPCs) into the organization of their language courses. The procedure they outline below was appropriate to the kind of intensive courses (3–5 hours per day) that they were teaching, in the UK, with small classes of mainly young adults.

1 The teacher or teachers offer the students the programme they think makes the best sense from Monday to Thursday of the first week of the course.

2 On Thursday the students are asked to come ready on Friday to discuss the week's work and to decide, as a group, what sort of work they wish to do the following week. It is made clear that the recommendations made by the group will be put into practice by the teachers ...

3 On the Friday morning the teacher sets aside 20–40 minutes for the SPC meeting. He/she leaves the students on their own and asks them to recall him/her once they have reached firm, majority decisions. You could suggest that they decide on a chairperson. The teacher then takes notes on the group's decisions. His/her role is to get a clear picture of what they want, rather than to oppose, self-defend or re-impose the teacher's authority. Sometimes it is hard for the students to offer a clear picture of what they

want ... [but] the main thing is that the teacher and the group end up with a clear understanding of what has been decided.

4 The SPC meets each Friday of the course, and is of course free to reverse the decisions of the previous week.

Leather and Rinvolucri 1989 p17

Activity

The above procedure was used on an intensive course with small classes of young adults who were motivated enough to make the trip to the UK.

If that is similar to your teaching situation, then:

- Have you tried anything like this?
- How did it go?
- What changes would you make to the procedure described above in order to make it suitable for your classes?

If this does not correspond to your teaching reality, then:

- Of all the decisions you make about planning your classes, can you identify the decisions that you could hand over to your students to make? Start with those that would be a low risk to hand over.
- Take a simple decision that you make at the moment (perhaps the order in which you do some exercises, or what would be the best class or homework activity to do next, etc) and work out how to invite the students to participate in the decision.

Adopting a person-centred approach to teaching means that there is trust between teacher and students. The students know that their questions and opinions will be heard and taken seriously, and through them the teacher obtains feedback on the effectiveness of her presence, both as a person and as a teacher. Sue Leather commented on her own experience of using student planning committees in the following way.

Although I do not fool myself that my students always feel they can say exactly what they would like to, I do feel that they have gained confidence in the validity of their own judgements. They have certainly become progressively bolder in their requests! I have gained the confidence of knowing that I am no less a teacher for hearing the criticisms of my students or of knowing that I will not react badly to their suggestions.

Sue Leather in Davis and Rinvolucri 1990 p57

10 Learning from other teachers

Teachers learn from each other in many ways. *Peer observation*, *team teaching* and doing *collaborative classroom research* are some of the ways in which this can happen.

Yet most teachers, most of the time, are on their own with their class. Michael Fullan and Andy Hargreaves have studied the way that teachers work in a number of schools and colleges. They believe that professional isolation limits access to new ideas and better solutions and is detrimental both to the individual teachers and to the institutions in which they work. They contrast this with a school environment in which 'interactive professionalism' is the norm, in which collaboration flourishes, teachers work together by habit, learn from each other and share their expertise as a community. Their research has shown conclusively that both individuals and institutions develop under these conditions.

Isolation means two things. Whatever great things individual teachers do or could do go unnoticed, and whatever bad things they do go uncorrected. Many of the solutions to teaching problems are 'out there' somewhere, but they are inaccessible. We can't see them ... Older experienced teachers are grossly under-utilized ... New teachers with their combination of idealism, energy and fear are also under-utilized, as the conservative tendencies of survival take their toll, and already begin to shape their careers towards the lower limits of what could be possible. Any solutions will have to tap into and propel what teachers at all stages of their careers have to offer. This unseen pool of expertise is one of the great untapped reservoirs of talent – it can fuel our improvement efforts, and it is right under our noses ...

Many teachers are very effective. Their problem is lack of access to other teachers. Access would mean that they could become even better while sharing their expertise. Many other teachers are competent but could improve considerably if they were in a more collaborative environment ... Interactive professionalism exposes problems of incompetence more naturally and gracefully [than punitive appraisal schemes]. It makes individuals reassess their situation as a continuing commitment.'

Fullan and Hargreaves 1992 pp17–19

Activity

Thinking about the institution in which you work at present:

- What opportunities are there for teachers to share their expertise and ideas?
- Can you think of a colleague who is particularly good at something, and whose skill or ability you admire?
- What aspects of your job are you particularly good at? Are there, or could there be, opportunities for you to pool this expertise to help your colleagues? (Look at the Activity on 'modelling new behaviour' in Chapter 7 for a way of doing this.)
- If professional isolation is a feature of your workplace, how do you experience this and what are its positive and negative effects?

---

11 Peer observation

One way in which teachers can learn from each other is by doing peer observation. Peer observation is intended to be supportive rather than evaluative. The teacher who is being observed decides what aspect(s) of her teaching will be the focus of the observation. The purpose is developmental in that the observer helps the teacher to focus attention on aspects of her classroom behaviour which have become habitual and perhaps no longer serve her well.

In the following extract Peter Maingay distinguishes between 'ritual teaching behaviour' and 'principled teaching behaviour' and explains how observation can have a developmental function in helping teachers to reassess the reasons why they do what they do in the classroom.

> Much of what a teacher does in a language-teaching classroom is ritual behaviour rather than principled behaviour; and I believe that the most important role of an observer in most, if not all, observations is that of making teachers think about what they do: of drawing their attention to the principles behind the rituals, of leading them away from ritual behaviour towards principled behaviour ...
>
> An EFL teacher – or any teacher for that matter – possesses a stock of techniques or procedures which he/she does not have to think about. Starting a class, correcting spoken error, arranging pair or group work, pre-teaching lexis, writing new lexis on the board with accompanying stress marks – the list could be endless – rapidly become rituals that can be performed without conscious thought ... Such classroom rituals enable teachers to gain some respite from the strain of teaching 25 classes a week, and free them to pay close attention to other matters in a lesson.
>
> However, there are two dangers in this use of ritual behaviour in class: in one situation a new teacher, just off a pre-service training course, may have picked up such rituals very efficiently, having watched his/her trainer or other experienced teachers perform them. This is obviously an important part of initial training ... but it is essential that at a fairly early point in that teacher's career, the principles behind the rituals are made clear to him or her in some way, so that rituals can generate fresh behaviour ... And in another situation, a more experienced teacher, who had a principled knowledge of his teaching, who has at some point chosen certain techniques for principled reasons, has lost sight of those reasons and his teaching has consequently set into unquestioned ritual.
>
> *Maingay 1988 pp119–20*

Maingay goes on to argue that the most important role for the observer is that of developer, and to distinguish this from the roles of trainer and assessor.

Activity

- What forms of 'ritual behaviour' characterize your teaching?
- How could an observer help you to look at some of these behaviours and perhaps think about changing them?

- Can you think of someone who would be able to give you supportive and helpful feedback without being judgemental?
- What would be the benefits to you of questioning your practice in this way?

Doing peer observation

Here is a simple model for conducting peer observation. The teacher:

- decides what aspect of his teaching he would like to get feedback on from a supportive colleague.
- arranges for a colleague to observe his lesson.
- prepares a lesson plan.
- meets with the observer before the lesson to discuss the lesson plan and tell the observer what he wants the focus of the observation to be, and how he would like the data to be collected (eg using a checklist, or diagram of the classroom, or in the form of a letter to the teacher. There are lots of task suggestions in Wajnryb 1992). It is important to be as specific as possible about what the observer will actually do, how long she will stay, where she will sit, etc.
- teaches the lesson.
- makes his own self-assessment of the lesson, for later discussion with the observer. (It seems that feedback is often more productive when it is delayed, and when the teacher has had time for his own private reflection.)
- meets with the observer to exchange feedback. This is best done by the teacher speaking first while the observer listens, and then changing over.
- decides what he will do next as a consequence of any new ideas that emerge for improving his teaching.

The observer:

- agrees to observe a lesson.
- meets with the teacher and clarifies with him the aims and focus of the observation, and what exactly the teacher wants her to do while the lesson is in progress.
- observes the lesson.
- makes her own assessment, for later discussion with the teacher.
- meets with the teacher to exchange feedback.

Some examples

In the introduction to her book *Classroom Observation Tasks*, Ruth Wajnryb describes some typical scenarios in which a teacher or group of teachers might set up a peer observation schedule.

Scenario 1

You are keen to explore your teaching and generally wish to find out more about how you teach. You invite a colleague into your classroom and ask them to collect data about a particular aspect of your teaching, for example, the way you use questions, the spread of your attention through the class, your use of the board, or the patterns of interaction through your lesson. Your observer will, at an agreed time, observe you in the classroom from the agreed perspective. Following this, the two of you will confer and the data collected will serve you to discover more about what happens when you teach.

Scenario 2

A group of teachers wishes to initiate and engage in a programme of action research investigating a particular form of classroom activity, for example, patterns of interaction in multilingual classes; the spread of teacher attention in co-educational classes; the effect of question-type on student response. You each choose to observe a number of lessons by different teachers using an agreed means of collecting and recording data. Apart from the actual observation of lessons, such a programme requires preliminary meetings to establish commonalities of purpose, allocate tasks, set guidelines and time frames; and follow-up meetings to de-brief, pool data, analyse and interpret findings.

Scenario 3

Two teachers decide to observe each other to look at a particular aspect of their teaching. This again would lead to a post-lesson conference where the teachers would exchange opinions and ideas on the areas of concern.

Wajnryb 1992 p18

Activity

What would be the implications of inviting a colleague to observe one of your classes? The following sentence completion exercise will help to focus your ideas:

- I would feel OK about having an observer in my class if

  ....

- The aspects of my teaching I would like to know more about are

  ....

- I would like a sympathetic observer to give me feedback on the way I

  ....

- I would prepare for the observation by

  ....

- The most useful way the observer could give me feedback would be

  ....

---

12 Giving feedback to other teachers

A non-directive approach

What are the most helpful strategies for the observer to use in giving feedback to a colleague? Donald Freeman believes that a non-directive approach derived from Rogerian principles (see Chapter 3) is most effective.

> As the post-observation discussion between the observer and the teacher begins, the observer must ask: What kind of relationship, what insights, can I provide which this person may use in his/her own development as a teacher? The observer's goal is to build a relationship with the teacher which is supportive in the fullest sense. The objective is not to judge or to evaluate, but to understand ... and to clarify. The observer starts from the assumption that the teacher's own experiences and goals must provide the primary source of learning ... [and] the teacher always retains the choice of acting on or ignoring the observer's input. The teacher is in control throughout the process of observation and discussion ...
>
> The Non-Directive Approach is a process of reflection and self-evaluation. Taking the teacher's 'world' as a starting point, and based on what s/he has seen, the observer helps the teacher to compare what happened in the class to his/her goals. The observer facilitates this process through the use of counselling responses, followed by comments, questions, and suggestions which reflect the teacher's world and are not evaluative or judgemental. The approach seeks a delicate level of understanding and trust between both people. It asks the teacher to be open about what s/he wanted to happen in the class, his/her hopes and intentions, and to measure what actually took place against that standard with the help and perspective of the observer. At the same time, it asks the observer to suspend his/her own world for a limited time, to accept the primacy of the teacher's world and so to contribute to the process of self-development.
>
> *Freeman 1982 pp24–6*

The essence of this lies in the observer's willingness to understand and help the teacher clarify her experience of the lesson, so that she can be open with herself, rather than to judge or evaluate the lesson or the teacher. Our experience is that this is powerful and effective so long as the observers demonstrate a non-judgemental attitude as well as non-judgemental behaviour. Behaviour that appears supportive, along with an attitude that primarily wants to get on and tell the teacher what she should do to be a better teacher, can be confusing and self-defeating.

Activity

Try to observe yourself on the next two or three occasions when you are helping a colleague who is facing some small difficulties.

- How much of your intention is concerned with understanding and clarifying the issue for the benefit of the colleague?
- How much of your intention is concerned with solving the issue, getting rid of the problem, by giving advice?

It does not matter what you find. This activity is about *observing* your helping strategies. If you observe them well (again without judging yourself), you will later be able to change things.

Using language facilitatively

Language can be a powerful instrument when giving feedback. Evaluative, judgemental statements about the way a lesson has been taught have the effect of closing down the teacher's options by implying that there is a right and a wrong way of teaching. Tessa Woodward, who is interested in how language can be used to give helpful and unhelpful feedback messages, gives these examples of the kind of unhelpful feedback which closes down options:

Observer says to teacher:	Teacher says to himself/herself:
You should have …	I should have …
You shouldn't have …	I shouldn't have …
Why didn't you …?	I could have …
You could have …	Where I went wrong was …
I wouldn't have …	I don't know why I …
I would've …	It was terrible …
Where you went wrong was …	
Everything was okay until you …	
It wasn't terrible but you …	

By simply changing the way we use language, feedback can be made supportive and facilitative. Tessa Woodward illustrates the kinds of openings which offer options and possibilities:

Observer says to teacher:	Teacher says to himself/herself:
I noticed that you …	I chose to …
Another option available in that situation is …	The advantage was …
The advantage there might be …	The disadvantage was …
The disadvantage there another time could be …	Another time I could …
Another time you could choose to …	And if I did the good thing would be …
What do you feel was the advantage of taking that option?	But a disadvantage would be … so I'll have to weigh it up.

Woodward 1989 p21 (adapted)

In the latter, the discussion focuses less on what the observed teacher should have done and more on what he or she could have done, discussing a range of different tactics and times when they might work well or badly. Options are not closed down and discarded. They are discussed, weighed up, and kept in mind for future use in different situations.

Activity

This is like the previous activity, but this time the aim is to observe the language that you use when helping or offering feedback.

- Observe the language you use on the next few occasions when you are helping or giving feedback. You could audio record the session and listen to your language afterwards, or you could get another observer to observe you giving feedback!
- Analyse your language, either in terms of Tessa Woodward's 'opening up' and 'closing down' distinction, or in terms of 'more helpful' and 'less helpful', or some other distinction of your own.
- But don't stop at that. Analyse the *intention behind* your choice of what to say, because this can reveal something else that is useful to know.
- The more you can do this, the more you will get to know your typical language patterns, and you can ask yourself: Are any of my language habits not serving me well? Are there alternatives that I would like to adopt more?

In his book *Learning in Groups* David Jaques offers the following advice on handling feedback:

Feedback must always be handled with sensitivity and judgement. It is more effective if:

1 It is descriptive rather than evaluative. Describing one's own reaction leaves the other individual free to use it as he sees fit. Avoiding evaluative language reduces the need for the other individual to react defensively.

2 It is specific rather than general. To be told that one is 'confusing' will probably not be as useful as to be told 'when you ask us a question you seem to rephrase it so many times that we get confused'.

3 It takes into account the needs of both the receiver and the giver of feedback. Feedback can be destructive when it serves only *our* needs and fails to consider the needs of the person on the receiving end.

4 It is directed toward behaviour that the receiver can control. Frustration is increased when a person is reminded of some shortcoming over which he or she has no control.

5 It is solicited, rather than imposed. Feedback is most useful when the receiver has asked for it *and* accepts it without argument.

6 It is well timed. In general, feedback is most useful at the earliest opportunity after the given behaviour (depending, of course, on the person's readiness to hear it, on support available from others, etc).

7 It is checked to ensure clear communication. One way of doing this is to

have the receiver try to rephrase the feedback he has received to see if it corresponds with what the sender had in mind.

8 When feedback is given in a group, both giver and receiver take the opportunity to check with others in the group on the accuracy of the feedback. Is this one person's impression or an impression shared with others?

(Adapted from Kolb, Rubin and McIntyre, 1979.)

Feedback is probably the best way of getting evidence on the effectiveness of our communication. It enables us to learn about how others see us and about how we affect them. It is thus a vital ingredient in the process of evaluation.

Jaques 1984 pp54–5

13 Team teaching

Having an outsider observing your lesson, even a colleague you trust and feel comfortable with, can make you feel anxious, because whether or not they are actually evaluating your lesson, you probably feel that they are. Simply having an observer there makes you judge yourself more! Team teaching offers an alternative way of organizing a peer activity which allows teachers to work together on a more equitable basis. In team teaching, the two teachers both participate actively in planning, teaching and evaluating a lesson.

Here is an account by Marzenna Gwozdzinska, a teacher of English in Poland, of how she came to participate in team teaching for the first time, what it involved, and how she developed through it.

What one teacher does in a class seems a bit of a mystery to other teachers. If you have regular meetings with those teaching at the same level there is a valuable exchange of information, but this still does not reveal what actually happens in class.

Since a considerable number of foreign language teachers seem to suffer sporadic lapses of confidence, few of us like imposing our presence in another teacher's class. Being a passive observer in a class can make you feel awkward and out of place. So, although it is possible to find justifications for observing, the best reason for being in another teacher's class seems to be taking an active part in it ...

The team teaching project consisted of preparing a seven day residential course for intermediate adult learners, where most of the classes were to be run by teams of two or three teachers. All the teachers had approximately the same amount of experience, although only two of them had done any team teaching before ... I have to admit that the preparation of the course was both painful and time-consuming. All of us found we had to have plenty of stamina, patience, flexibility and, above all, resourcefulness and willingness to contribute ... At the stage when all of us were generating ideas, I realized that mine were as good as anybody else's. It allowed me to have my say in the initial planning. I also discovered that contradicting someone does not cause offence, but on the contrary, actually helps the development of ideas. I also think my co-operative skills have improved. While we were negotiating the classes I had to listen to other teachers, but I was also listened to. I had an opportunity to volunteer and share tasks with other teachers. During the course itself I felt as responsible for the course as a whole, as for my individual contribution to it. As a result, I had the feeling that all of us were giving far more support to the course leader than on other courses.

In class, at first, I found the presence of another teacher inhibiting. In some cases I felt our plan was not detailed enough, especially as it was the first experience of this sort of teaching for some of us. During class I found I had to be very sensitive to what the other teacher was saying and doing and to adapt quickly to the unexpected. I would have liked to have a tighter plan with less room left for improvisation, which is not one of my strong points.

Nevertheless I regard this experience as having been a good testing ground for my teaching. I believe that the classes I run single-handedly have improved in some respects. First of all, my rapport with my students has changed for the better. I feel much more relaxed in class. I have also become more aware of the need to build up my students' confidence. As a result, they are more willing to co-operate with one another and so contribute far more.

I have also realised now that whenever the other teacher felt uncomfortable I noticed it, so whenever I felt uncomfortable the other teacher must have noticed it too. Therefore, if I am uncomfortable in class my students must sense it and may start feeling the same way. I have started to look at them in a slightly different way ...

Another great plus is that I have got to know my colleagues better, both as people and as teachers, and similarly they have got to know me. As a result of this I have started to pay more attention to getting to know my students better.

All in all, it was an extremely beneficial experience. It was one of those rare occasions when I was not entirely on my own, which is my usual way of doing things. I think I can also say that I would now happily welcome any of the teachers I was on the team with into my class, provided we could have a good chat about it first.

Gwozdzinska 1990 pp5–6

My (Pauline's) first experience of team teaching was when I was teaching on a teacher refresher course. It helped me gain a lot in confidence. Rather than worrying about what might happen, I found it a relief to share the planning and follow-up review of sessions, and as well as learning new ideas from my team partner I found that my own opinions and ideas were valued by another person. At first I felt vulnerable and sometimes possessive of ideas that I considered 'mine'. However, seeing other people use and adapt them opened my eyes to new possibilities. The exchange of ideas and feedback became easier as the course progressed and as I learned to confront, rather than hide from, issues of power and control in the team which challenged my instinctive need to be in charge. Now each time I participate in team teaching I enjoy it even more, as I'm not only meeting new ideas but also developing the skills that make collaboration really effective. As a result of this team teaching experience, I now feel that I have a truly open door to my classroom.

14 The teacher as researcher

In *A Teacher's Guide to Classroom Research*, David Hopkins defines classroom research as:

> .... an act undertaken by teachers either to improve their own or a colleague's teaching or to test the assumptions of educational theory in practice. Classroom research generates hypotheses about teaching from the experience of teaching, and encourages teachers to use this research to make their teaching more competent ...
>
> *Hopkins 1985 p1*

Hopkins goes on to acknowledge the contribution of Lawrence Stenhouse, who popularized the concept of the 'teacher as researcher' in British secondary school education through his advocacy of student-centred approaches and enquiry/discovery teaching methods.

> Teachers are too often the servants of heads, advisers, researchers, text books, curriculum developers, examination boards, or the Department of Education and Science, among others. By adopting a research stance, teachers are liberating themselves from the control position they so often find themselves in ... Stenhouse ... encouraged teachers to follow the specification of a curriculum but at the same time to assess it critically: to assume that the curriculum proposal was intelligent but not necessarily correct and to monitor its effectiveness in the classroom. By adopting this critical approach, by taking a research stance, the teacher is engaged not only in a meaningful professional development activity but also engaged in a process of refining, and becoming more autonomous in, professional judgement.
>
> *ibid p3*

Hopkins proposes the following five principles to guide any research activity undertaken as a form of teacher development.

> 1 The teacher's primary job is to teach, and any research method should not interfere with or disrupt the teaching commitment ...
>
> 2 The method of data collection must not be too demanding on the teacher's time ...
>
> 3 The methodology employed must be reliable enough to allow teachers to formulate hypotheses confidently and develop strategies applicable to their classroom situation ... [and] to be rigorous about their methodology. It is no excuse to claim that rigour is unnecessary because the research is practitioner oriented, small scale, or used solely to improve individual practice ...
>
> 4 The research problem undertaken by the teacher should be one to which he

or she is committed ... [and] the problem must in fact be a problem; that is, the problem must be capable of a solution, else by definition it is not a problem. If a teacher chooses a topic that is too complex or amorphous then frustration and disillusionment will soon set in.

5 Teacher-researchers [need] to pay close attention to the ethical procedures surrounding their work ...*

ibid pp41–3

*[eg observe protocol, negotiate with those affected, obtain explicit authorization before you observe or examine documentation of any kind, accept responsibility for maintaining confidentiality; the full list of ethical principles is contained in Hopkins pp 135–6].

Here are some stories of classroom research by secondary school teachers, reported by Henry and Kemmis, who have long experience of working on research projects involving teachers in the School of Education at Deakin University, Australia.

A woman teacher interested in gender issues in her classroom asked a trusted colleague to keep a record of who she talked to. In a half-hour session, she discovered that she talked twice as often to boys as to girls, though the class was roughly half boys and half girls. She changed this pattern, but only gradually: she had to help the students themselves change their expectations and their sensitivity to gender questions in the classroom.

A year 12 physics teacher interested in student understanding in the classroom found that his classroom questioning gave students little opportunity to talk about their ideas and understandings. He changed his style of interaction with dramatic effect, so that he reduced the time he was 'on air' in classroom talk from about 85% to about 40% in a single lesson, then discovered he had to change the questions he asked so that students had more opportunity to develop their understandings by using them in more complex discussions with him and with fellow students.

A teacher had problems with an unruly year 9 group. She recorded the incidence of control statements in her usual teaching and discovered that she was creating discipline problems through keeping on at students about discipline. She negotiated classroom rules with the students and the 'problem' simply disappeared. She went on to explore the possibilities of negotiating the curriculum more generally with the students, and made further discoveries about the value of teaching strategies which actively used students' knowledge as the basis for further learning.

Henry and Kemmis 1985 p2

Activity

- What 'true stories' do you have where you discovered something about your own teaching that enabled you to make a simple and beneficial change?
- How did you make the discovery that enabled the change?

- And how did you come to make the discovery then and not earlier? Take a bit of time with this question; it's useful to know this.

Research procedures in 'exploratory teaching'

The idea that teachers themselves have a very important contribution to make to research into the classroom has gained increasing acceptance among academics in recent years. Dick Allwright, whose interest in bridging the gap between teaching and research extends over many years, believes that 'teachers, researchers and learners have a lot in common and therefore can learn a great deal from each other'. He proposes an 'exploratory teaching' model as a way forward for teachers.

The teacher is the researcher's link with learners, and also the learners' link with research. The teacher is contracted to help learners learn, but can do so better by knowing about previous research and by using the procedures of classroom research to understand better what is happening in his or her own classroom. In this way the exploratory teacher will not only improve achievement but will also contribute to our general research knowledge about how language classrooms work. This is what we mean by 'exploratory teaching' – teaching that not only tries out new ideas but that also tries to learn as much as possible from doing so. In fact, you do not even have to try out 'new' ideas to be an exploratory teacher. Any good experienced teacher will no doubt spend a lot of class time on ideas that are tried and trusted. Turning that 'good' teaching into 'exploratory teaching' is a matter of trying to find out what makes the tried and trusted ideas successful. Because in the long run it is not enough to know that ideas do work; we need also to know why and how they work ...

Allwright and Bailey 1991 p197

Reporting on his work with language teachers in Brazil engaged in 'exploratory teaching', Allwright proposes the following list of general research procedures. He also comments on what his experience has revealed about the steps which teachers find most difficulty in implementing.

Step 1 Identify a puzzle area

This is the starting point, with the term 'puzzle' deliberately chosen in preference to the more usual 'problem' to avoid the potential threat to self-esteem that admitting to having 'problems' might represent, and to capture the important possibility that productive investigations might well start from poorly-understood successes just as much as from poorly-understood failures.

Step 2 Refine your thinking about that puzzle area

This is increasingly establishing itself as a key stage ... It revolves around developing the ability to mentally 'explore' an issue, and not to accept a first interpretation of it ...

Step 3 Select a particular topic to focus upon

This is also a key step, and one that ... might be a terminal one for some teachers, who might feel paralyzed by the complexities revealed at the puzzle refinement stage ... It is clear that choices of focus may sometimes have to be dictated by immediate practicalities, rather than by the centrality of the chosen subtopic to the overall issue at the origin of the work.

Step 4 Find appropriate classroom procedures to explore it

In my experience, teachers have not found it difficult to list a good number of classroom procedures, pedagogic activities they already know and trust, that they can imagine exploiting for investigative as well as for narrowly pedagogic purposes ... [For example]

1 Group work discussions
2 Pair work discussions
3 Surveys
4 Interviews
5 Simulations
6 Role-plays
7 Role exchanging
8 Diaries
9 Dialogue journal writing
10 Projects
11 Poster sessions
12 Learner to learner correspondence

Step 5 Adapt them to the particular puzzle you want to explore

This seems to be a relatively unproblematic stage, consisting simply of putting learning 'on the classroom agenda' by, for example, substituting discussion of the chosen puzzle for more traditional (but not necessarily more engaging) topics such as 'pollution', or 'holidays' ...

Step 6 Use them in class

Again this seems to be a relatively unproblematic stage, although I am not convinced that we have done nearly enough work on helping teachers develop the monitoring skills they will probably need if they are to use activities both for their pedagogic potential and simultaneously for what are essentially data collection purposes.

Step 7 Interpret the outcomes

This stage is seen as at least as problematic as that of refining puzzles in the first place. My only comfort is that effort expended in these two areas ... can be of real practical value to the teachers (and hopefully also to the learners) involved, since it is central to learning from any experience ...

Step 8 Decide on their implications and plan accordingly

There seem to be four ... possibilities for work following an initial exploratory investigation. The most obvious is that the original plan will have been refined in the process of investigation, and that it will now seem necessary to move on to some slightly different conception of it – a new puzzle emerging from the old one. The second possibility ... is that enough will have been learned to justify moving in some other direction with an entirely new puzzle. A third possibility is that enough will have been learned to justify trying out pedagogic changes in the classroom (if these have been indicated) ... The fourth possibility, compatible with any or all of the others, is that enough will have been learned, in some sense at least, for the teacher or teachers involved to

> want to share their work with others ... The teachers at the Cultura Inglesa in Rio de Janeiro have approached this set of possibilities by converting their annual conference into a collective poster session, and by using their in-house newsletter (Views and News) to keep each other in touch with what they are all doing ...
>
> *Allwright 1993 pp132–4*

Activity

Here is a way of starting your own research project:

1 Agree with a colleague or colleagues to carry out a simple piece of classroom research.

2 Choose a puzzle about your own teaching that you would like to explore.

3 Refer to the list of steps suggested above and decide how you and your colleague will carry out each step.

A classroom research project in Uruguay

Teachers of English at the Alianza Cultural Uruguay Estados-Unidos in Montevideo set up a programme of collaborative classroom research as an integral part of their response to changes that were being introduced in their institution. Four teachers were appointed to the role of *counselors*, responsible for implementing and supporting the research programme. The following report by the counselors describes how the programme was set up and how it gradually gained credibility among the staff.

> Four teachers were appointed last March to the role of counselors. We would at the same time continue to teach our own classes. With the very clear concept that change is a process, not an event, we presented an action plan of continuing education for teachers through research. The first step in the plan was to get people interested in doing collaborative teacher research. We held a meeting for teachers in late April to explain why research is important, and noticed immediately how people started reading and discussing such topics as: the role of the teacher and students, cooperative learning, student centred activities, evaluation, learning strategies, and teachers' and students' self-assessment and portfolios. We encouraged research by means of diary studies, field notes, self-monitoring, recording of classes, peer observation, and team teaching. Little by little several colleagues started sharing ideas with the counselors, or exchanging different points of view, and we even received some invitations to attend classes either because the teacher wanted someone else to observe a certain aspect of their teaching situation, or just because they wanted to see how the new system worked. We need hardly say how enriching these opportunities were for both participants.
>
> One of the first-term objectives was to collect evidence from teachers involved in collaborative research. They prepared portfolios in whatever way they chose, and shared their experiences with colleagues at a meeting. Teachers

who had already worked with a counselor explained why they had done so and how they felt about it.

As counselors we have also been involved in our own research, by following these steps:

1 We presented an action plan when we were still in the planning stage.

2 We have been reading different books, not only about research but about other topics as well. We have been answering questions, sharing ideas with teachers, reading projects written by students (when teachers asked us to do so) to see whether we agreed with the teacher about the level of the work. We have also been in contact with materials writers, who have developed thematic units which were given to us to analyse and comment on.

3 We are now observing how things are going, and planning for the next stage of the action plan, which will include a questionnaire to teachers about their feelings during the first stage.

We all know that educational change is a slow process which requires time and effort, and we agree with the notion that teachers should try to be experts in learning. Our research is not done with the objective of finding an absolute solution, but in the belief that the best possible solution has to be based on personal choice.

Albertini de Garateguy et al 1993 p9

In a footnote to the same article, Maria-Elena Perera de Perez offered these personal insights into what classroom research means to her.

1 Classroom Research is Teacher Development made explicit.

2 You can be your own expert.

3 Create the psychological environment to take risks.

4 Concentrate on learning, rather than on teaching.

5 Be willing to understand, to investigate, not to judge.

6 Don't punish yourself for your errors.

7 When you find barriers, try to do the same thing again.

8 Use the information around you, don't let it defeat you.

9 Use all the knowledge you have to devise the best strategies to support managers. In an institution, as well as in the classroom, you have to be highly pragmatic to communicate better.

10 Don't say 'unless you do it this way, it's not action research'.

Maria-Elena Perera de Perez, Orientadora Pedagogica

15 Acknowledging the whole person

'We teach what we are.' (*Postman and Weingartner 1969*)

The focus of teacher education, action research, appraisal and development has tended to be very practice-oriented. Yet it is important to acknowledge that not all teachers regard work as the area of their life in which they want to invest the main effort of their personal development; and for such teachers, to start by focusing on questions which directly challenge their classroom practice may not be the best way to improve it. In encouraging teachers to address meaningful issues in their development we need to acknowledge the whole person, and not merely that part of the whole person that happens to teach. This is recognized by Michael Fullan and Andy Hargreaves when they write:

> Teachers ... are more than mere bundles of knowledge, skill and technique. There is more to developing as a teacher than learning new skills and behaviours. As teachers sometimes say to their students, they are not wheeled out of a cupboard at 8.30 am in the morning and wheeled back in at 4.00 pm. Teachers are people too. You cannot understand the teacher or teaching without understanding the person the teacher is. And you cannot change the teacher in fundamental ways, without changing the person the teacher is, either. This means that meaningful or lasting change will almost inevitably be slow. Human growth is not like rhubarb. It can be nurtured and encouraged but it cannot be forced. Teachers become the teachers they are not just out of habit. Teaching is bound up with their lives, their biographies, with the kinds of people they have become.
>
> *Fullan and Hargreaves 1992 p36*

Ivor Goodson believes in 'capturing the teacher's voice' through dialogue with teachers which allows them to talk about every aspect of their lives as people.

> In the research in schools in which I have been involved ... the consistency of teachers talking about their own lives in the process of explaining their policy and practice has been striking. Were this only a personal observation it would be worthless, but again and again in talking to other researchers they have echoed their point ... Listening to the teacher's voice should teach us that the autobiographical, 'the life', is of substantial concern when teachers talk of their work ... Life experiences and background are obviously key ingredients of the people that we are, of our sense of self. To the degree that we invest our 'self' in our teaching, experience and background therefore shape our practice.
>
> *Goodson 1992 p114*

Activity

Ivor Goodson suggests some areas of life experience that can also provide a rich source of insight into issues in your own development. A summary is given below. You may like to explore some of these areas in your own reflection and self-appraisal.

- The use of autobiographical comments to explain your policy and practice of teaching.
- The influence of the life experiences and background, key ingredients in our sense of self, on our practice and the degree to which we invest our 'self' in our teaching.

- The influence of your lifestyle, both in and out of school, and your identities with certain groups and cultures.
- Your perspective from your particular stage in your life cycle: whether you are caught up in forming or reformulating your dreams in the light of experience, whether you are attending to family matters, what you have learned about life so far, whether you have new priorities because of your age; how much energy you have or wish to expend on teaching and so on.
- Your career stage and career decisions.
- Critical incidents, persons and phases in your life and work.*
- Yourself in relation to the history and politics of your time and your society or your school and its management policies. It can illuminate the choices, contingencies and options open to you.

ibid pp115–19 (in summary)

*These can illuminate themes such as drop-out and stress and burnout (see Chapter 5) as well as the issues of effective teaching, the take-up of new initiatives and working conditions. Use a time events line like the one on p2, Chapter 1.

16 Workplace relationships

The nature of workplace relationships can significantly influence the extent to which you are able to develop yourself and to deal with change . The contribution you make to a school is measured in all kinds of intangible ways, and the fact that you spend so much time with the people you work with means that the relationships you form there have a significant effect on the level of job satisfaction you experience. Understanding how you relate to the other people who work within your school is one aspect of knowing where you are and of identifying your whole-person needs.

Activity

Professional space diagram

This activity aims to help you identify your range of personal and professional relationships in a school.

Read the instructions one by one and complete the professional space diagram.

1 List the names of the adults with whom you work.
2 Using the professional space diagram, write the initials of the people you have listed, placing them at distances away from the dot at the centre of the sheet. The distances represent the closeness of your relationship and the extent to which you know and rely on the person in your working situation.
3 Consider the overall pattern. Are there groups of initials where the people have things in common with each other as well as with you? Draw a line around these initials to cluster them: you might have to reposition some of them.

Professional space diagram

date ....

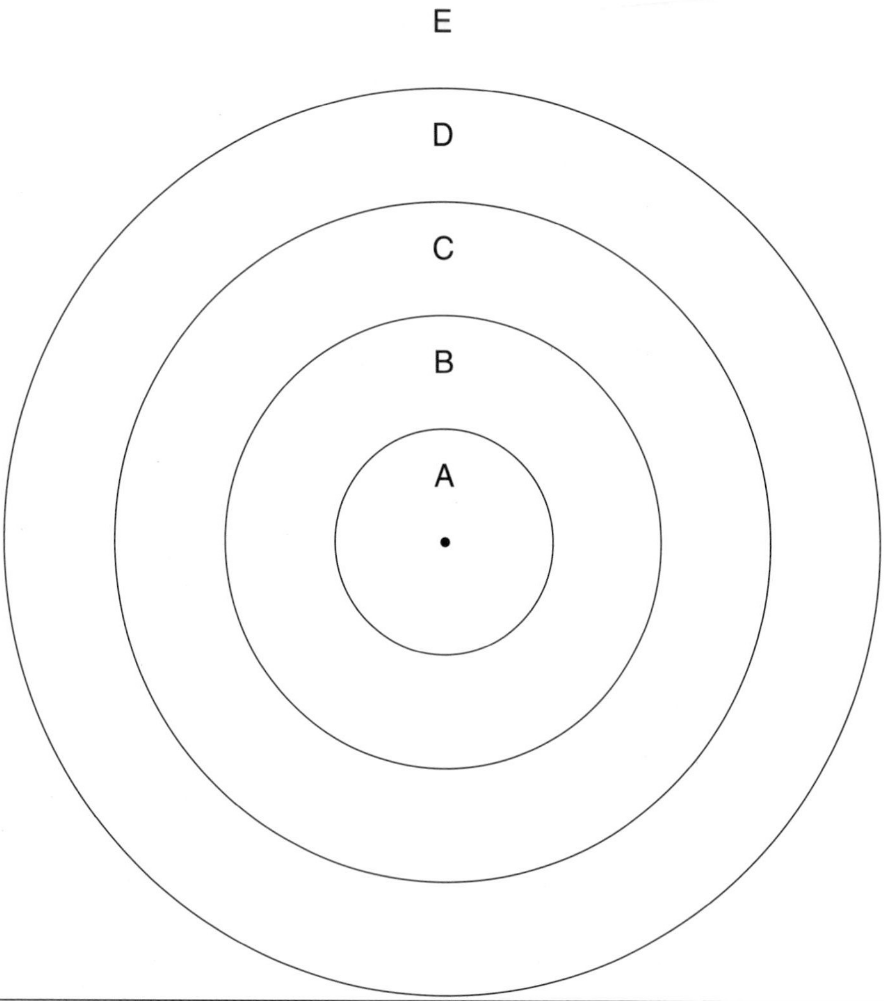

E

D

C

B

A

•

other people

Hancock and Settle 1990 p73

4 Consider the pattern of names in terms of roles. Which of these people are 'above' you in terms of the hierarchy of your organization or are directly responsible for you? Mark these with a B for Boss.

5 If you are a manager in some sense yourself, look where the people you are responsible for are placed. Are they grouped in any way? If they are, put a line around them or reposition them if you feel they should have been grouped. Mark each of these people with a BC (Boss Colleague).

6 Are any of them your friends? Rearrange them if you feel they should be in a group, and mark them with an F for Friend.

7 Consider the group in terms of support. Try to distinguish between support and friendship: our support group are key people whom we trust and on whom we rely for assistance and guidance. Such colleagues provide support outside the context of friendship. Mark them with an S for Support.

8 If you consider yourself to be a support for some of your colleagues, mark those with the letter SC.

9 Are any of them coming closer as sources of support or friendship? Mark them with an arrow pointing inwards to the centre of the paper. For others, who are moving away from you and providing less support, mark an arrow pointing away from the centre.

10 Identify those people who hold positions of formal authority within the staff. Mark them with the letters FA. Are there other people, not in positions of formal responsibility, who seem to have informal authority within the staff? Mark them with the letters IA.

11 Finally, is there anyone not on the sheet who has authority over you and is in a position to exert influence over you and your future development? Write their name(s) in the box at the bottom of the sheet.

Now you have a diagram representing the complex pattern of inter-relationships in your workplace. You also have some food for thought.

Think about the questions below and discuss them with one or two colleagues:

- What is the range of your professional relationships? Are you satisfied with it?
- What is the range and level of support you receive? Are you satisfied with it?
- Do you have a range of friendships at work? How do you feel about that?
- How closely do you relate to authority figures? Do you wish to change this?
- Do you have formal (or informal) authority? How do you use it?
- What changes, if any, would you like to see in your professional space diagram?

Activity adapted by Rosie Tanner from 'Professional Space Diagram' in Hancock and Settle 1990 pp71–5. She used this on a British Council teacher development course in Hastings in June 1993.

17 Self-appraisal and formal appraisal

As formal appraisal systems are being increasingly introduced into institutions, your level of preparedness for your own appraisal will help to ensure that you benefit as much as possible from the exchange of views. Being well prepared means not only that you show yourself in a good light, but also that you have taken time to reflect on your work in an organized way, and bring to the appraisal the information and insights gathered from this reflection. As a result you are more likely to get a good hearing and not to repeat any negative experiences you may have had before.

> Self-appraisal is an essential part of the effective teacher's normal way of working. The process of reflecting on performance: definition of objectives; analysis of outcomes; checking outcomes with objectives; re-thinking content and method of approach; and talking about teaching and learning with teachers and pupils, makes for better performance ... Self-appraisal prepares the appraisee to be in a stronger position to enter the appraisal process supported by clearer insights into the quality of personal worth and understanding of personal and professional development needs.
>
> The formal appraisal process in turn benefits from this information and in return creates the necessary structure of relating self-perception to the perception of others, thereby reinforcing shared perceptions and challenging differences in perception. Schools' formal appraisal systems also provide the rigour of required attention to needs in stated time frameworks. The process is both the sharp edge of professional judgement on performance and the source of personal and professional support for growth and development.
>
> Personal aims and objectives relate essentially to both processes. They provide a clear statement of personal expectations and aspirations as part of the formal appraisal process. They inform the appraisee in so far as they give insight to the match or mismatch with the teacher's current level of performance, and hence assist the appraiser in helping the appraisee to gain an accurate picture of their potential and future capacity for greater responsibility. Statements of aims and objectives also provide necessary guidelines for self-appraisal and act as a source of drive and motivation for the appraisee.
>
> In return self-appraisal supports the growth of self-confidence to reassess personal aims and objectives if they are too limited; or to accept them when they are truly challenging. The formal appraisal process, in the hands of a skilled and sensitive appraiser, further assists the appropriate adjustment of personal aims and objectives by helping us to see more clearly how others see us and value us.
>
> *Hancock and Settle 1990 p54*

Activity

Recall an experience you have had of being formally appraised. This could include assessment at school as a student.

- What do you remember most about the experience?
- What outcomes were there?
- What were your feelings before, during and after the appraisal?
- Were these similar, or quite different from each other?

Are you regularly appraised by someone in authority in your present job?

- Do you find these appraisals worthwhile?
- If not, what would improve them for you?

---

18 Conclusion

In this chapter we have emphasized the need for development to be monitored, and we have illustrated ways in which this can be managed. We have drawn a distinction between evaluative and developmental aims of appraisal. We have suggested that the habit of ongoing professional reflection leads to realistic self-appraisal and the setting of achievable development objectives. Feedback from students, although difficult to obtain and to evaluate, can be an important source of information about how well we are doing. Colleagues can provide a powerful support system for each other through the exchange of ideas and feedback. We have described activities involving peer observation, team teaching, and collaborative classroom research which facilitate creative professional interaction, and we have noted other research findings which confirm that institutions develop when collaborative teacher development initiatives are encouraged and supported. On a more general scale, relationships at work can also affect opportunities for development and appraisal of one's own position in the overall scheme. Finally, we have observed that any full self-appraisal needs to take account of the teachers' wider life priorities, which influence the attention they can pay to different aspects of their life at different times, and their readiness to get involved in the exciting and risky business of questioning, change, and the development of personal potential.

Conclusion This book and beyond

Metaphors can be very useful. We have referred to their usefulness several times already in this book. One of the metaphors we used in the Introduction to describe the book was that of a jigsaw. What we wanted to imply was something about the way in which the readings and ideas have been pieced together into chapters, and also about the kind of fitting and shaping process involved in writing them. But the metaphor breaks down, as they always do, because a jigsaw, once completed, contains all the pieces that make up the complete picture. Our picture of teacher development is not complete; it couldn't ever be, because teacher development can be about almost anything that meets a teacher's desire or need for fresh ideas and positive, fulfilling, personal change. And it couldn't be complete, also, because we cannot be objective about teacher development. This book is the product of our own understanding and experience, informed by the many sources and personal contacts that have enriched this understanding and experience.

At the same time, we have tried to offer as broad a focus to the area as possible in order to reach out to people in different teaching situations and help them make choices that are appropriate to their own situation and personality. The most difficult part can be getting started, since it is likely to involve giving up the safety of old habits, and thinking as well as acting in new and unfamiliar ways. Yet once you have made the decision to act and taken the first step, you are likely to find that the support systems are already there and that the process of change generates its own internal energy to build your self-confidence and enlarge your expectations.

Whatever you can do, or dream you can, begin it.
Boldness has genius, power and magic in it.

Goethe

We said in the Introduction that we hope this book will prove to be an added resource. This is because it is important to acknowledge that reading about development can never be as effective as experiencing it either for yourself or through the enthusiasm and commitment of other people. The letters we received from teachers who were invited to suggest readings for this book mentioned this again and again. Although all of them were interested in the book and keen to contribute, different people told us:

Probably the most powerful force for self-development for me has been and continues to be collaboration with colleagues ... For me this is an essential part of my development, of being a healthy, happy, interested and creative teacher.

Far more important than books in my own development ... have been encounters with people: either learners who have stopped me in my tracks, or colleagues who have enriched my thinking through collaboration, conversation, insights ... people who have helped me to see my own practices and principles clearly, and to question and clarify my values and beliefs.

What helped us to develop as teachers ... was mostly people! Listening, talking, drinking together ...

And one teacher, writing about his own difficulty in identifying the particular texts and authors that had inspired him, observed:

... of pieces I can remember being impressed by at the time – well, do they still enshrine eternal verities or were they (much more likely) temporary enthusiasms, staging posts on a journey?

Whether you have found a lot to impress you, or only a little, in the readings we have selected for this book, we hope we have helped you to map out your territory of teacher development and identify where you are, or want to be, on it.

The end of all our exploring
Will be to arrive where we started
And know the place for the first time.

T S Eliot

Appendix Useful addresses

IATEFL
3 Kingsdown Chambers
Kingsdown Park
Tankerton
Whitstable
Kent CT5 2DJ, UK

Six Category Intervention Analysis

(and other training in personal and group facilitation)
The Human Potential Research Group
Department of Educational Studies
University of Surrey
Guildford
Surrey GU2 5XH, UK
Tel: (0)1483 259237
Fax: (0)1483 300803

Neuro-Linguistic Programming

A range of NLP titles can be obtained by mail order from:
The Anglo-American Book Company Ltd.
Underwood St
Clears
Camarthen SA33 4NE
Wales, UK
Tel/Fax: (0)1994 230400

For a list of accredited NLP courses contact:
Association of Neuro-Linguistic Programming (ANLP)
P.O. Box 78
Stourbridge DY8 2YP, UK
Tel: (0)1384 443935

The activity on p166 was based on a technique learned on an NLP course given by
ChangeWorks, 5 Newbold St
Leamington Spa
Warwickshire CV32 4HN, UK

Voice work

Rowena Whitehead, a trained language teacher, is also trained to give workshops for those who wish to support and develop their voices and for those who feel they would like to be able to sing. Although based in the UK, she can also offer workshops abroad.
Rowena Whitehead
32 Harvey Goodwin Avenue,
Cambridge CB4 3EV, UK
Tel: (0)1223 573288

For contacts of voice teachers in many countries contact:
The Centre for Performance Research
Market Street
Cardiff CF5 1QE, UK
Tel: (0)1222 345174
Fax: (0)1222 340687

For voice teachers in the United States, contact:
Voice and Singing Teachers of America
Janet Rogers
2424 West Main St.
Richmond
Virginia VA 23220, USA

The Feldenkrais Method

For lists of teachers worldwide, contact:
The Feldenkrais Guild UK
PO Box 370
London N10 3XA, UK

The Alexander Technique

For a list of teachers worldwide, contact:
The Society of Teachers of the Alexander Technique
10 London House
266 Fulham Road
London SW10, UK

Bibliography

Chapter 1

Bolitho, R. 1986 Teacher development – a personal perspective. In *Teacher Development Newsletter 1* p2

Bolitho, R. 1988 The emergence of a teacher development movement in ELT in the UK. (Unpublished paper)

Fullan, M. 1993 *Change Forces*. London: The Falmer Press

Holly, M. L. 1989 Writing to Grow. Portsmouth, New Hampshire: Heinemann

Maley, A. 1990 Teacher development explained. In *Practical English Teaching* vol.10, no.4 p67

Marks, J. 1990 Teacher development ... right from the start. In *Teacher Development Newsletter 12* pp8–10

Pennington, M. C. 1990 A professional development focus for the language teaching practicum. In Richards, J. C. and Nunan, D. (eds.) *Second Language Teacher Education*. Cambridge: Cambridge University Press

Rossner, R. 1992 Where there's a will – facilitating teacher development. In *Teacher Development Newsletter 18* pp4–5

Underhill, A. 1986 Editorial. In *Teacher Development Newsletter 1* p1

Underhill, A. 1988 Training, development and teacher education. In *Teacher Development Newsletter 9* p4

Woodward, T. 1991 *Models and Metaphors in Language Teacher Training*. Cambridge: Cambridge University Press

Chapter 2

Aldred, C. Opening the 'can'; how about the worms? (Unpublished paper)

Dewey, J. 1938 *Education and Experience*. New York: Collier Macmillan

Fanselow, J. 1987 *Breaking Rules*. New York and Harlow: Longman

Freeman, D. 1992 Three views of teachers' knowledge. In *Teacher Development Newsletter 18* pp1–3. See also Research and what teachers know. In Bailey, K. and Nunan, D. (eds.) 1996 *Voices from the Language Classroom*. New York: Cambridge University Press

Gallwey, T. 1974 *The Inner Game of Tennis*. London: Pan Books

Kolb, D. A. 1984 *Experiential Learning*. Englewood Cliffs: Prentice Hall

Lundquist, T. 1990 The scarecrow, the tinman, the lion and me ... empowerment on the Yellow Brick Road. In *Teacher Development Newsletter 13* pp13–15

Moskowitz, G. 1978 *Caring and Sharing in the Foreign Language Class*. Cambridge, Massachusetts: Newbury House

Ricketts, K. 1986 I plead not guilty. In *Teacher Development Newsletter 3* p9

Schön, D. 1983 *The Reflective Practitioner*. London: Temple Smith

Underhill, A. 1986 Confidence in class. In *Teacher Development Newsletter 4* p9

Wallace, M. J. 1991 *Training Foreign Language Teachers: A Reflective Approach*. Cambridge: Cambridge University Press

Weintroub, E. 1993 The ghost instrument. In *The Teacher Trainer* vol.7, no.3 pp24–5

Woodward, T. 1989 Breaking rules. In *Practical English Teaching* vol.9, no.4 p19

Chapter 3

Brandes, D. and Ginnis, P. 1986 *A Guide to Student-Centred Learning*. Oxford: Blackwell

Brandes, D. and Ginnis, P. 1990 *The Student-Centred School*. Oxford: Blackwell

Gibran, K. 1992 *The Prophet*. Harmondsworth: Penguin Books

Hadfield, J. 1992 *Classroom Dynamics*. Oxford: Oxford University Press

Heider, J. 1985 *The Tao of Leadership*. New York: Bantam Books

Holt, J. 1984 *How Children Fail*. Revised edition. Harmondsworth: Penguin Books

Kolb, D. A. 1984 *Experiential Learning*. Englewood Cliffs: Prentice Hall

Moskowitz, G. 1978 *Caring and Sharing in the Foreign Language Class*. Cambridge, Massachusetts: Newbury House

Rogers, C. 1983 *Freedom to Learn for the 80s*. Columbus: Merrill

Rogers, C. 1990 Questions I would ask myself if I were a teacher. In *Teacher Development Newsletter 12* p6 (first published in *Education* vol.95, no.2)

Stevick, E. 1980 *Teaching Languages: A Way and Ways*. Rowley, Massachusetts: Newbury House

Underhill, A. 1989 Process in humanistic education. In *English Language Teaching Journal* vol.43, no.4 pp250–60

Underhill, A. 1991. Teacher Development. In *Teacher Development Newsletter 17* pp2–5

Underhill, A. 1994 Teacher Development: a person-centred view. (Unpublished paper)

Chapter 4

Bolton, R. 1986 *People Skills*. New York: Simon & Schuster

Brandes, D. 1982 *Gamesters' Handbook Two.* Cheltenham: Stanley Thornes

Brandes, D. and Ginnis, P. 1977 *Gamesters' Handbook.* Cheltenham: Stanley Thornes

Brandes, D. and Ginnis, P. 1986 *A Guide to Student-Centred Learning.* Oxford: Blackwell

Davis, P. and Rinvolucri, M. 1990 *The Confidence Book.* Harlow: Longman

Edge, J. 1992a *Cooperative Development.* Harlow: Longman

Edge, J. 1992b Cooperative development. In *English Language Teaching Journal* vol.46, no.1 pp62–70

Heron, J. 1990 *Helping the Client.* London: Sage Publications

Kiratli, G. 1993 Working towards self-development. In *Teacher Development Newsletter 23* pp7–9

Moskowitz, G. 1978 *Caring and Sharing in the Foreign Language Class.* Cambridge, Massachusetts: Newbury House

Luft, J. 1984 *Group Processes: An Introduction to Group Dynamics.* 3rd edition. Mountain View CA: Mayfield Publishing Company

Tangalos, B. 1990 When you get lemons, make lemonade. In *Teacher development Newsletter 14* pp10–12

Tanner, R. 1992 Believe in yourself. In *Teacher Development Newsletter 22* pp1–4

Chapter 5

Andreau, M. S. 1993 A Fueguian short story. In *Teacher Development Newsletter 24*

Brandes, D. and Ginnis, P. 1986 *A Guide to Student-Centred Learning.* Oxford: Blackwell

Cheng He 1989 One step toward Teacher Development. In *Teacher Development Newsletter 11*

Ellis, M. 1987 Are you being developed? In *Practical English Teaching* vol.8, no.2

Greenland, S. 1986 Caring and sharing at work. In *Teacher Development Newsletter 2*

Hadfield, J. 1986 *Intermediate Communication Games.* London: Nelson

Heider, J. 1985 *The Tao of Leadership.* New York: Bantam Books

Heron, J. 1989 *The Facilitator's Handbook.* London: Kogan Page

Houston, G. 1990 *The Red Book of Groups.* 3rd edition. London: Rochester Foundation

Jaques, D. 1984 *Learning in Groups.* London: Croom Helm

Levy, S. 1988 A staff development session on stress. In *Teacher Development Newsletter 8*

Parreiras, M. 1991 Teacher development – is there time for much of it? In *Teacher Development Newsletter 17*

Plumb, K. 1987 How we started. In *Teacher Development Newsletter 6*

Plumb, K. 1994 Teacher development: the experience of developing within a peer-group. In *Teacher Development Newsletter 25*

Tangalos, B. 1990 When you get lemons, make lemonade. In *Teacher Development Newsletter 14*

Underhill, A. 1992 The role of groups in developing teacher self-awareness. In *English Language Teaching Journal* vol.46, no.1

Wright, A. 1987 *Roles of Teachers and Learners.* Oxford: Oxford University Press

Chapter 6

Barduhn, S. 1989 When the Cost of Caring Is Too High. In *Teacher Development Newsletter 11*

Beels, C., Hopson, B. and Scally, M. 1992 *Assertiveness: A Positive Process.* London: Mercury

Bond, M. 1986 *Stress and Self-Awareness: A Guide for Nurses.* London: Heinemann

Brandes, D. and Ginnis, P. 1990 *The Student-Centred School.* Oxford: Blackwell

Bucklow, T. 1992. The Alexander Technique. In *Teacher Development Newsletter 18*

Cranwell-Ward, J. 1987 *Managing Stress.* Aldershot: Gower

Dickson, A. 1982 *A Woman In Your Own Right.* London: Quartet Books

Gelb, M. 1994 *Body Learning: An Introduction to the Alexander Technique.* London: Aurum Press

Gray, P. 1992 Co-Counselling: How it is useful to me in the classroom. In *Teacher Development Newsletter 18*

Holly, M. L. 1989 *Writing to Grow.* Portsmouth, New Hampshire: Heinemann

Humphrey, J. and Humphrey, F. 1990 *How to Get More Done.* London: Kogan Page

Jensen, E. P. 1988 *Superteaching.* Del Mar, California: Turning Point Publishing, Box 2551, Del Mar, CA 92014, USA

Kickx, C. *Awareness: The Feldenkrais Method* (pamphlet)

Lofts, J. *The Alexander Technique* (pamphlet)

Maley, A. 1993 Finding the Centre. In *The Teacher Trainer* vol.7, no.3

Mars, A. 1993 Singing, Health and Happiness. In *Rapport* Autumn issue

Maslach, C. 1982 *Burnout – The Cost of Caring.* Englewood Cliffs: Prentice-Hall

Mulligan, J. 1988 *The Personal Management Handbook.* London: Warner Books. © Marshall Editions Ltd

Olsen, J. W.-B. 1989 Burnout: Beyond The Limits. In *Teacher Development Newsletter 11*

Postle, D. 1988 *The Mind Gymnasium*. London: Macmillan

Struna, M. with Church, C. 1983 *Self-Massage*. London: Hutchinson

Welyczko, S. 1989 Development and Diaries. In *Teacher Development Newsletter 10*

Chapter 7

Bandler, R.1985 *Using Your Brain – for a Change*. Moab, Utah: Real People Press

Brandes, D. and Ginnis, P. 1990 *The Student-Centred School*. Oxford: Basil Blackwell

Byomantara, D. G. N. and Mace, S. 1996 The Psychology of Successful, Sustainable Staff Development. In Kenny, Candlin and Savage (eds.) *Language and Development; Teachers in a Changing World*. Harlow: Addison Wesley Longman

Cranwell-Ward, J. 1987 *Managing Stress*. Aldershot: Gower

De Mello, A. 1990 *Awareness*. London: Fount Paperbacks

Edwards, G. 1991 *Living Magically*. London: Piatkus

Fanselow, J. F. 1987 *Breaking Rules*. New York: Longman

Fullan, M. 1991 *The New Meaning of Educational Change*. London: Cassell Educational

Fullan, M. 1993 *Change Forces*. London: The Falmer Press

Fullan, M. and Hargreaves, A. 1992 *What's Worth Fighting For In Your School*. Buckingham: Open University Press

Greenland, S. 1986 Beliefs and Antidotes. In *Teacher Development Newsletter* 3

Mulligan J. 1988 *The Personal Management Handbook*. London: Warner Books. © Marshall Editions Ltd

Olearski, J. 1993 Applying NLP to Foreign Language Teaching. In *Teacher Development Newsletter 22*

Pirsig, R.1974 *Zen and the Art of Motorcycle Maintenance*. London: Vintage

Chapter 8

Albertini de Garateguy, N., Lores de Luisi, A. M., Anido, T., Bergamino de Quintas, M. and Murguía de Welters, L. 1993 Teachers' research in a language institution in Montevideo, Uruguay. In *Teacher Development Newsletter 22* p9

Allwright, R. 1993 Integrating 'research' and 'pedagogy': appropriate criteria and practical possibilities. In Edge, J. and Richards, K. (eds.) *Teachers Develop Teachers Research*. Oxford: Heinemann pp125–35

Allwright, R. and Bailey, K. 1991 *Focus on the Language Classroom*. Cambridge: Cambridge University Press

Bobb Wolff, L. 1990 So what do the students think of your lessons? In *Practical English Teaching* vol.10, no.3

Brandes, D. and Ginnis, P. 1986 *A Guide to Student-Centred Learning*. Oxford: Blackwell

Davis, P. and Rinvolucri, M. 1990 *The Confidence Book*. Harlow: Longman

Freeman, D. 1982 Observing teachers: three approaches to in-service training and development. In *TESOL Quarterly* vol.16, no.1 pp21–8. See also Intervening in practice teaching. In Richards, J. and Nunan, D. (eds.) 1990 *Second Language Teacher Education*. New York: Cambridge University Press

Fullan, M. and Hargreaves, A. 1992 *What's Worth Fighting For In Your School*. Buckingham: Open University Press

Goodson, I. F. 1992 Sponsoring the teacher's voice. In Hargreaves, A. and Fullan, M. (eds.) *Understanding Teacher Development*. London: Cassell

Gwozdzinska, M. 1990 A loner in a team: reflections on team teaching. In *Teacher Development Newsletter 13*

Hancock, R. and Settle, D. 1990 *Teacher Appraisal and Self Evaluation*. Oxford: Blackwell

Henry, C. and Kemmis, S. 1985 A point-by-point guide to action research for teachers. In *The Australian Administrator* vol.6, no.4

Hopkins, D. 1985 *A Teacher's Guide to Classroom Research*. Buckingham: Open University Press

Jaques, D. 1984 *Learning in Groups*. Beckenham: Croom Helm

Kolb, D., Rubin, I. and McIntyre, J. 1979 *Organisational Psychology: An Experiential Approach*. 3rd edition. Englewood Cliffs, New Jersey: Prentice Hall

Leather, S. and Rinvolucri, M. 1989 Letting go of your power. In *Practical English Teaching* vol.10, no.1

Maingay, P. 1988 Observation for training, development, or assessment? In Duff, T. (ed). *Explorations in Teacher Training: Problems and Issues*. Harlow: Longman

Nunan, D.1988 *The Learner-Centred Curriculum*. Cambridge: Cambridge University Press

Postman, N. and Weingartner, C. 1969 *Teaching as a Subversive Activity*. Harmondsworth: Penguin Books

Underhill, A. 1995a Self and peer assessment. (Unpublished paper)

Underhill, A. 1995b Mapping constraints to development. (Unpublished paper)

Underhill, A. 1995c Intentional action planning. (Unpublished paper)

Wajnryb, R.1992 *Classroom Observation Tasks*. Cambridge: Cambridge University Press

Woodward, T. 1989 Taking the threat out of discussing lessons. In *The Teacher Trainer* vol.3, no.2 p21

Index of topics

Index of quoted authors

Acknowledgements

The authors and publishers would like to thank the following for permission to reproduce copyright material: the *Teacher Development Newsletter* and the authors who have allowed their articles to be used; *The Teacher Trainer* for the extract on p190 from 'Taking the threat out of discussing lessons' by Tessa Woodward, reprinted from *The Teacher Trainer* vol. 3, no. 2, for the extract on p26 from 'The ghost instrument' by E. Weintroub, reprinted from *The Teacher Trainer* vol. 7, no.3 and for the extract on pp 119–20 from 'Finding the centre' by Alan Maley, reprinted from *The Teacher Trainer* vol. 7, no. 3; Cambridge University Press for the extract on p13 from 'A professional development focus for the language teaching practicum' by M. C. Pennington, in Richards, J. C. and Nunan, D. (eds.) *Second Language Teacher Education*, the extract on p9 from *Models and Metaphors in Language Teacher Training* by Tessa Woodward, the activity on pp23-4 from *Training Foreign Language Teachers: A Reflective Approach* by M. J. Wallace, the extract on p179 from *The Learner-Centred Curriculum* by D. Nunan, the extract on p177 from *The Language Teaching Matrix* by J. Richards, the extract on p187–8 from *Classroom Observation Tasks* by R. Wajnryb and the extract on p196 from *Focus on the Language Classroom* by R. Allwright and K. Bailey; the extracts on pp27–8 are from *The Inner Game of Tennis* by W. Timothy Gallwey, published by Jonathan Cape Copyright © 1974 by W. Timothy Gallwey. Reprinted by permission of Random House UK Ltd and Random House Inc; Heinle & Heinle for the extracts on pp31, 44–5 and 80 from *Caring and Sharing in the Foreign Language Classroom* by Gertrude Moscowitz and for the extracts on pp43–4, 58–9 and 60 from *Teaching Languages: A Way and Ways* by Earl Stevick; Chris Aldred for the extracts on pp 32–4; Stanley Thornes (Publishers) for the extracts on pp 61–4, 82–5, 87–8 and 100 from *A Guide to Student-Centred Learning* by D. Brandes and P. Ginnis, the extracts on pp 64–5, 151–2 and 170 from *The Student-Centred School* by D. Brandes and P. Ginnis and the extracts on pp 202 and 204 from *Teacher Appraisal and Self Evaluation* by R. Hancock and D. Settle; the extracts on p41 from *Classroom Dynamics* by J. Hadfield (1992) and on pp110–11 from *Roles of Teachers and Learners* by A. Wright (1987) are reprinted by permission of Oxford University Press; the extract on pp49–50 is from J. Holt *How Children Fail* (from pages 32–4), © 1964, 1982 John Holt. Reprinted by permission of A.M. Heath and Addison Wesley Longman Inc; the extract on pp 76–7 is reprinted from Heron, J. 1990 *Helping the Client* by permission of Sage Publications Ltd; Kogan Page Ltd for the extract on pp 105 and 112 from *The Facilitator's Handbook* by J. Heron, London: Kogan Page 1989; Routledge for the extracts on pp 100–101, 103–4 and 191–2 from *Learning in Groups* by D. Jaques, published by Croom Helm; Gaia Books Ltd for the extract on pp 123–4 from *The Mind Gymnasium* by D. Postle; the extract on pp 147–8 was taken from *A Woman In Your Own Right* by Anne Dickson, published by Quartet Books Ltd in 1982 and the extract on p149 from *Stress and Self-Awareness: A Guide for Nurses* by M. Bond, published by Heinemann in 1986, was based on material from *A Woman In Your Own Right* and is used with the permission of Quartet Books Ltd and Butterworth Heinemann; Gower Publishing Limited for the extracts on pp 130 and 168–9 from *Managing Stress* by Jane Cranwell-Ward; *Rapport* magazine for the extract on pp 139–41 from 'Singing, Health and Happiness' by A. Mars; Abner Stein for the extract on pp131–2 from *Self-Massage* by M. Struna with C. Church, published by Hutchinson; HarperCollins *Publishers* Limited for the extract on pp152–3 from *Awareness* by A. De Mello; Cassell for the extracts on pp172–3 from *The New Meaning of Educational Change* by M. Fullan; Open University Press for the extracts on pp 173–4, 185 and 200 from *What's Worth Fighting For In Your School* by M. Fullan and A. Hargreaves, Open University Press 1992 and the extract on pp 194–5 from *A Teacher's Guide to Classroom Research* by D. Hopkins, Open University Press 1985 (2nd edition published in 1993); Tony Duff for the extract on p186 from 'Observation for training, development or assessment?' by P. Maingay, in T. Duff (ed.) *Explorations in Teacher Training* Longman 1988; the extract on p189 is from 'Observing teachers: Three approaches to in-service training' by Donald Freeman, 1982, in *TESOL Quarterly, 16* (pp21–28). Copyright 1982 by Teachers of English to Speakers of Other Languages Inc. Used with permission; the extract on pp 42–3 from 'Process in humanistic education' by A. Underhill, in *English Language Teaching Journal* vol. 43, no. 4 and the extract on p97 from 'The role of groups in developing teacher self-awareness' by A. Underhill, in *English Language Teaching Journal* vol. 46, no. 1 are reproduced by permission of Oxford University Press; Aurum Press for the extract on pp 135–6 from *Body Learning: An Introduction to the Alexander Technique* by Michael Gelb, published by Aurum Press, 1994; Mary Glasgow Magazines for the extract on p6 from 'Teacher development explained' by A. Maley, *Practical English Teaching* vol.10, no. 4, the extract on p29 from 'Breaking rules' by T.Woodward, *Practical English Teaching* vol.9, no. 4, the extract on pp108–9 from 'Are you being developed?' by M. Ellis, *Practical English Teaching* vol. 8, no. 2, the extract on p182–3 from 'So what do the students think of your lessons?' by L. Bobb Wolff, *Practical English Teaching* vol.10, no. 3 and the extract on pp 183–4 from 'Letting go of your power' by S. Leather and M. Rinvolucri, *Practical English Teaching* vol. 10, no. 1; Falmer Press for the extracts on pp16, 17 and 150–1 from *Change Forces* by M. Fullan, Falmer Press 1993; Piatkus Books for the extract on pp 153–4 from *Living Magically* by Gill Edwards, Piatkus Books 1991; the Johari Window on p79 is from *Group Processes: An Introduction to Group Dynamics, Third ed.* by Joseph Luft. Copyright © 1984 by Joseph Luft. Reprinted by permission of Mayfield Publishing Company; the extract on pp159–60 by D.G.N. Byomantara and S. Mace is taken from Kenny, Candlin and Savage (eds.) *Language and Development: Teachers in a Changing World* published by Addison Wesley Longman. Reprinted by permission of Addison Wesley Longman.

It has not been possible to trace the copyright holders of all material used, and in such cases the publishers would welcome information from them.